Roosevelt the Reformer

Roosevelt the Reformer

Theodore Roosevelt as Civil Service Commissioner, 1889–1895

RICHARD D. WHITE JR.

THE UNIVERSITY OF ALABAMA PRESS
Tuscaloosa and London

*51867890

Copyright © 2003
The University of Alabama Press
Tuscaloosa, Alabama 35487-0380
All rights reserved
Manufactured in the United States of America

Typeface: Stone Serif and Stone Sans
∞

The paper on which this book is printed meets the minimum requirements of American National Standard for Information Science–Permanence of Paper for Printed Library Materials, ANSI Z39.48-1984.

Library of Congress Cataloging-in-Publication Data

White, Richard D. (Richard Downing), 1945–
  Roosevelt the reformer : Theodore Roosevelt as civil service commissioner, 1889–1895 / Richard D. White, Jr.
      p.   cm.
Includes bibliographical references and index.
  ISBN 0-8173-1361-3 (alk. paper)
  1. Roosevelt, Theodore, 1858-1919. 2. United States—Politics and government—1889-1893. 3. United States—Politics and government—1893-1897. 4. Civil service reform—United States—History—19th century. 5. United States Civil Service Commission—History. 6. United States Civil Service Commission—Biography. 7. Presidents—United States—Biography. I. Title.
  E757 .W575 2003
  352.6'3'092—dc21

                                                            2003005508

British Library Cataloguing-in-Publication Data available

For Cynthia, Chad, Andrew, and Elissa

Contents

Roosevelt the Reformer

Introduction

"AT TIMES I FEEL an almost Greek horror of extremes," Theodore Roosevelt once confessed to an English friend. Roosevelt could not decide whether he was a conservative radical or a radical conservative.[1] The twenty-sixth president of the United States was a complex, often contradictory, and almost always controversial man. Revealing stark contrasts, Roosevelt seemed at times altruistic, idealistic, and driven by a high-minded progressive desire to improve the fate of mankind. He demonstrated boundless energy, moral intensity, and in many ways perpetual adolescence. Often he could be quite childlike, a friend once remarking that one had to remember that Theodore's age was "about six." In the blink of an eye, however, Roosevelt could be politically ruthless, blindly ambitious, xenophobic, and to some, even racist. There are no lukewarm descriptions of Roosevelt. His supporters adored him as a champion of reform, while his enemies branded him either a traitor to progressivism or a traitor to conservatism. Henry Adams, one of the more discerning chroniclers of his time, quipped that Theodore possessed "the quality that medieval theology assigned to God—he was pure act."[2]

As the memory of Roosevelt fades over time, leaving mostly a toothsome and bespectacled caricature of the man, history has a more difficult time grasping Roosevelt's life and career. Roosevelt's interests were many and varied. He held strong views on almost every conceivable subject, including international relations, national defense, immigration, conservation of the wilderness, bird collecting, marriage and children, and, a central focus of this study, civil service reform. Roosevelt's life was so full that it is difficult, one hundred years later, to comprehend how one man could do so much in such a short span of time. In a life so packed with monumental accomplishments and colorful exploits, it is easy to overlook the more mundane periods of Roosevelt's life. While not as exciting as his presidency, these periods exerted a significant influence upon his life and contributed greatly to national progress. This book is about such an overlooked period, the six years he served as commissioner of the United States Civil Service.

As president, Roosevelt exerted a commanding force upon the modernization of American governance at the dawn of the twentieth century. For nearly eight years he wielded the powers of the presidency as few men have before or since. When Roosevelt entered office, the federal government was slow-moving and conservative, was dominated by the legislature, ceded most important decisions to the states, pursued an isolationist foreign policy, and stood militarily weak. When he departed, the administrative state had become progressive, powerful, centralized, globally focused, interventionist, and in many respects, a close resemblance of today's modern government. In two presidential terms, Roosevelt's vigorous leadership shifted the center of power from the statehouse to the White House.

What was the source of Roosevelt's dominant influence as president? What legacy did he bequeath to the modern administrative state? Much of Roosevelt's effectiveness as president was due to the abundance of administrative skill and experience that he brought to the White House. He previously spent three years as a New York State assemblyman, two years as New York City police commissioner, one year as assistant secretary of the navy, four months as a Rough Rider colonel, two years as New York governor, and six months as vice president. From 1889 to 1895 Roosevelt served as a U.S. Civil Service commissioner, providing the longest period, other than his two terms as president, that he stayed in one job. The six years he served as commissioner is a period of his life that historians frequently brush aside or ignore. The neglect of these years is understandable. At first glance, the civil service years appear quite dull when compared to such flamboyant exploits as Roosevelt's charge up San Juan Hill, his staccato speeches as a young legislator crusading for reform, or his side-busting rides across the Dakota Badlands. Many political insiders, including Roosevelt himself, saw the commission as a political dead end. However, a closer look reveals that Roosevelt's tenure at the Civil Service Commission significantly influenced the future president. During his commissionership he honed his extraordinary skills as an administrator and as a politician. His achievements in civil service reform were substantial and, taken alone, would serve as the capstone of any public servant's career.

Roosevelt's first six years in Washington fell within a dramatic period of American history. As the wounds from the Civil War healed and the twentieth century rapidly approached, unprecedented change embraced the country. Industrialization was rapidly gaining speed, railroads were reshaping both landscape and society, and the closing of the frontier signaled the country's transformation from a weak, agrarian, and provincial nation into an emerging world power. While Roosevelt served at the commission, the country experienced one of its severest depressions, dealt with labor disputes, and faced new waves of populist and anarchist unrest. A huge economic disparity existed in American society, where the richest 1 percent had more total income than the poorest 50 percent. As unveiled in Dreiser's *Sister Carrie,* a small few of the nation's wealthy lived in luxury. However, the vast population lived hand-to-mouth, eking out bare survival in urban sweatshops and gruesome factories, hopelessly sharecropping the small, barren farms across the South, or struggling to homestead the dry and lonely plains.

The Gilded Age, the Victorian Era, and the Gay Nineties were fading quickly, and the first rays of the Progressive Era were dawning. Abolition of slavery no longer festered as the central political issue, while women's suffrage and prohibition of alcohol would not gain notoriety until after the turn of the century. Instead, the burning political issue during Roosevelt's first six years in Washington was civil service reform, an issue in which he was deeply and passionately immersed.

Civil service reform was a battle that pitted those, including young Roosevelt, who wished to create a professional government bureaucracy staffed with competent officials chosen on merit against those who wished to retain the traditional patronage system whereby elected politicians selected government officials based on party allegiance. Roosevelt and his reform colleagues waged open warfare with patronage politics, known at its worst as the "spoils system," and called for the establishment of a merit-based civil service as the answer to the rampant corruption, inefficiency, and incompetency that plagued American governance. The reformers strove to improve the federal service through the introduction of competitive examinations for entrance into the civil service, to purify politics by reducing the number of positions subject to patronage abuses and by eliminating political coercion and political assessments, and to secure efficiency and economy through selected and improved personnel.[3] However, civil service reform was a much bigger issue than merely improving the government bureaucracy. Passionately debated by Democrats and Republicans alike, civil service reform made and broke presidents, would-be presidents, and a number of lesser political figures.[4] The life of Theodore Roosevelt cannot be understood fully without an appreciation of both the effect civil service reform had upon him and the effect he had upon civil service reform.

When Roosevelt arrived in Washington in the spring of 1889, the Civil Service Commission was just six years old. Congress had passed the Pendleton Act in 1883 as "an attempt to correct a vice that should never have been allowed to be born."[5] The act created the three-person commission, introduced a merit system for federal employees based on competitive examinations, and banned political assessments, a common practice whereby politicians demanded that government workers contribute part of their salaries to political parties. With the expansion of the merit system, civil service reformers expected an end to the excessive use of political patronage that bred government corruption and inefficiency since the days of Andrew Jackson. However, during the early years neither the civil service reformers nor the Pendleton Act thwarted the spoils system. At the time of Roosevelt's arrival, the commission controlled only a quarter of federal jobs, leaving the other three-quarters fair game for the spoilsmen. Spoils politicians controlled both houses of Congress; cabinet members were generally hostile to the commission, while presidents were indifferent on crucial occasions. Over the next six years, Roosevelt and his colleagues would face an uphill battle in expanding the federal civil service and abolishing the widespread and corrupting use of political spoils.

The commission years were important in Roosevelt's personal life, covering a period when he achieved his greatest scholarship, three of his six children were born, his brother died tragically, and he suffered financial difficulty. Only thirty when he arrived in the nation's capital, Roosevelt cultivated important friendships and allegiances, flourished intellectually, strengthened his progressive convictions of social justice, and hardened his theories of nationalism and foreign relations. While commissioner, he grew politically and learned the ropes of Washington intrigue. Unlike New York City, where a well-defined boundary separated politics and high society, no such separation existed in the nation's capital, where politics *was* society. "In Washington, there is no life apart from government and politics," wrote one observer at the time. "[Politics] is our daily bread; it is the thread which runs through the woof and warp of our lives; it colors everything."[6]

Theodore and his family soon adapted well to the Washington lifestyle, and in most respects their first years there were happy ones. Roosevelt especially enjoyed the political challenges he faced each day, sparring with powerful cabinet officers and congressmen and surviving their attempts to destroy him. His views toward the role of government also developed. "By the time I was ending my career as civil service commissioner I was already growing to understand that mere improvement in political conditions by itself was not enough," Theodore later wrote. "I dimly realized that an even greater fight must be waged to improve economic conditions, and to secure social and industrial justice, justice as between individuals and justice as between classes."[7] By the end of those remarkably industrious six years, a more mature Theodore Roosevelt emerged and his career began to accelerate dramatically.

In analyzing Roosevelt's years as civil service commissioner, several interrelated questions loom. First, what influence did Roosevelt's tenure as commissioner have on the commission and the early civil service reform movement? When Roosevelt arrived in 1889, the commission was new and controversial and its future was uncertain. Many politicians, dependent upon the spoils system for votes and cash, favored its abolishment. An earlier attempt to create a civil service commission during Grant's administration had failed in 1876, and the likelihood that the second commission would follow suit remained high. Roosevelt's influence upon the survival of the Civil Service Commission is an important issue to identify and explore.

Next, what influence did Roosevelt's commission years have upon the Roosevelt presidency a decade later? As president, Roosevelt exhibited considerable administrative talent and political savvy. The six years he spent as civil service commissioner were arguably meaningful in the training of the future president. To a large degree, Roosevelt honed his administrative and political skills as commissioner.

Finally, what influence did the Roosevelt presidency have on civil service reform? As president and as a former commissioner, Roosevelt had the unique opportunity to put his Progressive rhetoric into action and to implement lasting reform upon the civil service system. He grasped the inner workings of the administrative state as well as any president before or since, and his experience at the commission provided a solid foundation for the exceptional administrative skills he would wield in the White House. However, President Roosevelt, also a shrewd and realistic politician, at times turned to the spoils system to gain political leverage for his own programs and personal ambition. His ability to deal with the tension between his reform zeal and his practical politics offers another important dimension to explore.

The collective answer to these and other questions helps to measure the impact of Roosevelt's tenure as civil service commissioner. It also provides a deeper insight into the administrative legacy Roosevelt leaves to the modern presidency. Despite volumes written on Roosevelt, little attention has focused on his administrative talents and accomplishments. However, the answer to each of the questions is difficult to acquire accurately. Intuitively, Roosevelt's tenure at the Civil Service Commission should have been quite influential on the future president, as six years of anyone's life, especially in his mid-thirties, will leave dramatic imprints. In many ways, the commission period was the "most active and fruitful" of his administrative career.[8] Would the progress of civil service reform have been the same if Roosevelt had *not* been commissioner? Would he have been a different president had he not gained the administrative experience as commissioner? A more detailed investigation of Roosevelt's record in civil service reform is in order.

Roosevelt was a complex man whose professional endeavors, political ambition, and family affairs were intricately intertwined. He loved a great many things, "birds and trees and books, and all things beautiful, and horses and rifles and children and hard work and the joy of life."[9] It is impossible to understand his accomplishments as civil service commissioner without also understanding the impact of his wife and children, his travels and experiences, and the terrible personal tragedies he endured. Clear explanations of Theodore are difficult, as "you cannot explain him any more than you can explain electricity or falling in love."[10]

The six years Roosevelt spent as civil service commissioner were eventful ones in his private life. Trying to analyze his accomplishments in civil service reform and their impact upon his later presidency without considering the influence of private events would do a disservice to the Rooseveltian saga. Roosevelt's relentless energy, his often-blind ambition, and his tendency to reduce complex issues to simply a battle between "the forces of the Lord and of the Devil" are examples of his personality that compelled his actions as commissioner and later as New York governor and finally as president. Roosevelt's behavior as an administrator must be also understood in a particularly personal spirit. With this in mind, this study is careful to examine both the professional and personal aspects of Theodore Roosevelt's tenure as civil service commissioner in the hope that a harmony will emerge which provides a much more insightful view into an altogether fascinating, but previously overlooked, period of the life of America's most energetic president.

1

1889

Arriving in Washington

ON A SPARKLING spring morning in 1889, Theodore Roosevelt hurried along the smoothly paved avenues of Washington, D.C. His pace was quick, and for most people it would be a run. As he walked, Roosevelt soaked up the color and fragrance of Washington in full bloom, a city even more enchanting after a weekend rainstorm carpeted the sidewalks with pungent locust blossoms.[1] While a student at Harvard, Roosevelt once planned to become a biologist, and he never lost his fascination with nature's beauty. He especially had a love of trees, and could recall the Latin nomenclature of a *Quercus alba* shading a street corner or a *Platinus occidentalis* lining a boulevard. Washington charmed him, as some sixty-five thousand carefully tended trees added a green lushness to the city. Each avenue displayed its own unique foliage. Massachusetts Avenue had its lindens, New Hampshire Avenue its stately elms, and Connecticut Avenue flaunted sycamores most of the way but changed to sturdier pin oaks near the countryside.[2]

In 1889 Washington had the trappings of a small southern city. With roughly 190,000 residents, the capital enjoyed a friendly mood and unhurried pace. This favored a young, energetic man like Roosevelt, who came to Washington to make his name. "In four-and-twenty hours he could know everybody; in two days everybody knew him."[3] One English visitor spoke of an air "of comfort, of leisure, of space to spare, of stateliness you hardly expected in America. It looks the sort of place where nobody has to work for his living, or, at any rate, not hard."[4] Office workers breakfasted between eight and nine, arrived at work about ten, at noon had a cup of coffee and a sandwich, and when government offices closed at four o'clock, went home to hearty dinners or dined at a restaurant.[5] Washingtonians had their own concept of time. City merchants seldom delivered goods promptly or when promised. One northern visitor complained, "when they say noon in New York it generally means a little before; when they say noon in Washington, it means from one to four hours later."[6] The times were still simple, an era when bicycles were a novelty, telephones a rarity, and phonographs an outright revelation.

Impressive government buildings dominated the Washington cityscape. Most visitors admired the capital's grand architecture, although a visiting Henry James complained at the time that the city was "overweighted by a single Dome and overaccented by a single Shaft."[7] On the west side of the White House stood the ornate State, War, and Navy Building, or as Henry Adams described it, "Mr. Mullett's architectural infant asylum."[8] To the east loomed the Greek-columned Treasury, and just a couple of blocks up Pennsylvania Avenue stood the new granite Post Office, a massive Romanesque structure with an imposing Gothic clock tower. On this morning in May, Roosevelt headed for another of Washington's landmarks. As he approached Judiciary Square, a dozen blocks north of the White House, two large buildings caught his eye. At the north end of the square on G Street stood one of Washington's newest and most controversial structures. The Pension Building, just two years old, overwhelmed the viewer with its dazzling red brick facade, a dramatic departure from the traditional white sandstone of most government buildings. Many visitors winced at the brashness of the structure, which vaguely resembled an Italian Renaissance palace, and General Sherman once quipped that the only problem was that the building was fireproof. Most agreed, however, that the interior was magnificent, featuring a great hall fifteen stories high and flanked by eight colossal Corinthian columns.[9] The great hall, capable of hosting twelve thousand partygoers, served as the site for every presidential inaugural ball since its completion, as it would for Roosevelt fifteen years in the future.[10]

Standing at the south end of Judiciary Square was City Hall, the other dominant building to catch Roosevelt's eye. A dramatic contrast to the Pension Building, City Hall was one of Washington's oldest and more stately buildings, a classic white Grecian monolith with six Ionic columns topped with a graceful dome.[11] Built in 1820, City Hall no longer served as the seat of local government but now housed an assortment of federal agencies, including Roosevelt's destination, the

United States Civil Service Commission. For the commission's clerks, the temple-like City Hall offered a pleasant place to work, with large, quiet offices, high ceilings, and windows with relaxing views of lawns and trees. Across the street stood Harvey's, a popular restaurant where politicians and bureaucrats discussed the nation's affairs over plates covered with the cook's specialty, splendid fried oysters.

It was still early when Roosevelt bounded up the steps of City Hall and headed for the commission. The clerks working at their desks were surprised as he burst into the office. They looked up to see a young man about thirty, of average height and build, and dressed in Brooks Brothers finery. He had thick, blondish-brown hair parted near the middle, and a face "adorned by nature with a light moustache and artificially with a pair of gold-rimmed eyeglasses."[12] Snapping blue eyes and a dazzling smile with its prominent white teeth were his most vivid features.[13] Roosevelt, in a distinctive high-pitched Dundreary drawl, announced with authority to no one in particular, "I am the new Civil Service Commissioner, Theodore Roosevelt of New York. Have you a telephone? Call up the Ebbitt House. I have an engagement with Archbishop Ireland.[14] Say that I will be there at ten o'clock."[15]

⌐

Theodore Roosevelt's selection as civil service commissioner began roughly a year before he arrived in Washington. During the presidential election of 1888, Roosevelt, a loyal Republican, campaigned energetically for Benjamin Harrison. Theodore admired the incorruptible Harrison, a stodgy little former Civil War general, keen-minded lawyer, senator from Indiana, grandson of President William Henry Harrison, and "frigid Presbyterian deacon."[16] Four years earlier, while fighting the nomination of James G. Blaine at the 1884 Chicago Republican convention, Roosevelt allied himself with Louis Michener, an Indiana power broker. Now, Michener managed Harrison's campaign and Roosevelt volunteered his services to the Republicans.[17] Roosevelt appeared enthusiastic in a letter to his sister Anna in July 1888. "We have a first class ticket; Harrison is a clean, able man, with a good record as a soldier and a Senator," wrote Theodore. "I do'not [sic] like some points of our platform altogether; but on civil service reform, it is sound, while the Democratic platform is not. I suppose I shall be on the stump a short while this fall."[18]

Roosevelt spent August and September of 1888 in the West hunting elk in Idaho's rugged Kootenai country. On October 6 he returned to his home at Oyster Bay, New York. On the next day, with his wife, Edith, at his side, Theodore boarded the *Chicago Limited* and headed west again for an exhausting twelve-day trip campaigning for Harrison.[19] Giving speeches in Chicago, Detroit, and St. Paul, Roosevelt praised the Republican platform that favored civil service reform and attacked the "thoroughly rotten" spoils system that rewarded political loyalty with government jobs. He was happy to be in the midst of a political campaign. "I always genuinely enjoy [politics] and act as target and marksman alternately with immense zest," he wrote his friend Cecil Spring-Rice after the election. "But it is a trifle wearing."[20]

The election was close. In November, Harrison lost the popular vote to the incumbent, Grover Cleveland, but won the electoral college ballot and the presidency. Four months later, on March 4, 1889, President Harrison delivered his inaugural address while sheltered beneath an umbrella amid a cold downpour so heavy that it caused "ladies bangs to come out of curl and hang loose around their foreheads."[21] Nearly half a million people braved the weather to watch, for the nation also celebrated the one-hundred-year anniversary of George Washington's taking the oath of office.

Roosevelt wanted a job in the new administration. Although outwardly hostile to the spoils system, he saw no irony in seeking an appointment from Harrison as a reward for his campaign efforts. Early in 1889, Congressmen Thomas Reed[22] and Henry Cabot Lodge asked Harrison to appoint their friend Roosevelt as assistant secretary of state. To Roosevelt's chagrin, the new secretary of state was James G. Blaine,[23] the man whose presidential nomination Roosevelt fought in 1884. Blaine refused to accept Theodore as his assistant. "I do somehow fear that my sleep [while vacationing] at Augusta or Bar Harbor would not quite be so easy and refreshing if so brilliant and aggressive a man had hold of the helm," Blaine explained to Lodge. "Matters are constantly occurring which require the most thoughtful concentration and the most stubborn inaction. Do *you* think that Mr. T. R.'s temperament would give guaranty of that course?" It is doubtful that Blaine seriously considered Roosevelt for the post, as at the time he was trying vainly to convince Harrison to appoint his son, Walker Blaine, as assistant secretary.[24]

Undaunted by Blaine's refusal, Theodore pressed for an appointment in another bureau. By spring 1889, Harrison's advisers suggested that Roosevelt, as "persistent as a mosquito on a summer night," be appointed as one of three civil service commissioners.[25] The commissionership offered only a minor post but one that might placate the irrepressible Theodore. Politically, placing Roosevelt at the commission appeared an ideal choice for Harrison. The new president at least nominally supported civil service reform, and a Roosevelt commissionership would satisfy the progressive side of the Republican Party, which favored an attack on the spoils system. Besides, a Roosevelt commissionership did not waste a more desirable political plum such as a departmental assistant secretaryship reserved for old-guard stalwarts.

Ideologically, Roosevelt suited the commissionership and its reform mission. The commission's primary function was to reform the federal bureaucracy by replacing an inefficient and often corrupt patronage system with a professional civil service based on merit, not politics. Despite his youth, Roosevelt was a well-seasoned reformer. Ten years before, as a student at Harvard, he supported many popular reform causes, including civil service reform. Shortly after graduation, Theodore joined a local Republican association in New York City and led a resolution favoring nonpartisan administration of the street-cleaning department. The resolution failed.[26]

Between 1881 and 1884, Roosevelt served three terms as the youngest legislator in the New York State Assembly, where he championed a series of reform bills attacking corruption and professionalizing New York State government. During his second term in Albany, Theodore joined forces with then-governor Grover Cleveland to pass a bill making New York the first state to replace its patronage system with a merit-based civil service.[27] Roosevelt and his reform allies also enacted legislation requiring merit systems for the twenty-three New York cities with populations of twenty thousand or more.[28] While running unsuccessfully for mayor of New York in 1886, he campaigned on a reform ticket that promised to clean up the city's corrupt patronage system.

Roosevelt expressed a serious interest in the civil service job as early as April 1888, writing to Lodge that he hoped "the President will appoint good Civil Service Commissioners."[29] At first Roosevelt was optimistic about the new president's resolve for civil service reform. In his inaugural speech, Harrison promised that his administration would "enforce the civil service law fully and without evasion" and personally vowed "to do something more to advance the reform."[30] As a senator in 1883, "Little Ben" mildly supported civil service reform and voted for the Pendleton Act, although he believed a government employee should be allowed to make unrestricted contributions to political campaigns.[31]

Roosevelt was not reluctant to offer advice to the president-elect. "You will doubtless have forgotten me; I think that any New Yorker can tell you who I am," Roosevelt wrote Harrison soon after the election. Theodore complained that appointing New York political boss Thomas Platt to a cabinet post would have "a very unfortunate effect on our politics here" and stated that "honest politics and a clean, non-partisan civil service can only come from Republican men."[32] In the next month Roosevelt noted that the new president's commitment proved not as strong as the campaign rhetoric suggested. Roosevelt wrote Harrison to object to his earliest appointments that, in Roosevelt's eyes, smacked of spoils politics at its worst. In the New York City post office, Harrison replaced Postmaster Henry Pearson, to Roosevelt an honest and efficient official, with the spoils politician and machine loyalist, Cornelius Van Cott. The new president also replaced Silas Burt as surveyor of the Port of New York and Leverett Saltonstall as collector of customs in Boston.[33] Roosevelt wrote Harrison twice to protest Van Cott's appointment, but the new president never responded.[34] Theodore complained to Lodge soon after writing his second letter to the president. "I learn that Harrison thinks of making an ordinary ward politician, Van Cott, a Platt henchman, postmaster; a horrible contrast to Pearson," wrote Theodore. "It would be an awful black eye to the party here; a criminal blunder. Platt seems to have a ring in the President's nose as regards New York . . . curse patronage."[35]

While Roosevelt's complaints brought no action, they must not have angered the president. In April 1889, Lodge called on the president's secretary, Elijah Halford, and urged that Theodore be appointed commissioner. Later that day, Halford and the president took a walk after finishing their office work and Halford suggested the Roosevelt appointment. After mulling over the idea for a few days, Harrison had Halford wire Roosevelt to come to Washington.[36] Shortly thereafter, Roosevelt took the train south from Oyster Bay and, on May 7, met with Harrison in the White House. The young New Yorker apparently impressed the president. A decade later, when Roosevelt served as New York governor and was rumored to be a candidate for vice president, Harrison recalled that "the only trouble I ever had with managing [Roosevelt] was he wanted to put an end to all the evil in the world between sunrise and sunset."[37] When Harrison offered the commissionership, Roosevelt promptly accepted.[38] The next day he wrote a friend, Baltimore reformist Charles Bonaparte,[39] "I hated to take the place, but I hardly thought I ought to refuse. I was a good deal surprised at the offer."[40]

President Harrison would not have appointed Roosevelt civil service commissioner without the political maneuvering of Henry Cabot Lodge.[41] Theodore relied heavily on the advice of Cabot, who over the years became "the most loyal friend that ever breathed."[42] Tall and spare, Lodge dressed impeccably and wore "his close-fitting suits with the trouser pockets foppishly cut on the horizontal."[43] He was "English to the last fiber of his thought."[44] With a spike of a beard underscoring his angular face, Lodge seemed unbearably superior and fastidious, cold and calculating. But the Boston aristocrat also was fiercely loyal to his friends.[45] Theodore and Cabot began their close relationship during the 1884 Republican convention when they fought Blaine's presidential nomination, then refused to break from the party with the radical Mugwumps and supported Blaine.[46] Liberal reformers attacked Roosevelt and Lodge for standing behind their party, describing them as immature delegates who "pouted and sulked like whipped schoolboys."[47] According to Roosevelt, "from that time on [Cabot] was my closest friend, personally, politically, and in every other way, and occupied toward me a relation that no other man has ever occupied or ever will occupy."[48]

The two men differed in significant ways. Eight years older than Theodore, Lodge held wide-ranging interests and, while more intellectually agile and polished than Roosevelt, lacked his friend's breadth, flexibility, and charisma.[49] Like Theodore, he loved history and literature, long walks, horses, and Harvard. In public both men appeared humorless, but their correspondence to each other often revealed wit and whimsy. In many ways, Lodge became the big brother Theodore never had.[50] An outspoken supporter of civil service reform, Lodge also shrewdly took advantage of his patronage privileges when politics demanded.[51]

Until Roosevelt's death in 1919, the two men maintained an unbroken correspondence that remains a priceless chronicle of the presidency, politics, literature, and turn-of-the-century society, as well as a rare glimpse into their eventful times and eclectic lives. Roosevelt recognized the uniqueness of their relationship soon after becoming commissioner. "What funnily varied lives we do lead, Cabot! We touch two or three little worlds, each profoundly ignorant of the others," Roosevelt wrote Lodge from New York City. "Our literary friends have but a vague knowledge of our actual political work; and a goodly number of our sporting and social acquaintances know us only as men of good family, one of whom rides hard to hounds, while the other hunts big game in the Rockies."[52]

⌐⌐

Roosevelt went to work immediately at the Civil Service Commission. The day after he arrived, Theodore and the two other commissioners paid a call on the president and, while leaving the White House, encountered several of Harrison's new cabinet members. Secretary of the Navy Benjamin Tracy, a former New York Appeals Court judge, recognized Roosevelt. "You haven't any power over my place, anyway," joked Tracy, hinting that the commission would have little control over the Navy Department. "Hush, don't say a word," Roosevelt countered in jest. "If I had been compelled to pass a civil service examination, I never should have got my place."[53]

Another cabinet member was the new postmaster general, John Wanamaker, a brawny man whose robust, beefy face radiated vitality.[54] Roosevelt and Wanamaker were cordial when they met, but each must have known that their new jobs soon would plunge them into heated battle. Roosevelt's job was to eliminate political spoils; Wanamaker's was to dispense them.

Meanwhile, Roosevelt's appointment to the commission met approval with the more extreme reformers. The Civil Service Reform League elected Theodore to its executive committee shortly before he arrived in Washington, but he resigned soon thereafter so there would be no hint of conflict of interest.[55] Two days after Roosevelt accepted Harrison's offer, the *Nation*'s E. L. Godkin, himself a tireless advocate of reform, described Theodore as "erratic and impulsive, but energetic, enthusiastic, and honest and may be relied on to see that the law is faithfully executed. The commission as now constituted is the best we have had." A week later the *New York Times* reported that "Mr. Roosevelt, young as he is, has already done good service to promoting this reform. If his judgment should prove equal to his zeal, the politicians who seek to use the business offices of this country as rewards for their henchmen will find him a formidable opponent."[56] A *Washington Star* editorial also approved. "It is pleasant to find a civil-service commissioner speaking out with such directness as Mr. Roosevelt does when he says 'the law must be obeyed.'"[57]

Roosevelt was one of three commissioners. His two colleagues, Hugh Thompson and Charles Lyman, were quite competent and equally responsible for the day-to-day bureaucratic chores necessary to build and manage the merit service. A former Confederate officer, Thompson served as governor of South Carolina from 1882 to 1886 and assistant treasury secretary from 1886 to 1889. Appointed the same week as Roosevelt, Thompson served on the commission until June 23, 1892.[58] Lyman, a former Union officer from Connecticut, served for three years as the commission's chief examiner before being appointed commissioner in 1886.[59] Lyman provides an unusual example of a successful career civil servant who managed to survive the years of rampant spoils.[60] He became a government clerk in 1864 and worked his way up through the bureaucracy, eventually becoming chief of appointments in the Treasury Department during Roosevelt's presidency three decades later. During the first months, Commissioner Roosevelt became impatient with his reliable but slow colleague, writing Lodge in September 1889 that "Lyman is a good, honest, hard-working man, very familiar with the law; but he is also the most intolerably slow of all the men who ever adored red tape."[61] Soon, Theodore's regard for his colleagues deteriorated and he began to trust only his own abilities. "Of course, excellent though Thompson is (and I can not be glad enough he is my colleague) I hardly dare trust him in such work," Roosevelt wrote Lodge a month later. "As for Lyman, he is utterly useless; I wish I had one more good Republican on the Commission. I wish to heaven he were off."[62]

Despite his eagerness, Roosevelt had his doubts about accepting the commissionership.[63] Like many of his Washington colleagues, he regarded the commission as a political graveyard and later admitted he gave up all hope of a political career when he took the position.[64] When he arrived the commission regulated about twenty-eight subordinate federal jobs, still a small percentage of the total federal workforce. Likewise, little prestige came with the office, and its duties caused such controversy that efficient, honest performance by a commissioner only created bitter political enemies. To the combative young Roosevelt, the new job seemed ideal.

⤹

The presidential inaugural of 1829 was a riotous occasion. Andrew Jackson, hero of the War of 1812, arrived in Washington after a landslide victory and firmly took the reins of power. Over six feet tall and slender, his long-jawed, high-browed face topped with a bristly mass of gray hair, the seventh president of the United States commanded awe and respect. Still mourning the death of his wife, Jackson stepped to the podium at the Capitol with a ribbon of black crepe wrapped around his tall hat and hanging down the back of his plain black suit. In his brief address, the new president promised to give the government back to the people. Jackson vowed to create a populist and more democratic government that changed hands more often, with government jobs rotated frequently between the common man. Declaring that "no man has any more intrinsic right to official station than another," Jackson ushered in a new era of patronage politics.[65] He confirmed his affinity for the common man that evening, when he opened the doors of the White House to his raucous followers for his official reception. A huge drunken mob descended upon the mansion, smashing priceless presidential china and glassware and forcing Jackson to escape through a window for his own safety.

With promises of political spoils, many thousands of office seekers descended upon the capital in hopes of being given a government job as reward for supporting Jackson. In their eyes, the political spoils were "delicious slices of pie to be grabbed and devoured by the greediest and strongest person in sight."[66] In Washington and across the nation, thousands of post office workers, clerks in customshouses, Indian agents, and other federal workers found themselves, almost overnight, fired from their jobs and replaced with Jacksonians. As Henry Clay explained, ousted government workers seemed "like the inhabitants of Cairo when the plague breaks out; no one knows who is next to encounter the stroke of death." Though hardly the first use of the spoils system in American history, the huge number of dismissals unquestionably intensified a process that would plague American democracy for years to come.[67]

Jackson's sweeping spoils appointments provoked immediate criticism and soon spawned a nationwide movement to reform government. As early as 1832, only three years after Jackson took office, the eloquent Daniel Webster, outraged at the rampant and corrupt use of patronage, stood upon the floor of the Senate and colorfully described the emerging American political scene,

> There is no civilized country on earth in which on a change of rulers there is such an inquisition for spoil as we have witnessed in this free republic. When, Sir, did any British Minister, Whig or Tory, ever make such an inquest? When did he ever get down to low-watermark to make an ousting of tide-waiters? When did he ever take away the daily bread of weighers, and gaugers, and measurers? When did he ever go into the villages to disturb the little post-offices, the mail contracts, and everything else in the remot-

est degree connected with Government? A British Minister who should do this and should afterward show his head in a British House of Commons would be received by a universal hiss.[68]

Over the next half century the movement to abolish the spoils system and create a professional civil service system became one of the foremost political issues debated within the country. Any reform, however, would be difficult and slow, as the spoils system was lodged deeply in all levels of government. Besides, the spoils system may have been beneficial during its earlier years, for it helped create the mass political parties that were essential for the democratization of American politics. After the Civil War the parties had grown in size and power and had become the dominant force on the political landscape. Powerful party bosses chose thousands of public officials, from cabinet officers in Washington, to clerks in rural post offices, to lighthouse keepers on remote islands. Often a congressman controlled federal patronage in his district by maintaining a close relationship with the editors of pro-spoils newspapers who supported his election. The congressman, in turn, would give postmasterships to these editors, who continued to manage their papers while dipping into the public trough. Early in Benjamin Harrison's administration, for example, Kansas alone had thirty-three editors who had been given postmasterships.[69]

The Civil War increased the fervor over spoils as the bureaucracy expanded. One of Abraham Lincoln's most distasteful duties as president, but one that he skillfully used to increase power, was to satisfy thousands of requests from congressmen and party bosses for patronage appointments. Often Lincoln awoke to find a swarm of office seekers buzzing around his bedroom door, waiting for a chance to lobby him for one of the valuable spoils appointments, of which there never seemed to be enough. "I have more pegs than holes to put them in," lamented Lincoln.[70]

As rampant spoils appointments went unchecked, government efficiency suffered from high turnover, incompetence, and widespread corruption. The small professional bureaucracy labored under a primitive personnel system. Examinations were farcical, nepotism was common, no real promotion policy existed, no training program was available for the newest employees, and no retirement benefits were provided for the oldest.[71] Over the years, the flaws became more serious and obvious. Political leaders required their patronage appointees to devote more time and money to party affairs and less to managing the government. After each election, hungry office seekers besieged successful candidates, and wrangling between the president and Congress over patronage became increasingly endemic. The growth of the federal bureaucracy compounded the problems of the spoils system. In Jackson's time there had been 20,000 persons on the federal payroll. By end of the Civil War the number had increased to 53,000; by 1884, 131,000; and by 1891, 166,000.[72] At the same time, government had become more technical and complex. Despite Jackson's claim that any man could fill a government position, new government jobs required special skills. The use of typewriters, introduced in the early 1880s, meant that mere literacy and decent penmanship no longer sufficed for a clerk's job.[73] With the creation of more technical agencies, such as the Interstate Commerce Commission, the Geological Survey, and specialized agricultural bureaus, many jobs required scientific expertise. The spoils system was incapable of providing the professionals and specialists necessary to run an increasingly complex government.

The attack on the spoils system slowly built in intensity. Many civil service reformers looked upon the efforts to abolish the spoils system as a religious crusade, much like the abolition movement years before and the suffrage and Prohibition movements in years to come. Other, less idealistic reformers saw the destruction of spoils as a way for disenfranchised political elements, namely northeastern Republicans, to replace entrenched party machines, mostly big-city Democrats. Thus the reform movement was in part a nativist, class-bound reaction against the success of foreign, mainly Irish Catholic, working-class groups in urban politics.[74] Meanwhile, many businessmen began to carry the reform banner, for they realized that honest and competent government officials would serve their interests better than the old, obnoxious spoilsmen and political hacks.[75] As early as 1867, the National Manufacturers' Association, believing that the reform movement promised greater governmental efficiency that would lead to lower taxes, adopted a resolution "heartily" endorsing civil service legislation.[76] Many, including business leaders, began to realize that government was getting bigger and needed more competent officials to manage its increasing complexity.

Reformers also argued that abolition of the spoils system would crush the political boss, weaken the linkage between Congress and the patronage, and, in the long run, increase the power of the presidency.[77] Presidents began favoring civil service reform, as it provided a weapon in the executive's unending struggle with Congress and as a reprieve from the onerous task of filling spoils appointments. Like most presidents of his era, Garfield saw firsthand the problems caused by the spoils system, once complaining that a host of hungry office seekers often descended upon him "like vultures for a wounded bison."[78]

Despite a groundswell of support, civil service reform did not happen overnight. As early as 1811, Congress failed to pass a bill to limit patronage.[79] Beginning prior to the Civil War and continuing through the Progressive Era, the reform movement was beset with powerful opposition and underwent several failures before finally overpowering the spoils system in the early twentieth century. In April 1864, Senator Charles Sumner introduced a futile bill to require examinations for admission into the civil service. Between 1865 and 1869, Congress defeated four successive civil service bills.[80]

The prime mover for civil service reform during this period was Thomas Jenckes, a Republican congressman from Rhode Island.[81] A skilled lawyer from a prominent family and backed by a political constituency that kept him in Congress from 1863 until 1871, Jenckes spent much of his career devoted to reforming the administration of the federal government and eliminating the obvious inefficiencies of an overgrown and nonprofessional bureaucracy. Civil servants, whose number doubled between 1860 and 1865, were still "haphazardly recruited and haphazardly expelled."[82] Approaching the question of administrative reform scientifically, Jenckes studied the civil services in Prussia, England, France, and China. Although Congress failed to pass the bills he authored, he laid a pattern for civil service reform from which reformers drew heavily in shaping permanent legislation.

Reformers achieved temporary success early in Grant's administration when Congress created the first Civil Service Commission. Key to the success was a new crop of reformers, notably George William Curtis, Carl Schurz, and Dorman Eaton, who lobbied vigorously for new legislation. On the last day of the last session of 1871, Illinois senator Lyman Trumball tacked a rider upon an appropriation bill.[83] The rider consisted of one lengthy sentence giving the president wide latitude in creating a professional civil service.[84] Grant appointed a seven-member commission, directed them to draft regulations for the new reform, and chose Curtis[85] as the first chairman. Curtis resigned in protest after two years when Grant appointed a spoils politician and ex-general as surveyor of the Port of New York.[86] Eaton replaced Curtis as chairman. The Grant commission lasted for three years, drawing up competitive examinations and holding them in New York, Washington, Cincinnati, St. Louis, and Savannah.[87] Although both Congress and Grant allowed the first commission to expire in 1875, the same year Thomas Jenckes died, the early experiment established valuable precedents, such as the "rule of three," and created many of the concepts and terminology and thus much of the groundwork for later reforms.[88] Nevertheless, the movement for a civil service law made little headway before 1880. Civil service reform lacked organization, had no central direction, and failed to excite popular support.[89]

After the Grant commission expired, Curtis, Eaton, Schurz, and their fellow reformers continued their crusade for permanent civil service legislation. Their work made little progress, however, until July 1881, when a disgruntled office seeker named Charles Guiteau assassinated President Garfield. The assassination galvanized public opinion against the spoils system. A month after Garfield was shot, George Curtis, then editor of *Harper's Weekly,* and E. L. Godkin of the *Nation* met with other reformers in Newport, Rhode Island, and created the National Civil Service Reform League. For the next two years the league lobbied aggressively for an end to the spoils and spurred a flood of petitions from across the country. Republican losses in the 1882 congressional midterm election, during which civil service reform was a central issue, also added to the political climate favorable for passage of civil service reform legislation. The timing was finally right that winter. Congress approved a new civil service reform bill, drafted by Eaton, Curtis, Schurz, and members of the New York Civil Service Reform Association and named the Pendleton Act after its sponsor, Democratic senator George Pendleton. The reformers remained nervous after passage, however, as the bill needed the approval of the new president, Chester Arthur, a man who had a reputation as a notorious spoilsman. Arthur, to the reformers' relief, signed the bill, and the Pendleton Act became law on January 16, 1883.[90] Remarkably, Arthur appointed a competent group of civil service commissioners, including Eaton as the chairman, and during his administration gave general support to the enforcement of the Pendleton Act.[91]

In passing the Pendleton Act, the reformers intended to replace the spoils system with a professional government workforce. The act created a merit-based civil service, outlawed political assessments and other election skullduggery, and provided some job security and insulation from political influence. As an aside, the authors of the act revealed their zeal for another cause by prohibiting employment of persons who "habitually use intoxicating beverages to excess."

To enforce its provisions, the act established a bipartisan three-person commission of which "not more than two of whom shall be adherents of the same party." The act aimed to improve the federal workforce by upholding the concepts of merit, tenure, and neutrality. First, it created a merit system for federal employees that relied upon a widely expanded system of practical examinations. Competitive rankings, not political affiliation, determined who was hired into the classified civil service. The reformers also attacked nepotism, prevalent at the time, by denying employment to persons "whenever there are already two or more members of a family in the public service." Second, the act guaranteed tenure in office and some degree of job security for classified employees by prohibiting removal for solely political purposes. Prior to the act, an employee could be fired at will for political affiliation or, for that matter, any other reason or prejudice. Even if his party remained in power, an employee could fall prey to factional struggles within the party. Third, the act demanded partisan neutrality of classified civil servants by forbidding a government worker from forcing the political action of another person, as well as forbidding the extortion of political assessments from government employees.[92]

With the Pendleton Act in place, civil service reformers expected an early death of the spoils system. They soon were disappointed. When passed in 1883 the Pendleton Act failed to provide a complete remedy to spoils. Aside from federal offices in Washington, the act applied only to customshouses and post offices in the largest cities.[93] The new civil service regulations failed to protect the vast majority of federal employees, while no legislation existed for most state and municipal workers. Passed the year that Theodore first ventured west to the Dakota country, the Pendleton Act covered 13,900 federal employees out of a total of 132,800.[94] When Roosevelt arrived six years later, the commission controlled a quarter of federal jobs, while the rest remained fair game for the spoilsmen.

Despite the reformers' early expectations, the spoils system remained alive and well, and years would pass before the Pendleton Act made serious progress. Well into the next century, ward heelers continued to reward their party faithful with government offices and "take the boys in out of the cold to warm their toes."[95] State and local governments were particularly slow to reform. By 1905 only four states—New York, Massachusetts, Illinois, and Wisconsin—had passed civil service legislation.[96] At the federal level, the majority of positions remained unclassified and subject to spoils. Congressmen dictated most of the spoils appointments in their districts, selecting loyal party workers as customs agents, U.S. marshals, postmasters, or census takers. Reformers had an uphill battle, as the number of federal patronage positions actually in-

creased from 1883 to 1901, rising from 118,000 in 1884 to 150,000 in
1901, an increase due to the overall expansion of the government workforce.[97]

When Roosevelt arrived, the commission operated under extreme
handicaps. Cabinet members, not the commission, controlled promotions, demotions, and firings of civil servants. The commission could
only make recommendations, and cabinet members frequently ignored
suggestions that interfered with the spoils system.[98] The commission
possessed no authority to transfer patronage positions into the merit
system. Screening applicants for federal appointment remained the
commission's chief function. For several years the Pendleton Act lingered as a weak law that effectively allowed each presidential administration to classify public offices as it chose.[99] Progress was slow. Twenty
years after the Pendleton Act's passage, President Theodore Roosevelt
saw the proportion of classified employees finally exceed 50 percent,
and not until another thirty years, during the Hoover administration,
did it surpass 80 percent.[100]

⌇

Emily Neyland was nervous. As soon as she realized that Benjamin Harrison had won the presidency in 1888, she knew her job was in jeopardy. Emily worked in the huge Interior Department building on F
Street in the General Land Office. As a senior clerk she earned $1,600 a
year, a comfortable salary for most government workers and unusually
high pay for a woman. The Land Office was still largely a man's domain
when Emily began work there, as a spittoon sat next to each desk.[101] An
efficient and responsible worker, Emily managed to save enough of her
earnings to spend three months on leave in Europe with two women
friends from work. With political ties to the Democrats, Emily had been
given her job at the Land Office job by President Cleveland four years
earlier. To her dismay, the Republicans were now in power, and for several months she waited for the ax to fall. "[I] lived the life of a toad
under a harrow," Neyland later wrote to Interior Secretary John Noble.
"Bets were made that I would be discharged."[102]

In the end, Emily was fortunate. She kept her job but was demoted
by a new Republican supervisor who "descended to an unmanly war
upon a delicate woman merely because she belonged to a family differing from him in the matter of political faith."[103] Thousands of Democrats were not as lucky as Emily and soon discovered that they were
out of work, replaced by the thousands of Republicans then invading

the nation's capital and looking forward to their turn at reaping the spoils.[104]

＄

As soon as he started work in his City Hall office, Commissioner Roosevelt, somewhat like Emily Neyland a few months before, confronted the spoils system at its ruthless political efficiency. President Cleveland, just prior to leaving office in March 1889, signed an order transferring five thousand Railway Mail Service workers into the classified service. The Railway Mail Service traditionally provided a refuge for spoils appointments. When Cleveland departed, however, the Civil Service Commission had not completed the necessary paperwork and delayed the railway transfers until May 1, 1889, after the Republicans took office and shortly before Roosevelt arrived. The Post Office Department, now run by Harrison appointees, took advantage of the hiatus and replaced nearly all of the incumbent Democratic postal workers with their own party faithful. Civil service reformers complained about the Republicans' political mischief, but the replacements were perfectly legal. The reformers expected the new president to be more supportive of reform and to disavow rampant spoils appointments, but Harrison refused to intervene. Having just arrived, Roosevelt was powerless and his complaints to the president and Postmaster General Wanamaker went unanswered.

Although frustrated with his own party's pillaging of the post office, Roosevelt did not sit idly by. During his first weeks in Washington he took several trips north to see Edith, who was then four months pregnant and remained with the two children at their Oyster Bay home, Sagamore Hill. A week after taking office, Theodore made the first of his commutes home. On May 20 he took the short train ride from Oyster Bay to New York City, where he joined fellow commissioner Hugh Thompson. The two headed for 55 Wall Street, headquarters of the spoils-ridden New York Customshouse, where they spent the day in the huge, Ionic-columned building investigating appointments and interviewing employees. The commissioners found "great laxity, negligence, and fraud" and discovered that customs officials manipulated the eligibility lists, had at least one applicant's examination written by another person, and sold copies of civil service examinations for fifty dollars apiece.[105] Meanwhile, customs bosses passed over competent applicants in favor of political appointees. Roosevelt discovered, for example, that "one Michael Hart passed an examination for opener and packer, standing at the very head of the list, with a mark of ninety-five percent, yet not only was he never informed that he had passed, but even his constant inquiry at the office failed to procure him the information."[106] The report of the two commissioners prompted the firing of three customs employees.[107] From New York City Roosevelt traveled to Troy, New York, where he annulled a special examination and quashed a partisan eligibility list.[108]

Roosevelt's foray into the New York Customshouse during his first week on the job astonished many of the spoilsmen and signaled that the civil service law was to be enforced aggressively. The successful customshouse investigation also gave Theodore a taste for uncovering political wrongdoing, a taste he savored.

After spending a week with his family at Sagamore Hill, Roosevelt returned to Washington, staying at Henry Cabot Lodge's spacious house at 1721 Connecticut Avenue. During the first week in June, all who could deserted Washington before the hellish heat of summer. After all, much of the city was still "a mere political camp, as transient and temporary as a camp meeting for religious revival."[109] The diplomats and lobbyists were long gone, the national press was thinning out, and Congress was about to adjourn.[110] Roosevelt ignored the heat and plunged into his work. On June 16, Theodore and the other commissioners departed on a ten-day inspection tour of federal offices in the Midwest. On the eve of their departure, Roosevelt announced the purpose of the trip to the press. "We have to do two things," he declared. "One is to make the officials themselves understand that the [civil service] law is obligatory, not optional, and the other is to get the same idea into the heads of the people."[111]

The commissioners inspected government offices in Indianapolis, Chicago, Grand Rapids, and Milwaukee.[112] In Indianapolis, Roosevelt investigated complaints against Postmaster William Wallace, described as a "well meaning weak old fellow."[113] Wallace, however, was a former law partner of the president and the brother of General Lew Wallace, author of *Ben Hur* and Harrison's biographer. At first Roosevelt charged the postmaster with illegally removing three workers, but eventually he found no fault with Wallace, who remained in office. While in Indianapolis, Roosevelt had several corrupt workers dismissed, and his actions began to attract criticism. Indiana attorney general Louis Michener, who previously managed Harrison's campaign, complained to the president. "It seems to me that [Roosevelt] should be given to understand that it would be well for him to have less to say to newspapers," wrote Michener. "When he was here, he was positively insulting to the

Republicans he met and extremely agreeable to every interest hostile to the Republican Party."[114] Roosevelt continued undeterred. In Minneapolis he found eight persons had been appointed without being certified and had them dismissed.[115]

The president never censured Theodore. Roosevelt was difficult to handle, and while Harrison, and later Cleveland, may have wanted to be rid of him, neither was prepared to face the hostile criticism from powerful reform forces.[116] Instead, Harrison let his appointee carry out his duties, an indication that the president, who possessed one of the country's keenest legal minds, favored at least modest reform. Reformers criticized Harrison harshly, but during his administration he allowed the merit system to expand, cleaned up several corrupt agencies (including the spoils-controlled Patent Office), classified the free-delivery postal service, and supported his secretary of the navy, Benjamin Tracy, who placed the entire labor force of the Navy Yards under the merit system and stopped the political ruse of hiring extra men in the yards sixty days before an election.[117]

During his first few months, Roosevelt began to feel pressure from above to relax his attacks on Republican spoilsmen, but he stubbornly dug in his heels. "As for me, I am having a hard row to hoe. I have made this commission a living force, and in consequence the outcry among the spoilsmen has become furious; it has evidently frightened both the President and Halford a little," Roosevelt wrote Lodge in June 1889. "They have shown symptoms of telling me that the law should be rigidly enforced where the people will stand it, and handled gingerly elsewhere. But I answered militantly; that as long as I was responsible the law should be enforced up to the handle every where; fearlessly and honestly."[118]

After Indianapolis, Roosevelt traveled to Milwaukee, where on June 20 he accused Postmaster George Paul of re-marking the tests of Republican office seekers. Writing to Lodge, Roosevelt described Paul as "about as thorough paced a scoundrel as I ever saw—an oily-Gammon, churchgoing specimen. We gave him a neat hoist."[119] Roosevelt planned to have Paul fired as an example to deter others from violating the law. After Wanamaker took no action on the postmaster, Roosevelt appealed to Harrison. An impatient Theodore fired off three letters to Elijah Halford, Harrison's assistant, in July 1889, pleading to see the president and attacking Paul as a "most flagrant wrong doer" and a "genuine phenomenon and liar."[120] Still seething over the retention of Paul, Roosevelt ran into the president near the end of July, a meeting he shortly thereafter described to Lodge: "Today I caught a glimpse of the President, and repeated to him the parable of the backwoodsman and the bear. You remember that the prayer of the backwoodsman was 'Oh Lord, help me kill that b'ar; and if you don't help me, Oh Lord, don't help the b'ar.' Hitherto I have been perfectly contented if the President would preserve an impartial neutrality between me and the bear, but now, as regards Postmaster Paul of Milwaukee, the President *must* help somebody, and I hope it won't be the bear."[121]

For two months, nothing was done as Harrison and Wanamaker delayed. Roosevelt was frustrated, as the Civil Service Commission did not have the power to remove employees—only the president or the postmaster general could fire postal workers. The president eventually allowed Paul to resign.[122] Afterward, Roosevelt revealed his inability to see the value of compromise. "Harrison in the Milwaukee Postmaster business followed his usual course of trying to hold the scales even between myself and the Bear (Wanamaker)," Theodore wrote Lodge in August 1889. "He accepted Postmaster Paul's resignation on the one hand, and notified him on the other that if he hadn't resigned he would have been removed. It was a golden chance to take a good stand; and it has been lost."[123]

The Midwest tour by the commissioners caused a sensation, for it departed from the more passive enforcement policies of previous commissions. By taking the law into the hinterland where the spoils system previously operated unchecked, the new commission gave notice that the Pendleton Act provided a real law to be enforced with vigor and impartiality. As the Civil Service Commission began to emerge as an important player in the Washington policy arena, it was Roosevelt who provided much of the commission's newfound energy and aggressiveness. He became a lightning rod for both its praise and criticism. Although three men served as commissioners, Roosevelt clearly dominated the public arena. He liked it that way. One of his sons later described his father's need for the limelight, remarking that Theodore "never likes to go to a wedding or a funeral, because he can't be the bride at the wedding or the corpse at the funeral."[124]

Soon after Theodore arrived, the weekly magazine *Puck* published a political cartoon showing a small Jack, alias Theodore Roosevelt, who brandished a sword labeled civil service rules and attacked a large giant, labeled the spoils system. Holding a leash attached to Roosevelt's belt was the president. The spoils system giant warned his attacker, "Calm yourself, Theodore. If you go too far, you'll find yourself jerked back mighty suddenly by President Harrison."[125] The cartoon omitted the other two commissioners.

Returning to Washington at the end of June, Roosevelt continued his work through the summer. His only break was a week at Oyster Bay in early July. Later that month, back at City Hall, he met with Herbert Welsh,[126] an activist with the Indian Rights Association. The two worked on a plan for transferring a number of personnel in the Indian Bureau into the merit system. In the years ahead, Roosevelt and Welsh developed a close friendship and collaborated on several projects aimed at improving living conditions on Indian reservations.

During his first summer at the commission, Roosevelt settled comfortably into his new position. He seemed glad that he had not become assistant secretary of state. "I could have done nothing [at State], whereas now I have been a real force," Theodore wrote Lodge. "I think I have helped the cause of good government and of the party."[127] Theodore's passion for reform, if it changed at all, intensified. "[I am] more than ever a most zealous believer in the merit system," he wrote to *Boston Journal* editor William Clapp that summer. "I do not see how any man can watch the effects of the spoils system, both upon the poor unfortunates who suffer from it and upon the almost equally unfortunate men who deem that they benefit by it. . . . It is a curse to the public service and it is a still greater curse to Congress."[128]

On July 10, Harrison summoned the three commissioners to the White House. At first Roosevelt feared the president was going to berate him because of the controversies stirred up during the recent midwestern trip. Harrison, however, made no mention of the trip. He treated the commissioners with chilled cordiality, sitting "like a marble statue" across from his guests with his arms folded across his chest and staring searchingly at them.[129] The following day Roosevelt wrote Lodge that Harrison "did not express the least dissatisfaction with any of our deeds or utterances . . . the old boy is with us, which was rather a relief to learn definitely." In the same letter, however, Theodore suggested that relations with the postmaster general had worsened. "We have done our best to get on smoothly with [Wanamaker]," wrote Theodore, "but he is an ill-conditioned creature."[130]

↝

In many ways, Theodore Roosevelt and John Wanamaker were polar opposites. Roosevelt was a Harvard-educated, Knickerbocker blue blood, an outspoken progressive Republican, but stretched financially. From rugged Pennsylvania Dutch stock, Wanamaker took pride as a self-educated dropout, devout Presbyterian elder, successful Philadelphia merchant, marketing genius, and millionaire. The two men, however, were alike in important ways. Both possessed excellent administrative abilities, inexhaustible energy, confidence, and obstinacy and were headstrongly moralistic. A collision between the two could be thunderous.

Wanamaker was a proud old-guard Republican who boasted he cast his first vote for Abraham Lincoln. He worked loyally with party leadership in every national campaign from 1888 to 1920. Like Roosevelt, Wanamaker detested the disloyalty of the Mugwump Republicans who bolted the party in 1884 to protest Blaine's candidacy.[131] During the presidential campaign of 1888, Wanamaker served as finance chairman for Harrison and raised $400,000, the largest sum up to that time. Wanamaker personally contributed $10,000.[132] He persuaded Republican Party bosses, including Mark Hanna, Tom Platt, and Matthew Quay, to squeeze Wall Street tycoons for huge sums, estimated close to four million dollars, and used the money to buy votes in the key swing states of Indiana and New York. So much money flowed during Harrison's bid that the 1888 election became the "boodle campaign."

During the campaign, Wanamaker organized the business community as a united political force within the Republican Party and helped transform the GOP into its more conservative modern-day counterpart. Using the protective tariff as a weapon, he solicited fellow businessmen for donations that would "fry all the fat out of them."[133] He sent a confidential circular to manufacturers saying that "we want money and we want it quick."[134] Like his innovations in retail merchandising, Wanamaker's political fund-raising techniques broke new ground.

Wanamaker, like Roosevelt, wanted a post in the Harrison administration. In October 1888 the *New York Times* reported that Wanamaker desired to be secretary of the treasury.[135] That winter, Harrison turned to Pennsylvania's Matthew Quay, a powerful member of the Republican Party's inner circle, for help in selecting a cabinet. "Boss" Quay, a cunning character with an eagle's beak of a nose and almond-shaped eyes, was among the country's ablest politicians. Quay was a true believer in the spoils system and once coined the phrase "shaking the plum tree" to refer to the bureaucratic fruits of electoral victory.[136] Describing his fellow Pennsylvanian as "the tower of saving strength," Quay vouched for Wanamaker's character and competence and recommended a cabinet post.[137]

In January, Harrison summoned Wanamaker to Indianapolis where the two met for several hours. Both Presbyterian Sunday school teachers, they took to each other immediately.[138] Harrison first asked the

Philadelphian to become secretary of the navy, but Wanamaker declined because he feared a conflict of interest in awarding shipbuilding contracts to Pennsylvania steel mills.[139] The vice chairman of the Republican National Committee, James S. Clarkson, suggested Harrison appoint Wanamaker as postmaster general. Clarkson, political boss of Iowa and a former editor of the *Iowa State Register,* would serve as Wanamaker's first assistant.[140] Harrison agreed, and in March 1889, two months before Roosevelt arrived at the Civil Service Commission, Wanamaker became postmaster general and the most powerful member of Harrison's cabinet. Wanamaker's appointment angered the civil service reformers, who saw him as another wealthy comrade of the spoilsmen. The *New York Times* was so scathing that the new postmaster general punished the newspaper by withdrawing Post Office Department advertisements of foreign mail departures and banning copies of the *Times* from Philadelphia YMCA reading rooms.[141]

Between 1889 and 1893, Roosevelt and Wanamaker waged almost continuous battle over control of thousands of positions in the postal service. Throughout this period, Roosevelt and the commission attempted to remove corrupt postal officials and replace the traditional spoils system with a process of merit selection. At the same time, Wanamaker, with the passive consent of Harrison, thwarted Roosevelt's efforts by replacing large numbers of postal workers with Republican loyalists.

Wanamaker viewed the patronage question as one demanding the use of common sense and, provided the privilege was not abused, supported the oft-quoted sentiment that the spoils belong to the victor. Nevertheless, for the first few months he followed customary practice and delegated most of the decisions to his efficient first assistant, Clarkson. While he eventually desired to improve the efficiency of the Post Office Department, Wanamaker convinced Harrison that he first must strengthen the Republican Party machinery without demoralizing or destroying it, reward loyal party members with patronage appointments, and avoid the more drastic anti-spoils measures preferred by the civil service reformers.[142] Of all the cabinet officers, the postmaster general had the most powerful patronage stockpile, controlling more than 100,000 postal jobs across the nation.[143] The postmaster general's powerful reach extended to hundreds of cities, towns, and villages and throughout every congressional district. The postal service employed nearly two thirds of the entire federal workforce.[144] Of the postal offices subject to patronage, more than 57,000 were fourth-class postmaster jobs, the most fruitful political plums for rewarding party faithful.[145]

Party bosses spread the patronage even wider, often dividing a position among several employees with each receiving a percentage of the salary.[146] Fourth-class postmasters earned less than $1,000 annually and the vast majority less than $100. Despite the poor compensation, party bosses used these positions to repay thousands of political debts. Under Hayes, 68 percent of the fourth-class postmasters changed hands; under Garfield and Arthur, 72 percent; and during Cleveland's first administration, 76 percent.[147]

Wanamaker's assistant, Clarkson, wasted no time. An unabashed spoilsman and shrewd politician, Clarkson thought civil service reform was "the toy of a child, the trifling thing of hobby riders."[148] When Roosevelt arrived at the commission two months after Harrison's inauguration, Clarkson was removing Democratic postmasters at the rate of one every three minutes.[149] Clarkson served as Washington's busiest spoilsman, answering during his eighteen months in office more than 100,000 letters and giving not less than 15,000 interviews to senators, congressmen, and hordes of political office seekers who "follow him home, and keep him up after midnight."[150] Clarkson resigned after only eighteen months at the Post Office but in that time performed his task with ruthless skill and energy. By November 1889, he and Wanamaker replaced 32,335 fourth-class postmasters with Republicans.[151] Added to this number were at least 500 Democratic postmasters who were asked to submit "voluntary" letters of resignation.[152] By 1891, the Harrison administration replaced 87 percent of its fourth-class postmasters. Civil service reformers were mad as hornets over the Republican actions. The National Civil Service Reform League investigated the removals and laid the blame on the White House. "It is the President, who appointed Wanamaker and Clarkson, and who permitted these things to be," concluded the league's report.[153] *Harper's Weekly* also voiced the reformers' anger, charging that "there never was in our history a grosser violation of distinct promises and pledges than the partisan devastation of the post offices under this administration."[154]

Wanamaker's skill in dispensing the spoils shocked Roosevelt, who feared the pillaging of the postal service demoralized the remaining workers. Shortly after becoming commissioner, Roosevelt asked the postmaster general to slow Clarkson's rampage. Wanamaker ignored him and Roosevelt appealed to the president, who also took no action.[155] Roosevelt, at first loyal to Harrison, assumed the president would make sweeping extensions in the merit civil service, but he became increasingly impatient with Harrison's delay and his acquiescence to Wanamaker. Roosevelt soon realized that the president generally ignored him and that almost every time a dispute arose between the commission and the postmaster general, Harrison sided with Wanamaker.[156] An exasperated Roosevelt complained to Lodge, "Oh, Heaven, if the President had a little backbone, and if the Senators did not have flannel legs!"[157]

↫

Early in the morning of August 6, a few days after chiding the president with his bear parable, Roosevelt left Washington and took the train north to New York. From the city he boarded a local that steamed eastward along Long Island to the village of Oyster Bay. As Roosevelt stepped from the train, he greeted his coachman, Hall, waiting outside the little clapboard station. Leaving the village, the two men crossed the peninsula known as Cove Neck that jutted like a huge thumb, half a mile wide and a mile and a half long, northward into Long Island Sound. Their carriage clattered past rolling pastures still green and lush in the summer heat and skirted along the shore of the bay, its pungent smell of salt marsh reminding Theodore that he neared home.

The carriage swung right, up an old wood road, then sharply to the right again, making short loops up a steep hill that slowed the horses, now sweating in the August heat, to a walk. At the top, a left turn and a hundred yards of straight promenade and finally to the house itself. The house loomed large, roomy, and solid, a colored jumble of red brick, oaken framing, and mustard yellow shingles. Under the peak of the southern gable, the wide antlers of an elk, weathered and gray, proclaimed to any visitor that this was the home of an outdoorsman, a hunter, and a man who cherished the rugged life.[158]

Theodore returned to Sagamore Hill in time to celebrate Edith's twenty-eighth birthday. He had little time, however, to spend with his wife and enjoy his children. Early the next morning he departed Sagamore and headed west for a monthlong hunting trip in the Dakota Territory, arriving at the Elkhorn Ranch near the Little Missouri River on August 10. Spending time in the West always provided a tonic for Roosevelt's health and spirit. "I am now on my way home," he wrote Cabot later that month from Helena, Montana. "By Jupiter I feel well; I have had a hard but a very successful trip . . . and never was in better condition."[159] While in the Montana foothills he made his proudest and most dangerous kill, a large grizzly bear.

By September 19, Roosevelt was back to work as a Washington bureaucrat. He rose at seven, breakfasted at eight, gulped down several cups of strong coffee, and arrived at his City Hall desk by nine to start his day tending to the commission's affairs. Theodore spent his mornings doing correspondence and receiving visitors, often took a long lunch with friends, and returned to the office in time to meet with the other commissioners. The three men reserved the afternoon for their formal meeting, held daily at three o'clock, when they decided upon the numerous personnel issues crossing their desks.[160]

During this period Roosevelt suffered harsh attacks from the press and Congress and from reformers and conservatives alike. Among his more bothersome liberal critics was the editor of the *Nation* and the *New York Evening Post,* E. L. Godkin.[161] Sixtyish, balding, with dark brooding eyes peering behind a full gray beard trimmed neatly to a point at his chin, Godkin emigrated from Ireland to New York in 1856 and quickly gained a reputation as a "hardworking, hardheaded, a trifle hardhearted, and very hardhitting" journalist. Godkin's unsparing attacks on every form of venality, hypocrisy, and corruption in public life made him the most hated and most admired publicist in America.[162]

As early as 1866, Godkin attacked the spoilsmen, labeling them "political eunuchs with not force enough to call their souls their own" and describing the corrupt New York Post Office as nothing more than an ill-managed "large hall for political reunions."[163] Godkin's and Roosevelt's views on civil service reform were not far apart, but the two men feuded bitterly until the editor died in 1902. The animosity began in 1884, when Roosevelt refused to join Godkin and other Mugwumps in opposition to Blaine's campaign for the presidency. It flared again in 1886 when Godkin aggressively fought Theodore's bid for New York mayor, and throughout Theodore's first six years in Washington it continued to burn. At one point Godkin refused to attend any dinner if Roosevelt was present. Meanwhile, Theodore had few kind words for the Irishman, once calling him a "brass rivetted liar."[164] After reading one of Godkin's flagrant editorials in the *Nation,* Theodore erupted. "So foolish, so malignant, so deliberately mendacious and so exultant," Roosevelt wrote to Lodge. "It fairly made me writhe to think of the incalculable harm to decency that scoundrelly paper, edited by its scoundrelly chief, Godkin, has done."[165]

Roosevelt also felt the wrath of the conservative, pro-spoils press. The editor of the *Washington Post,* Frank Hatton, printed a copy of Roosevelt's handwriting while Theodore vacationed in the West, "chasing the antelope over the plains." Hatton, a die-hard spoilsmen, claimed that "Mr. High Joint Civil Surface [*sic*] Reform Commissioner Theodore Roosevelt's" penmanship was so bad that he could not pass the civil service test for clerk typist. Hatton also inquired facetiously if Theodore's "great knowledge of the classics, his ability as a fractionist, his familiarity with metaphysics . . . would make him a fit copyist."[166]

Roosevelt agreed sarcastically and "confessed" he had neither the capability nor the intention of becoming a clerk.[167] If the attack from the *Post* wasn't enough, the *New York Sun* published an anonymous review in late September which charged that Roosevelt used a collaborator to write his latest volume of *The Winning of the West*. "It would have been simply impossible," the reviewer claimed, "for [Roosevelt] to do what he claims to have done in the time that was at his disposal." The reviewer turned out to be James R. Gilmore, a disgruntled historian whose own work had been superseded by *The Winning of the West*. Theodore fired back a long, detailed, and humiliating rebuttal that concluded, "there is a half-pleasurable excitement in facing an equal foe; but there is none whatever in trampling on a weakling."[168]

Congressional opponents also attacked the commission. During Roosevelt's first two years, dashing Kansas senator John Ingalls led the attack.[169] Wirily built, nattily dressed, goateed, and hair parted in the middle, Ingalls spoke eloquently, wrote poetry, and served as a powerful Republican political leader. To Roosevelt and many civil service reformers, Ingalls was "evil incarnate in the Senate chambers."[170] The fidgety, sharp-tongued Ingalls railed at Theodore and his colleagues, accusing them of "tea-custard and syllabub dilettantism and frivolous sentimentalism."[171] Despite Ingalls's prestige, Roosevelt openly labeled him the "mouthpiece" of the spoilsmen and a traitor to his party.[172] The two men skirmished until Ingalls left the Senate in 1891.

On the other side of the aisle, Roosevelt clashed with Maryland senator Arthur Pue Gorman.[173] Cold and urbane, with a clean-shaven, thin-lipped face and steel-gray eyes, Gorman was an imposing political heavyweight, former chairman of the Democratic National Committee, and Cleveland's presidential campaign manager in 1884. In 1883 Gorman absent-mindedly voted in favor of the Pendleton Act, a stance he regretted for the rest of his legislative career.[174] "I am no civil service reformer," Gorman bellowed on the floor of the Senate. "I do not believe in the system [where] hundreds and thousands of men had become barnacles and . . . under the civil service law they could not very well be removed and their places bettered."[175] When Gorman criticized Roosevelt's reform efforts on the Senate floor as "going beyond the bounds of propriety," Theodore ignored the political risks and swiftly counterattacked. "As there was not a word of truth in your allegations it was evident either that you were willfully stating what you knew to be false, or else that you had been grossly deceived," Theodore wrote to the powerful senator. "Your position was not a pleasant one, and it is no pleasanter now."[176]

At the same time, other legislators joined in the attack upon Roosevelt and the commission. Congressmen Henry Blair of New Hampshire cursed civil service reform as "humbug," Joe Cannon of Illinois, "an infernal nuisance," Thomas Browne of Indiana, "a cumbersome piece of political patchwork," and Bishop Perkins of Kansas, "a farce."[177] Roosevelt struck back hard at any legislator opposing civil service reform, thinly disguising his contempt for congressmen who "from the standpoint of pure intellect I should never be surprised to see . . . develop tails and swing from a bough."[178]

On October 10, Roosevelt received a telegram from Oyster Bay saying that Edith had gone into labor and given premature birth to their second son, christened Kermit. Theodore, both elated and concerned for his wife's health, took the first train north, arriving in New York City in the middle of the night. Arriving late at the East Thirty-fourth Street ferry and discovering that the next train to Oyster Bay would not depart until the next day, the impatient Roosevelt hired a private train for the last leg of his journey. Finally arriving at Sagamore Hill at four the next morning, he found Edith and the baby in good health, although his wife scolded him for wasting their money to hire the special train.

After spending two weeks with Edith and the children, now numbering three in his growing family, Roosevelt returned to Washington. For the rest of the year he continued to battle with Wanamaker, who was dispensing the last of the 32,000 fourth-class postmaster positions to Republican Party workers. With few successes in halting the widespread abuses of spoils appointments, Theodore confessed that the future of the commission and a merit-based civil service was uncertain. That winter he traveled to Boston to speak to the Massachusetts Civil Service Reform Association. "We are in serious jeopardy," Theodore warned the audience. "The law may be nullified; but woe to those who do it."[179]

2
1890
Attacked from All Quarters

WASHINGTONIANS AWOKE to a miserable winter morning on New Year's Day 1890. The temperature hovered just above freezing, and a cold drizzle seeped from the lowering gray overcast. The gloomy weather, however, failed to dampen the spirits of Theodore and Edith Roosevelt. Bundled warmly in their carriage, they rode along the glistening pavement of Connecticut Avenue and headed south toward the center of the city. The Roosevelts were excited, on their way to their first reception at the White House. Arriving shortly before eleven, they jostled their way through the crowd shivering in the rain. Theodore found their place near the end of the long line of top-hatted legislators, cabinet members, plumed diplomats, military officers, and fur-draped ladies. As a civil service commissioner, Roosevelt followed the strict protocol of Washington rank, trailing just behind the secretary of the Smithsonian, his friend Professor Samuel Langley, and just in front of members of the Interstate Commerce Commission.[1]

When the doors to the White House opened, the long line of dignitaries snaked through the East Room, where lush foliage plants decorated the mantels and tropical palms bordered the walls, while a scattering of scarlet poinsettias and pink azaleas cast a holiday brilliance about the room. Beneath the great sparkling chandeliers, each entwined with verdant smilax, stood the scarlet-coated Marine Band, conducted by John Philip Sousa,[2] which serenaded the guests with a medley of military marches. President Harrison, a short, square-faced man with cold, steel-blue eyes and a full sandy beard, stood alone in the nearby Blue Room greeting his visitors. Edith was disappointed at not meeting the president's wife, Carrie, who was in mourning over a relative's death.[3]

Despite his lowly rank in the Washington protocol, Theodore was already becoming a celebrity. "Mr. Roosevelt could hardly proceed to the Blue Room from the frequent delays caused by the friends he met on the way, who wanted to shake hands with him," reported a local newspaperman. The journalist, from a newspaper skeptical of reform, also remarked that "as the representatives of a crippled [civil service] reform entered the doorway of the Blue Room, the air played by the Marines became very plaintive, resembling a dirge. But no one got a heartier reception than the three commissioners. Mr. Roosevelt [is] being very demonstrative in his protestations of good wishes to the President for the coming year."[4]

The White House reception lasted only an hour, ending at noon when the mansion's doors opened to the public. For the Roosevelts and other official guests, the festivities had just begun. They spent the remainder of the day braving the cold drizzle and attending dozens of receptions hosted by foreign embassies and cabinet officers. At the top of their list were the receptions held at the British legation with its huge crystal-chandeliered ballroom, on Connecticut Avenue, and at Secretary of State Blaine's lavish new mansion on Massachusetts Avenue. They also could not miss the reception given by Roosevelt's friend, Speaker of the House Tom Reed, at his handsome apartments in the Shoreham Hotel.[5]

For Washington's elite, New Year's Day heralded the beginning of the capital's social season with its cluttered calendar of balls, receptions, and teas. Newcomers were dazzled with the social scene, prompting one visiting journalist to remark, "Washington in the winter is the gayest of the gay."[6] To Edith's delight, the highlight of the month was attending a sumptuous banquet held for twenty-eight guests at Vice President Levi Morton's home on Rhode Island Avenue. Once the home of Thomas Alva Edison, the Morton mansion vaunted a magnificent carved staircase and a grand salon graced with gilt French mirrors.[7]

For Theodore, January 1890 was a hectic month. His family now joined him in Washington, and many loose ends remained untied after the move. During his previous six months as commissioner, Edith and the children stayed at Sagamore Hill, but shortly after Christmas 1889 Theodore moved the family to Washington. Edith no longer allowed him to live alone. While opening a second household in Washington strained the family budget, Edith tired of her husband's long absences and insisted that the family be together. The previous fall, Theodore moved into a small house he rented at 1820 Jefferson Place in northwest Washington, just off Connecticut Avenue and within walking distance of the White House. When his sister Anna visited their cramped home, she had to sleep on a couch in Theodore's dressing room. The house, "with barely enough room for everybody when all the chinks were filled," bordered Rock Creek, a rugged park where Theodore began a Sunday ritual of leading family and friends on his point-to-point "scrambles" through the jagged gorge. Theodore made up the rules for the scrambles, which allowed fellow hikers to only go over, under, or through, but never around, the obstacles encountered. Roosevelt delighted in dragging his foreign diplomat friends through mud holes and briar patches, wading through ponds with green scum on top, climbing "the Crack," a sloping fissure in the vertical wall of a quarry on the west bank, squirming up "the chimney," two vertical rocks that hikers climbed with "an undulating and serpentlike movement," or crossing the "seal's walk," a stone ledge overhanging the river, which hikers nervously crossed by crawling on their stomachs and "moving as seals do."[8]

Theodore and Edith enjoyed the busy social season during their first winter in Washington, often going out five times a week. "Our evenings have been fairly occupied," Theodore wrote to Anna in January. "One night we dined at Cabot's to meet the Willy Endicotts; another night I gave a dinner to some historical friends. Last night we went to the theater, and supper afterwards with John Hay. It was to see 'The Senator' which was killingly funny. . . . Edith enjoyed it as much as I did."[9]

Edith's arrival pleased Theodore. Throughout their marriage, the strong-willed Edith exerted considerable influence on Roosevelt and his career. Edith, an attractive woman with lustrous auburn hair and bright, piercing blue eyes, appears to have been the perfect match for Theodore. Like his older sister, Anna, Edith was savvy in politics and provided a stable force on the sometimes volatile Theodore. He was outspoken and sometimes recklessly brash while his wife appeared clear-eyed, restrained, and wary.[10] On one hand, Edith was kind, considerate, and tactful, while on the other she seemed shrewd, calculating, and even ruthless. Well read and an authority on Shakespeare, fluent in French, she matched her husband's intellectual appetite.[11] At Sagamore Hill, Edith spent her mornings in her first-floor drawing room doing correspondence and overseeing the family's business and finances, or sometimes worked upstairs with her faithful old nanny, Mame, sewing clothes for the children. In the afternoons, however, she read vora-

ciously, needing books "as she needed air and food." When her husband was home the two went hiking in the nearby woods, rowing on
the Sound, or riding through the surrounding pastures on their favorite
horses, Diamond and Pickle.[12]

Most important, Theodore and Edith loved each other totally and devotedly. She stood by him in his darkest hours, including his disastrous
third-party bid for reelection in 1912. Edith disliked public appearances
and during Theodore's lifetime stayed out of the political limelight.
Years after his death, however, Edith emerged in 1932 in a rare appearance at the Republican Convention to endorse Herbert Hoover, much
to the enmity of the distant Roosevelt cousins, whose Franklin ran as a
Democrat.[13] Outliving her husband by twenty-nine years, Edith died
in 1948.

Edith and Theodore knew each other since childhood. During the
Roosevelt children's early years, Edith was one of very few nonfamily
friends and their closest companion. She grew up in a house on Livingstone Place, a few blocks from Roosevelt's Manhattan home. Edith was
the same age as Theodore's younger sister, Corinne, and their mothers
wheeled the two girls side by side in baby carriages around the park at
Union Square.[14] As ten-year-olds the girls attended Miss Comstock's
School on West Fortieth Street, and Edith vacationed frequently with
the Roosevelts.[15]

Young Theodore's attachment to Edith appears early. While the Roosevelts toured Europe in November 1869, eleven-year-old Theodore
mentions "Eideth," writing to her after climbing a snow-capped Mt.
Vesuvius and signing the letter, "Ever your loving friend, T. Roosevelt."
He missed her, recording in his diary in Paris that "In the evening
mama showed me the portrait of Eidieth Carow and her face stired [sic]
up in me homesickness and longings for the past which will come again
never, alack, never." His attention to Edith continued during his first
years at Harvard. In a letter to Corinne in June 1877 he mentioned that
during a recent visit "I do'nt [sic] think Edith looked prettier" and instructed his sister that "when you write to Edith tell her that I enjoyed
her visit *very* much."[16] During a summer at Oyster Bay, Theodore named
his rowboat after Edith.[17] Throughout his life, Theodore hated the more
sedentary sport of sailing but loved rowing, and a twenty-mile paddle
was not unusual. Rowing also provided solitude for husband and wife
when late in the afternoon he rowed Edith across the glassy waters of
Oyster Bay, where the couple took the opportunity to talk alone in the
light rowing skiff, to read poetry of Browning, prose of Thackeray, or
discuss the latest literary vogue, but mostly to enjoy the glory of sunset

and some time away from the maelstrom of their boisterous children, left ashore to run "like sand pipers along the beach."[18]

While they were at Harvard, relations between Theodore and Edith strained. He referred to Edith as "her Ladyship" and later asked Corinne to "give my love to Edith—if she's in a good humour; otherwise my respectful regards. If she seems *particularly* good tempered tell her that I hope that when I see her at Christmas it will not be on what you might call her off days." It appears he had a fight with Edith in August 1878 and the romance ended.[19]

They rekindled the romance seven years later. Theodore, widowed when his first wife died in 1884, visited his sister Anna at her home in New York City in August 1885. By chance, Theodore and Edith met in Anna's hallway as she was leaving.[20] Because the prevailing romantic code demanded that a widower never remarry, the two conducted their three-month courtship in secret. Theodore proposed on November 17, 1885, and the couple sealed their engagement with a ring and a watch.[21] The following April, Edith sailed to Europe with her mother on an extended vacation and remained there until the wedding. On November 6, 1886, four days after losing the election for mayor of New York, Roosevelt and Anna departed for England on the steamer *Etruria*. On December 2, a London day so thick with fog that Anna could barely see her way from her hotel to St. George's Church on Hanover Square, Theodore married his childhood sweetheart Edith Carow.[22] Edith's sister, Emily, served as bridesmaid, while Cecil Spring-Rice, a young British diplomat whom Roosevelt met on his voyage to England, stood as best man. The newlyweds spent fifteen weeks in Europe, touring Florence, Milan, and Sorrento. For the bookwormish Edith, the highlight of the tour took place during their final days in London, when the couple arranged a meeting with the renowned poet Robert Browning. Edith, since her youth a devoted fan of the aging poet, was overwhelmed. The couple returned to New York City in March 1887.[23]

The Roosevelts settled into their home, Sagamore Hill, a large half-brick, half-frame home overlooking the protected harbor of Oyster Bay on the north shore of Long Island. There, Roosevelt devoted his time to Edith and three-year-old Alice, Theodore's daughter from his first marriage. Finished two years before, their new home stood large but was not a mansion of the time. Of its twenty-three rooms, twelve served as bedrooms.[24] Throughout the house, shaggy animal skins were scattered across the floors and game heads of elk and bison and other beasts stared silently down from the walls, each a trophy of Theodore's annual journey to the West. On the first floor, next to the main entrance,

Theodore had an office where he wrote and conducted his correspondence. Across the hall was Edith's hideaway, a simply furnished parlor where she managed the family's business. The gun room, nestled in a third-floor garret, "which incidentally has the loveliest view of all," was Roosevelt's retreat and the place where he wrote many of his books. Theodore cherished Sagamore, where he came the closest to unwinding and slowing his frenzied pace.[25] The summers were especially refreshing, when he soaked up the smells of hot pine woods and sweet ferns in the scorching noon sun, of newly mowed hay, plowed earth, of stables, barns, and cow yards, and of salt water and low tide on the marshes surrounding Oyster Bay.

In that house overlooking the Sound, on September 13, 1887, just after two in the morning, Edith gave birth to their first son, Ted, "a fine little fellow about 8 1/2 pounds."[26] Roosevelt spent much of 1888 writing, and during that year he published *Ranch Life and the Hunting Trail* and the biography *Gouverneur Morris*. While writing filled Roosevelt's days, it did not fill his passion for the political limelight. Soon he stepped back upon the national stage, campaigning for Harrison in 1888 and accepting the appointment as civil service commissioner.

⌐

Back at his City Hall desk in January 1890, Commissioner Roosevelt had more on his mind than the festivities of the Washington social season. His job was in jeopardy. The Midwest inspection tour during the previous summer, while hailed by Roosevelt and the reform newspapers as a blow to the spoilsmen, created one of Roosevelt's more serious embarrassments and probably came closest to causing Harrison to fire him. To obtain damaging evidence against Postmaster George Paul, Roosevelt enlisted the help of Hamilton Shidy, a postal supervisor and secretary of the Milwaukee Civil Service Board. Shidy testified that Paul ordered the alteration of eligibility lists and the re-marking of examinations to ensure that their party members were hired. In early July, Roosevelt, back at Oyster Bay, learned that Postmaster Paul fired Shidy in retaliation. Having earlier promised Shidy protection if he testified, Theodore appealed to Wanamaker, who refused to intervene.[27] Returning to Washington amidst the stifling summer heat, Roosevelt persuaded Shidy to come to Washington and take the civil service examination, and later convinced the superintendent of the census to find a place for Shidy in the Census Bureau.[28]

Near the end of July, the *Washington Post*'s Frank Hatton began a vicious attack on Roosevelt and the commission. Hatton was a skillful politician, an outspoken critic of civil service reform, and a tough match for Roosevelt. After serving as a young officer in the Civil War, Hatton returned to Iowa, where he built the *Burlington Hawk Eye* into one of the most influential Republican organs in the Midwest. In 1881 his support for President Arthur garnered Hatton an appointment as assistant postmaster general and, for a short time, postmaster general. While still serving at the Post Office, Hatton took over the *Washington Post.* According to his critics, Hatton used the power of the Post Office Department to increase the newspaper's circulation, while at the same time he used the *Post* to attack civil service reform efforts in the Post Office and other federal departments.[29] A decade later, Hatton was still at the *Post* and pummeling civil service reform and Commissioner Roosevelt. He accused "the Fifth Avenue sport" of personally allowing violations of the civil service law and squandering large sums of federal money. Roosevelt retaliated in the *Baltimore Sun* and accused a "certain Cabinet officer" of blocking reform efforts.[30]

In October, amidst the overpowering sweetness and beauty of the Long Island autumn, Theodore spent two weeks with his wife after their son Kermit's birth. While at Sagamore, Roosevelt learned that the Milwaukee controversy heated up again in Washington. Hatton announced that Roosevelt used the spoils system he supposedly fought to secure the Census Bureau position for Shidy, the Milwaukee informer. Hatton called for a House investigation and the removal of "this pampered pink of inherited wealth." When Congress returned after the new year, Hatton's almost daily attacks on the commission produced results. On January 27, 1890, the House ordered an investigation of Roosevelt and the commission and appointed Representative Hamilton Ewart of North Carolina, an outspoken opponent of civil service reform, to lead the investigation, with Hatton, that "blackguard spoilsman," to assist him.[31]

On the evening of February 19, the House committee began its investigation in a large, poorly ventilated room in the lower basement of the Capitol.[32] Congressman Herman Lehlbach, a New Jersey Republican, sat at one end of the long council table and chaired the meeting, but Ewart and Hatton controlled the proceedings as chief prosecutors. Hatton's intention to attack Roosevelt was clear from the start, as he labeled Theodore's investigation an "underhand attempt to harass the administration."[33] For the next two months, the committee heard testimony from a score of witnesses, including a befuddled Shidy and an obstinate Wanamaker. For Hatton, the hearings provided a tempting opportunity to attack Roosevelt and the commission. The committee examined Roosevelt for several hours and, according to the pro-spoils *Post*, "made him squirm" and prompted Theodore to "give all sorts of excuses and indirect replies." Near the end of the hearings, Roosevelt began "to look worn and haggard under the strain of the charges . . . his buoyancy seems to have been crushed out of him by the weight of a great burden."[34]

After Shidy testified on February 28 that Roosevelt had arranged his job in the Census Office, Hatton struck with huge front-page headlines:

Roosevelt's Man Shidy

Dr. Jekyll and Mr. Hyde
Impersonated by the Reformers

One Committed Many Criminal Offenses

The Wise Commission Rewarded the
Villainy with a Place in the Census Bureau

Shidy Proves to be Both a Scoundrel and a Fool

Roosevelt Knowing His Infamous Character,
Forced Him into an Important Position

The Most Shameful Testimony Ever Offered

Even Roosevelt Hung His Head in Shame

"It was not a good day for the civil service reformers," reported the *Post*. By the end of Shidy's five hours of embarrassing testimony, Theodore was furious. "I do not care to talk to you anymore," Roosevelt growled at Shidy when he departed. "You have cut your own throat."[35]

The next day a bloodied Theodore fought back. Gesturing wildly to the committee members, Roosevelt launched a ceaseless barrage of high-pitched argument. Soon he dominated the hearings and turned the proceedings into grand theater. Theodore pounced on hostile witnesses mercilessly, including Wanamaker and ex-postmaster Paul, "helpless as a trussed turkey" when brought from Milwaukee for three days of testimony. Theodore argued that the investigation was "the most rancorous and mendacious—albeit singularly unintelligent—malevolence" and had failed to uncover one single fault with the commission.[36] By March 7, Roosevelt had worn everyone out and the committee adjourned. The House delayed issuing its report until June 1890, when it declared that "the public service has been greatly benefitted, and the law, on the whole, well executed" and that Commissioner Roosevelt had executed his duties "with entire fidelity and integrity."[37] Roosevelt was both surprised and elated at his exoneration.

ᔕ

While Congress investigated the Shidy incident, Roosevelt scampered the few blocks from the commission offices to the recently completed Library of Congress. There, among "a riot of rare material and rich ornament,"[38] he would dive into a pile of musty old books and documents. Earlier in the year he had agreed to write a history of New York City, and now his publisher pressured him to meet a summer deadline. Roosevelt used what little spare time he had to research the book. After some anguish, he completed the manuscript at the end of July.

For Theodore, writing was much more than an intellectual pastime. He feared that the civil service posting was a dead end to his political career, and his stormy relationship with the Harrison administration meant that he could be fired at any time. If he became unemployed, Theodore realized, he would need to write full-time to support his family.

Earlier that year, Roosevelt confessed to George Putnam that his commission duties and writing projects often conflicted. "My great work to which I intend steadily to devote myself is the *Winning of the West,*" wrote Theodore. "I half wish I was out of this Civil Service Commission work, for I can't do satisfactorily with the *Winning of the West* until I am; but I suppose I really ought to stand by it for at least a couple of years."[39] Despite the difficulty in balancing his writing and his official duties, Roosevelt pressed on in his fight for civil service reform.

As he worked to create a professional, merit-based civil service, Theodore received an abrupt and thorough education in the problems of managing a government bureaucracy.[40] He continued to face many imposing political and administrative challenges and soon learned the frustrations of government service. The future of the Civil Service Commission was by no means certain during the early years. New and controversial, the commission confronted a host of enemies, including powerful politicians who favored its elimination. Between 1888 and 1898, Congress carried out a series of critical investigations of the commission's efforts. On several occasions, patronage-bent legislators attempted to repeal the Pendleton Act, abolish the commission, deny funding for its operation, weaken the merit system by placing a fixed term of employment on all government workers, or strip the commission of its authority to administer examinations and return to personnel systems managed by individual agencies.[41] The first serious attempt at repeal took place in 1884, only a year after the Pendleton Act's passage, when Democratic congressmen J. F. Clay of Kentucky and Aaron Shaw of Illinois introduced legislation to abolish the commission. They argued the Pendleton Act was "tomfoolery," "a perfect farce," and "contrary to the spirit of our institutions."[42] Their attempt failed. The wrath of the spoilsmen spread to Senator George H. Pendleton, who sponsored the civil service legislation that carries his name. His support of civil service reform angered so many of his fellow Democrats that they urged his ouster from Congress. In January 1884 the Ohio legislature voted Pendleton out of office and replaced him with a die-hard spoilsman. President Cleveland later appointed Pendleton minister to Germany.

On several occasions opponents attempted to kill civil service reform by withholding funds from the commission. During Roosevelt's tenure, the most serious attempt to abolish the commission occurred during a House Committee of the Whole session when "Democratic wild horses took the bits in their teeth" and adopted an amendment to strike out the commission's entire appropriation. The *Washington Evening Star* labeled the attempt a "cowardly murder." The amendment passed by a vote of 109 to 71, but two days later cooler heads prevailed and, behind the leadership of Lodge and Reed, the House reversed its decision and appropriated the commission funds.[43]

Nevertheless, the commission continually needed both greater authority and more personnel to manage a growing civil service. The size of the government workforce was exploding. In 1859, just over twelve hundred government employees worked in Washington; by the turn of the century the number had grown to more than twenty-five thousand.[44] When Roosevelt arrived in 1889, the commission employed only three clerks to oversee the growing workforce, relying upon other agencies, over which it had no direct control, for most of its personnel. Often, "the tendency of the departments was to detail the deadwood to us."[45] Throughout Roosevelt's tenure at the commission there seems to have been too much work to do and too few clerks to do it. In June 1893 the commissioners complained to the president of being overworked and understaffed. "The public service of the country is not to be regarded as an asylum," Roosevelt and fellow commissioner George Johnston wrote to Cleveland. In the eleven-page letter the two commissioners complained that their clerks were five thousand examination papers behind. Of the twenty-two men detailed to the commission by other agencies, "only twelve are competent. . . . [T]he other ten are inferior clerks who are charged with the responsibility of marking examination papers when they themselves could not pass a creditable examination."[46]

Another pressing problem was inadequate funding for the commission and its staff. Invariably, "its larder was bare."[47] A letter from Roosevelt to the editor of the *American Architect* in May 1891 illustrates the financial straits:

> Sir:
> The Commission tenders the inclosed notice of examination for draftsman for publication, but has no means for paying for its publication, and neither such tender nor this letter must be regarded as in any sense creating a liability on the part of any one to pay for inserting the notice. It is simply hoped that you will regard it as an act of justice to those who wish to be examined for the public service to give them, as far as practicable, the information needed for that purpose, . . . Very respectfully, Theodore Roosevelt.[48]

Congressional opponents of the commission attempted to strangle reform by withholding funds. A hostile Congress easily could starve the commission into extinction, as was done to the first Civil Service Commission in 1875 during Grant's administration. On January 13, 1890, Roosevelt described the difficulties to Charles Collins. "Our present clerical force is wholly insufficient to do the work entrusted to us. If Congress is against the law and wishes to repeal it, well and good; but surely if we are to execute it we ought to be given the means wherewith to do it," wrote Theodore. "We are now three months behind in our work and we are falling steadily more behind every week. . . . In a very short while, if our present stinted means are not increased, we will be unable to meet the demands made upon us by the different governmental offices; and as the government can only get clerks through us, it will be seriously hampered in its work."[49]

Despite the obstacles, Roosevelt and the other commissioners found ways to make progress with Congress. On occasion the commission convinced recalcitrant legislators, especially those who threatened to withhold commission funds, to cooperate by refusing to hold examinations in their districts.[50] When voters complained that their local examinations had been canceled, legislators often yielded to voter demands, reversed their stance, and reluctantly supported the commission.

ᔆ

On a chilly Sunday evening in December 1877, after the rest of his family had gone to bed, Theodore Roosevelt's father relaxed in his small study in the family's town house on Manhattan's Fifty-seventh Street. Earlier in the day he had been visited by his artist friend Albert Bierstadt, who described his paintings of the buffalo during his latest trip to the West.[51] Now alone, Roosevelt's father sat at his desk and wrote his son. Theodore, then a student at Harvard, had yet to experience politics, and the elder Roosevelt, who had just lost an important political battle due to the viciousness of the spoils system, warned his son of a government that was tragically flawed. "I feel sorry for the country, however, as it shows the power of the partisan politicians who think of nothing higher than their own interests," the elder Roosevelt wrote young Theodore. "I fear for your future. We cannot stand so corrupt a government for any great length of time."[52]

In his efforts to uphold the civil service law, Theodore Roosevelt remained steadfastly honest and fair and could not fathom being otherwise. Undoubtedly, he inherited his exceptional moral values from his father, "the best man I ever knew."[53] Roosevelt's father, also named Theodore and called Thee by family and friends, was among New York's most prominent citizens and a man who "walked these streets the image and figure of the citizen which every American should hope to be."[54] Handsome, powerful, with a bearded lionlike face, Thee distinguished himself as a philanthropist and humanitarian. Vigorous and courageous yet tender, gentle, and unselfish, he befriended everyone he met, for "among them were bankers and newsboys, ambassadors and down-and-outers, society folks who rode to hounds and little Italians who went to Miss Slattery's night school."[55] Nicknamed Greatheart by an adoring sister-in-law, he cared for his fellow man with "a heart filled with gentleness," especially toward children.[56] Always immaculately dressed, Thee helped countless persons and charities in need, ranging from homeless newspaper boys to stray kittens that he sometimes carried home in his coat pockets.[57]

Thee Roosevelt was a sixth-generation member of one of New York's oldest and wealthiest Dutch families. His ancestors arrived in Manhattan in 1644, and many descendants still lived and worked in the city.

His father, Cornelius Van Schaack Roosevelt, lived six blocks away on Union Square. Known as CVS, the elder Roosevelt founded the Chemical Bank and headed the family business, Roosevelt and Son, a plate glass importing firm that had traded on Manhattan's Maiden Lane since 1797. When CVS died in 1871, he left his children and their families independently wealthy. Although Thee remained a partner in the family firm, he showed little interest in business. Instead, he devoted much of his time to his wife and children and traveled with them frequently. Said to handle a four-in-hand team of horses better than any other New Yorker, Thee always seemed to find time to play with the children, teaching them to ride horses and climb trees. Besides his family, he loved his intense philanthropic work. He sponsored the Children's Aid Society and the New York Orthopedic Hospital and spent every Sunday evening caring for waifs at the Newsboys' Lodging House. Alongside other members of New York's aristocracy, he helped promote New York's impressive system of parks and museums. On an April evening in 1869, Thee and other philanthropists met in the front parlor of Roosevelt's brownstone and approved the original charter of the Museum of Natural History. Thee donated the land upon which the huge museum stands at Seventy-ninth Street and Central Park West.[58]

For the vast majority of Americans of the era, the Civil War became the most significant event of their lifetime. The Roosevelt family was no exception. The war was equally painful for the elder Theodore, who was twenty-nine at the beginning of the war and physically fit to serve, but for a variety of reasons did not join the Union army. Foremost was his obligation to a wife and four small children. Mittie may have used her own delicate health to persuade her husband not to go to war, and the thought of Thee fighting against his wife's Confederate brothers seemed inconceivable.[59] Also, Thee possessed a strong strain of pacifism inherited from his Quaker mother. Before secession, he urged that war be avoided at all costs, personally appealing to Congress and organizing a huge antiwar rally in the city. Eventually, Thee paid a thousand dollars for a young German immigrant to serve for him in the army, a common and legal practice of the wealthy of the time.[60] Still, wanting to contribute to the Union cause, Thee turned to what he did best, providing humanitarian assistance to those in need. In his charity work he observed that many families were destitute since their breadwinning fathers and brothers were at war and unable to provide support. Thee became the driving force in establishing the Allotment Commission, a new institution created to assist soldiers in sending part of their pay back to their families. He received no pay for his work and spent nearly two years away from home, riding from camp to camp to interview soldiers. At Fredericksburg, Thee witnessed the slaughter of thousands of Union soldiers and took charge of the evacuation of many of the wounded. Later in the war he was injured in a railroad accident, and he nearly died of typhoid fever. According to a friend, Thee toiled tirelessly during his years with the Allotment Commission, "on the saddle often six to eight hours a day, standing in the cold and mud as long, addressing the men and entering their names."[61]

The Civil War left a lasting impression on young Theodore, spellbound by victorious Union troops marching through New York. On April 24, 1865, shortly after the war, two small boys, Theodore and his younger brother, Elliott, stood in the window of their grandfather's house at Union Square watching Abraham Lincoln's funeral procession passing down Broadway. To Theodore the Civil War provided a glamorized vision of warfare, a vision that deepened into the warrior spirit he embodied as an adult. As a youth he acquired much of his romanticized versions of the past from his remarkable mother. Martha Bulloch Roosevelt,[62] or Mittie to her family, was born into wealth and southern aristocracy and raised on a slave-holding plantation twenty miles north of Atlanta. In 1853 she married Thee in the dining room of her plantation home, Bulloch Hall, in a wedding so splendid that ice had to be shipped from Atlanta to make ice cream for the guests. Although Mittie moved north soon after her marriage, she remained southern in spirit. Supposedly a Dixie banner hung outside her bedroom window during a New York antislavery demonstration.[63] A petite, raven-haired beauty, Theodore's spirited mother gave him a sense of adventure and a love for the arts and letters. Mittie displayed creativity and grace, had a talent for music and poetry, and quoted Dickens and Shakespeare. Somewhat eccentric, she always arrived late and never seemed to be concerned with time, quite unlike her husband, who followed rigid Dutch punctuality. As a widow, Mittie defied the Victorian dress code and always wore white.

Mittie kept her children enthralled with her stories of the antebellum South. She captivated young Theodore with Civil War stories of her brother James, an admiral in the Confederate navy. Early in the war "Uncle Jimmy" sailed to England, where he masterminded the construction of Confederate commerce raiders, including the notorious *Florida* and *Alabama*. Mittie's brother Irvine also became a Confederate naval officer and served on the *Alabama* and later on another raider, the *Shenandoah*. Because neither uncle received amnesty after the war, both exiled themselves to Liverpool, England, where they spent the rest of their lives raising families and becoming wealthy cotton merchants.[64]

The Civil War left another lasting, but more negative, memory. Theodore regretted that his father did not take up arms and join the fight. Somehow, the younger Roosevelt never understood that Thee's humanitarian work probably provided much more benefit to the Union cause than his serving in uniform would have.

⌒

While Theodore was at Harvard, his father became active in politics. Thee always supported reform causes but refrained from actual political involvement. This changed in 1876, when he helped organize the Republican Reform Club, which demanded an end to corruption in city government. A number of distinguished citizens joined, including Henry Adams, Frederick Law Olmstead, William Graham Sumner, William Cullen Bryant, Peter Cooper, and a young Henry Cabot Lodge.[65] Also in 1876, Thee served as a delegate to the Republican convention in Cincinnati. Disappointed with the scandal-ridden Grant administration and particularly the New York machine politics of Senator Roscoe Conkling, Thee allied himself with the reform wing of the party, which included Carl Schurz, William Evarts, and George William Curtis. In a four-man presidential race, Thee supported Benjamin Bristow of Kentucky and vehemently opposed the nominations of Conkling and party favorite James G. Blaine. Although his candidate failed, Thee promoted the nomination and subsequent election of the dark-horse governor of Ohio, Rutherford Hayes.

After Hayes's inauguration in March 1877, Thee and the new president met in New York and forged a friendship. Later, Hayes nominated Thee as collector of customs in New York and created a heated battle over patronage and civil service reform. Months before, Hayes ordered an investigation of the customshouse which revealed that it served as a refuge for political workers and a power center for the dispensing of spoils. The customshouse was notoriously corrupt. During Jackson's administration, Collector Samuel Swartrout sailed off to Europe with a million dollars of federal collections in his satchel, and for many years the term "swartrouting" meant embezzlement.[66] A more recent investigation by Hayes's administration found hundreds on the customs payroll who gave no services to the government, inefficiency and competence running rampant, bribery and smuggling prevalent, and illegal fees routinely extracted from merchant shippers.[67]

By nominating Thee to clean up the customshouse, Hayes touched off a political firestorm. The nomination directly challenged the influence of Conkling, a powerful politician in Congress who dominated the New York City machine and patronage politics. Conkling's lieutenant, Chester Arthur, served as his handpicked collector of customs. Conkling viewed Hayes's attempt to replace Arthur as a personal attack on his prestige as well as an intrusion by the president into decisions traditionally reserved for the Senate. The New York collectorship, the most lucrative and politically powerful post in the nation, controlled over a thousand political appointments. Due to the moiety system, whereby the collector received a percentage of the fines and fees amassed, the post provided an annual salary several times more than the president's and equal to a half million of today's dollars.

Thee, to the delight of his reform colleagues, announced that he would accept the customshouse appointment without pay. At Harvard, Theodore had shown little interest in politics but knew of his father's political controversy, writing Anna on October 14, 1877, to "Tell Father I am watching the 'Controllership' movements with the greatest interest." On November 9 he confessed that he followed the developments more closely but was not optimistic. "At present it looks as if father would not get the collectorship," Theodore wrote Anna. "I am glad on his account, but sorry for New York."[68] To his father on December 8, Theodore wrote, "I am very much afraid that Conkling has won the day."[69] The customshouse controversy created a bitter fight that tested the powers of the president and the Senate. The Senate prevailed on December 12 in closed session, voting 31–25 to reject Thee's nomination.

During the final weeks of the fight over the New York collectorship, Thee fought another battle, this one more personal and deadly. He suffered severe intestinal pains which, unknown at the time, proved to be stomach cancer. Two weeks after the Senate rejected his customshouse nomination, the American Museum of Natural History held its grand opening, but Thee's failing health prevented him from attending an event that for eight years he worked to make happen.[70] In two months, Thee neared death. Word of his illness quickly spread through the city, with family and friends converging on the Roosevelt home and a somber crowd of ragged newsboys and orphans gathering on the steps to await news about the man who had done so much for them.[71] On February 9, 1878, Thee Roosevelt died at the age of forty-six.

The death devastated the Roosevelt family, especially Thee's younger son, Elliott, who tried desperately to ease his father's pain. The family kept many of the details of the last agonizing days from Theodore, then in his second year at Harvard. He knew his father was ill, recording in his diary on December 21, 1877, that he was "suddenly called on to New York. Dear Father very sick." But two days later he writes, "Father very much better,"[72] and after Christmas he returned to Harvard assuming that Thee was recovering. Summoned to New York at the last minute, he arrived shortly after his father passed away. A shocked Theodore later recounted that those "last days seem like a hideous dream"[73] and mourned "the blackest day of my life."[74]

It is likely that young Roosevelt linked his father's premature death to the customshouse defeat. Thee's nomination was Theodore's first experience with politics and also a very personal and tragic introduction to the harshness of the political machine and the spoils system. To Theodore, corrupt politics not only won the battle unfairly but helped destroy the most important man in his life. With almost the last words from his father being a protest against corruption in government, Thee's death likely contributed to the conviction and persistence with which young Theodore thereafter pursued the cause of civil service reform.[75]

Young Theodore returned to Harvard and, despite fits of depression over the loss of his father, threw himself into his studies with renewed energy and a new sense of independence. For the rest of his life Theodore questioned whether he lived up to his father's image. Success in his Harvard studies became just one of many ways he would measure himself. From his father, the young man inherited a passion for reform and uncompromising values of devotion to honesty, fairness, industriousness, and the betterment of mankind. Both Theodores hated idleness, and like his father, the younger Theodore became a loving and caring father and, despite imposing public duties throughout his life, always found time to romp with his children.

⏝

Desolate and dangerous, the Dakota Badlands earn their name. To one observer, the foreboding landscape is "like the work of an evil child."[76] On the edge of this inhospitable wilderness stood Theodore Roosevelt's ramshackle ranch house, perched on the brink of a low bluff overlooking the broad, shallow bed of the Little Missouri River, which, after a recent freshet, surged past in a foaming, muddy torrent. From the house, the river twisted down in long curves between narrow bottoms bordered by sheer cliff walls and meandered into the Badlands, a chaos of peaks, plateaus, and ridges that rose abruptly from the edges of the level, tree-clad, or grassy meadows. There were no neighbors for ten or fifteen miles on either side of the ranch. On the front of the one-story, rambling ranch house of rough-hewn logs stretched a long veranda that looked out upon a row of cottonwood trees with gray-green leaves that "quivered all day long if there was a breath of air." At night the ranchers could sit on the veranda and "hear the far-away, melancholy cooing of mourning doves, while little owls called tremulously from their tree perches."[77]

In late August 1890, Roosevelt again traveled west to his Dakota ranch on the Little Missouri. During his years at the commission, he seldom allowed his stretched finances, family problems, or official duties to interfere with his annual pilgrimage to the West. In July 1888, for example, he had been shaken by his wife's miscarriage but nevertheless departed a fortnight later for a six-week hunting trip to Idaho. Theodore's infatuation with the West began at three o'clock on a cool September morning in 1883, when he stepped from a Northern Pacific train in the town of Medora, Dakota Territory, then a bustling little cattle outpost with eighty-four buildings. He had come west to ease a recent bout of asthma, but he soon fell in love with the area's rugged beauty and soon thereafter invested in two cattle ranches on the Little Missouri River.[78]

"After the first year I built on the Elkhorn ranch a long, low ranch house . . . with, in addition to the other rooms, a bedroom for myself, and a sitting-room with a big fire-place," Roosevelt wrote in his autobiography. "I got out a rocking-chair—I am very fond of rocking-chairs—and enough books to fill two or three shelves, and a rubber bathtub so that I could get a bath. . . . We had buffalo robes and bearskins of our own killing. . . . Sometimes from the ranch we saw deer, and once when we needed meat I shot one across the river as I stood on the piazza."[79]

On his visit in 1890 he did not travel alone. Roosevelt took Edith; his sisters, Anna and Corinne; Corinne's husband, Douglas Robinson; and Henry Cabot Lodge's teenage son, Bay.[80] In the predawn hours of September 2 the party arrived in Medora, North Dakota,[81] amidst a pelting rain that soaked the ladies' dresses.[82] Taking two months, they visited Yellowstone, which eighteen years before had become the first national park. Amid the delightful weather of early September, they took a two-week pack trip along the Continental Divide among the sheep, deer, antelope, and great herds of elk, "which are shyer than the smaller beasts."[83] During the trip, a horse threw Edith, an otherwise excellent horsewoman, who escaped with only bruises. The group returned to New York in the middle of October.

Back at work in December, Roosevelt exploded when he learned that the Seventh Cavalry massacred more than three hundred Sioux at Wounded Knee. From his experiences in the West, Roosevelt took special interest in the fate of American Indians. His friend Herbert Welsh, an activist with the Indian Rights Association, provided firsthand reports of the carnage. Throughout his years at the commission, Roosevelt remained determined to reform and professionalize the spoils-ridden Indian Service. "The Indian problem is difficult enough, heaven only knows, and it is cruel to complicate it by having the Indian service administered on patronage principles," Theodore wrote a friend. "To my mind the most important step that could be taken to solve the Indian problem would be to make the service absolutely non-political."[84] In 1891, Roosevelt recommended that "civilized" Indians be put to work in "farming, blacksmithing and the like, and should extend the present system of paid Indian judges and police."[85]

In dealing with the Indian problem, Roosevelt revealed one of his many contradictions. By modern standards, his words and writings appear outwardly racist and anti-Indian, such as the rhetoric of his *Winning of the West* or a typical speech he made in 1886. "I don't go so far as to think that the only good Indians are dead Indians, but I believe nine out of ten are, and I shouldn't like to inquire too closely into the case of the tenth," said Roosevelt. "The most vicious cowboy has more moral principle than the average Indian."[86]

On the other hand, and despite his racist slurs, Commissioner Roosevelt supported the improvement of living conditions for Indians and contributed to the reform of the Indian Service. Soon after arriving in Washington, Roosevelt lent his support to the Indian Rights Association, an organization that aggressively fought for Indian causes, including better education and health services and eventual assimilation into the mainstream of American society.[87] In a May 1893 *Century* article, Roosevelt suggested that the federal government provide pensions to Indians. He persuaded Harrison to grant civil service classification to 626 teachers, doctors, and administrators in the Indian schools but failed to gain Indian preference for most of those jobs.[88] A decade later, President Theodore Roosevelt ordered all Indian Service agents into the classified service.

3
1891

Building Valuable Friendships

LATE ON A BLUSTERY March afternoon, Theodore Roosevelt rushed the few blocks from old City Hall to the Baltimore and Potomac railroad station at Sixth and B Streets.[1] Ten years before, on a steamy July 2, 1881, President James A. Garfield passed through this same station on his way to a summer's vacation. As Garfield, who took office only four months before, walked through the waiting room, a deranged attorney named Charles Guiteau leapt from a crowd of bystanders and fired two bullets into the president's body, one in the arm and one, fatally, in the back. For weeks before, Guiteau had beseeched the White House for a spoils appointment as consul to Paris, but both Garfield and Secretary of State James Blaine spurned the office seeker.[2] An outraged American public blamed the assassination on the spoils system, and the resulting public outcry forced Congress to pass permanent civil service legislation in 1883 and, ultimately, create Roosevelt's job at the commission.

It is unlikely, however, that Roosevelt dwelled on the irony of the tragic events that had taken place in that train station a decade before, for he brooded over a more immediate problem. He boarded the first train headed north and, six hours later, arrived in Jersey City, where he caught the steam ferry across the Hudson River to Manhattan. As he stepped onto the city's streets that evening, gusts of wind and shivery rain slapped him in the face. A storm had moved in from the south and now sat off the East Coast, brewing a late-winter northeaster. Undaunted by the weather, Theodore hurried to his destination, a meeting of the New York Civil Service Reform Association. Roosevelt burst into the meeting and glanced around the room to make sure no newspaper reporters were present. Satisfied that only trusted friends could hear, he let his anger fly. Theodore talked fast and seemed to explode his words, which flew in short, staccato volleys.

"Damn John Wanamaker," cursed a crimson-faced Roosevelt. His audience flinched to hear the often high-strung but always moralistic Roosevelt swear angrily. Even when furious, Theodore's harshest expletives were little worse than "By Jove," "My Heavens," or "By Godfrey." It was equally unusual for a thirty-three-year-old civil service commissioner to attack a senior cabinet officer who in this case was the postmaster general and one of the nation's more powerful and rich politicians.[3] Still angered, Roosevelt went on for another hour describing his two years of futile battle with Wanamaker over spoils patronage.

In early 1891 Roosevelt and Wanamaker again collided. On March 24, John Rose, counsel for the Maryland Civil Service Reform League, visited Roosevelt at the commission and reported serious violations of the civil service law in Baltimore. Rose accused the Baltimore postmaster of illegally influencing Republican voters who were to elect delegates to the state convention. According to Rose, the postmaster forced each postal worker to contribute five to ten dollars to finance pro-Harrison candidates. Roosevelt, not wishing another Post Office dispute, asked Wanamaker to investigate. When the postmaster general did nothing, Roosevelt took action. Early on the morning of Monday, March 30, 1891, Roosevelt took the train to Baltimore, eager to observe any election-day shenanigans. He was not disappointed. "We certainly struck pay gravel," Roosevelt wrote Charles Bonaparte the following week. "We will be able to show plainly how a federal office is used to influence a primary election."[4] The commissioner saw firsthand an almost ludicrous election, where the total votes cast vastly outnumbered the total voters. Roosevelt observed party hacks paying voters in cash and ushering them into saloons for further coercing. When he returned to Washington, he reported the blatant violations and recommended the postmaster general dismiss twenty-five Baltimore Republican appointees.[5] Again, Wanamaker took no action, explaining that he was not responsible for events in Baltimore because he distributed the nonclassified positions among the various wards and the ward leaders nominated the men to fill them.[6] An exasperated Roosevelt complained to Lodge. "[Wanamaker] intends to prove the falsity of my report. Now that fool Wanamaker is quite capable of trying this, for his sloppy mind will not enable him to see that his case is weak," wrote Theodore. "He may involve me against my will, in such a muss that the President will have to turn me out simply because he can't turn out Wanamaker. If only the President would take me into confidence!"[7]

Republican party bosses fumed at Roosevelt's trip to Baltimore. On April 4, a group of Maryland politicians visited the White House and demanded Roosevelt's removal.[8] The pro-spoils press also attacked, spewing a torrent of billingsgate at the young commissioner. "The removal of Theodore Roosevelt from the Civil Service Commission is among the possibilities of the near future," predicted the *Boston Post* on April 1. Hatton's *Washington Post* dubbed Roosevelt "the rollicking ranchman of bogus reform" and reported that "Mr. R. is not helping the administration coaching party by throwing bricks at Driver Wanamaker."[9] An editorial in the *Albany Evening Journal,* a paper critical of Roosevelt for years to come, declared, "Go it, Roosevelt. If any man can repeal the Pendleton law during the coming four years his name is Teddy. If Teddy Roosevelt is not chained down, no power under heaven can prevent the repeal of the law before President Harrison's term shall have expired."[10] An editorial in Jay Gould's *New York World* called for "[t]he Democratic House [to] refuse to vote one dollar to pay the expenses of the Civil Service Commission while this ranting young humbug [Roosevelt] is a member of it. He has made the very name of reform redolent of hypocrisy."[11]

Roosevelt remained undaunted by the criticism and likely delighted in it. He remained enthusiastic. "I have pretty hard work, and work of rather an irritating kind; but I am delighted to be engaged in it," Theodore wrote his friend Brander Matthews. "The last few years politically for me have been largely a balancing of evils, and I am delighted to go in on a side where I have no doubt whatever. . . . I intend to hew to the line, and let the chips fall where they will."[12]

Despite pressure to remove Roosevelt, Harrison delayed. The president announced that he would wait for an official report of the Baltimore investigation before acting. The pressure was now on Roosevelt to justify his actions and to give Harrison no alternative but to keep him in office. Theodore returned to Baltimore several times to gather more evidence, interviewing over two hundred employees.[13] He drafted his report carefully and with great detail. Pacing back and forth across his office and pounding his fist into his palm for exclamation points, Roosevelt dictated relentlessly to his weary young stenographer, Orville Swank. Swank, a $900-a-year clerk, served Roosevelt efficiently through his political crises, receiving praise from the commissioners for being "punctual in his attendance, industrious in the performance of duty, excellent in his habits, and of sufficient quality and aptitude."[14]

The final report that Swank typed was typical Roosevelt overkill. Theodore filled 146 pages with his *Report of Commissioner Roosevelt Concerning Political Assessments and the Use of Official Influence to Control Elections in the Federal Offices at Baltimore, Maryland.* He refuted every conclusion, seriatim, of the internal Post Office investigation of the incident ordered by Wanamaker that acquitted the men accused by Roosevelt. Spewing a torrent of evidence, Roosevelt argued that he acted completely within his powers as commissioner. His report incriminating several of his own Republican Party members was so critical that he began to have second thoughts regarding its release. His fellow commissioners recommended he delay the report until the summer, when Washington was deserted and few would hear the explosion of the latest Roosevelt bombshell. On August 4, Theodore forwarded the document to Harrison.[15] On August 17, the White House released a censored, abbreviated version of the report, but one still critical enough to make front-page news. To Roosevelt's relief, Harrison and Wanamaker vacationed at the time.

By March 1892, a year after Theodore's trip to Baltimore, Wanamaker had not acted on the commission's recommendations. Still angry, Roosevelt traveled to New York to give his "Damn John Wanamaker" tirade. After returning to Washington, he gave several critical interviews to the press and, bypassing the president, sent his scathing report directly to the House Committee on Civil Service. The House, now dominated by Democrats, happily began an investigation of the Baltimore episode. During testimony before the committee, bitter exchanges erupted between Roosevelt and Wanamaker that wrought political embarrassment for Harrison, watching powerless as two of his appointees fought tooth and nail. Wanamaker attacked Roosevelt's investigation, calling it "unfair and partial" and the conclusions "unjustifiable and malicious."[16] On May 16, 1892, Roosevelt fired off a letter to Wanamaker again refuting the postmaster general's report and denying that he had been malicious or had "calculated to deceive and mislead" during his Baltimore investigation. Theodore also sent a copy of the Wanamaker letter to the president. "I have used every effort to avoid a conflict with the Post Office Department," Roosevelt confessed to Harrison. "It has now become merely a question of maintaining my own self respect and upholding the civil service law."[17]

On the last day of the congressional investigation, May 25, Theodore delivered one of his more commanding performances. With long lists of typewritten notes, he launched a "merciless and humiliating" barrage, refuting almost every item of Wanamaker's nine-hundred-page report of the Baltimore incident. The press had a field day. "The Harrison administration is not big enough to hold both Commissioner Roosevelt and Postmaster General Wanamaker," suggested the Plymouth, Massachusetts, *Free Press*. "He must get rid of one of them."[18]

In June 1892 the Democratic majority of the committee found in favor of Roosevelt and lightly censured the Baltimore postmaster for not removing the workers. The committee criticized Wanamaker as "evasive" and "garbled" and concluded that his actions were "indicative of a determination not to enforce the law."[19] The three Republicans on the committee approved Wanamaker's actions.[20] Theodore, still at work and complaining that "I have been boiling in Washington lately,"[21] was elated at his victory over Wanamaker, a victory that surprised many of Washington's political insiders.

⟿

The winter of 1891, besides being filled with collisions with John Wanamaker, offered another busy social season for the Roosevelts. New Year's Day 1891, like that of the year before, began wretchedly. Theodore and Edith, along with hundreds of other official dignitaries, suffered through fog and cold showers to make their morning trek to the White House reception. Snow from the week before still lay on the ground, and the cold rain softened the slush into a slippery mess. No one thought to clear the long, circular driveway from Pennsylvania Avenue to the executive mansion, and the horses pulling the carriages slid through the muck. The reception began promptly at eleven, with Sousa and the Marine Band serenading the guests with a medley of marches.[22] The Roosevelts walked through the tile-covered vestibule where a Louis Tiffany masterpiece, an opalescent stained-glass screen decorated with four bejeweled eagles, dominated the entrance from floor to ceiling.[23] In the Blue Room, President Harrison greeted the Roosevelts gruffly, shaking Theodore's hand with a grip "like a wilted petunia."[24]

For Theodore and Edith, the first months of 1891 were a hectic assortment of social engagements. Until the beginning of Lent on Ash Wednesday, they dined out three or four times a week and often invited guests to their home. While the Roosevelts did not live outlandishly, they lived comfortably and seemed to fit well in Washington society. To make ends meet, they did much of their entertaining by hosting less expensive Sunday-evening high teas. To Theodore's chagrin, his wife no longer served expensive champagne at dinner.[25] In early February, Roosevelt reported to his sister Anna the latest happenings in their busy life. "We have been going out a good deal during the last week. One evening we dined at the Vice Presidents [Levi Morton]; another at [Congressman John] Andrews; and then again we dined at the Riggs," wrote Theodore. "My pleasantest dinner was one in Baltimore at Charles Bonaparte's, to meet Cardinal Gibbons. The latter was very entertaining; the cultivated Jesuit, with rather kindly emotions, and a thorough knowledge of the fact that his church must become both Republicanized and Americanized to retain its hold here."[26]

While Theodore socialized at night, he fought during the day. His efforts at destroying the spoils system created a host of enemies besides Wanamaker. The political fray also became much more intense, as congressional elections held the previous November proved disastrous for the Republicans. Two years before, the Republicans captured the White House and both houses of Congress, but in 1890 they lost their majority in the House, where their membership plummeted from 166 to 88. Democrats defeated a number of important incumbents, including Congressman William McKinley.[27] McKinley had sponsored an unpopular tariff bill which many Americans believed caused consumer prices to rise.[28] Roosevelt blamed the tariff for the Republican losses of 1890, writing Lodge that "as you know I never liked that measure."[29]

Roosevelt's close friend, Congressman Thomas Reed,[30] lost his Speakership to the Democratic majority. With the presidency and the Congress now split between the parties, Theodore found himself more than ever caught between powerful political forces. That February he predicted that "there will soon be another battle over civil service reform." Seeming to face enemies from all directions, he appeared frustrated and uneasy. "I have been continuing my civil service fight, battling with everybody . . . the little gray man in the White House looking on with cold and hesitating disapproval," Theodore wrote his sister Anna. "I think I have done good work, and a man ought to show that he can go out into the world and hold his own with other men; but I shall be glad when I get back to live at Sagamore."[31]

↩

With a magnificent white beard drooping to his waist and a reputation as a fiery orator with an acid tongue and sharp wit, Charles Grosvenor was a nineteenth-century political icon.[32] Looking like an eccentric undertaker in his dark wool suit, Grosvenor was a major power on the national scene in 1891. Eventually serving ten terms as a Republican congressman, he marched in step with the conservative ranks of his fellow old-guard stalwarts. Back home in Athens, Ohio, Grosvenor was a full-fledged hero, a former Civil War general and veteran of Chickamauga. The irascible old general, known as "Old Figgers," championed spoils politics and fought civil service reform almost as fiercely as he opposed efforts to lift the South out of Reconstruction. It was only a matter of time before Charles Grosvenor and Theodore Roosevelt tore into each other.

In February 1891, during House budget hearings, Grosvenor attacked the Civil Service Commission's appropriation and attempted to withhold funds for ten new clerks needed to process an increasing backlog of civil service examinations. After Grosvenor "enumerated [Roosevelt's] sins in picturesque rather than accurate fashion," Theodore erupted. To Roosevelt, Grosvenor "proved to be a person of happily treacherous memory, so that the simple expedient of arranging his sentences in pairs was sufficient to reduce him to confusion."[33] A bitter debate took place in the House for two days. Grosvenor, Joe Cannon, and "similar cattle" led the attack on the commission, while Lodge and other reform Republicans defended it. Representative Louis McComas, a reform Republican from Maryland, spoke up for Roosevelt, and Congressman Benjamin Butterworth,[34] an Ohio Republican, fought for the commission funding by warning that "we can stop the engine by withholding wood and coal and water." Butterworth argued that the clerks were essential to the commission's survival. "He takes my life who takes away the means by which I live," he concluded.[35]

With the influence of Congressman Tom Reed, a compromise eventually funded the commission. Representative Nelson Dingley of Maine proposed an amendment to the appropriations bill giving $36,400 to the commission for the clerks. The bill passed 95–71.[36]

Earlier, Grosvenor, proud of his Union army record, fumed when he learned the commission recruited clerks in Louisiana and Arkansas to fill the quotas of those states. On the floor of the House he rose and exhorted his colleagues. "I want, as an ex-Union soldier and on behalf of the ex-Union soldiers of this country, to express my unqualified condemnation of that act," bellowed Grosvenor. "That alone will forever damn the Civil Service Commission. . . . I want to abolish this board. It is abnormal, and it is a growth that was never contemplated by the Constitution."[37] Roosevelt struck back at Grosvenor when he testified before a House committee. "[Theodore] was to have gone to his ranch for the fall and he had his cowboy spirit of dash and daring," reported a local newspaper with tongue in cheek. "Two or three times as he smelt the air of the plains—or the blood of the anti–civil service Congressmen—the cowboy yell arose to his lips." According to the *Washington Evening Star,* Roosevelt and Grosvenor argued for two hours, and when the hearing ended Theodore "was left champion of the field."[38] Roosevelt later boasted that he bettered the crusty Ohio legislator. "I did not leave enough of Grosvenor to be put in a coal shuttle," Theodore wrote to Lodge. "Before I was half way through he took refuge in what he called his constitutional right not to be questioned. . . . The committee screamed with laughter."[39]

While Roosevelt fought his battles with Grosvenor and other spoils politicians, he remained busy on the home front. As summer approached in 1891, Edith and the children moved from the house on Jefferson Place and returned to Sagamore Hill. Edith, in the last months of pregnancy, wished to have her baby amid the breezes of Long Island Sound and far from the torrid heat of Washington. While Edith enjoyed the bustle of Washington, she craved the tranquillity of the large house on the bluff overlooking the Sound, where, dressed in cool white muslin and wearing a straw sailor hat, she could relax under a sycamore and read Elizabeth Gaskell or Jane Austen or another of her many favorite novelists.

The following November, as the city's maples blazed red and yellow, Theodore moved his family back to Washington. They took a large frame house at 1215 Nineteenth Street, located between Connecticut and New Hampshire Avenues and about six blocks from Rock Creek. They needed more room for their rapidly growing household. When he arrived in Washington in 1889, his oldest daughter, Alice, had just turned five. Alice was named for her deceased mother and Theodore's first wife, Alice Lee Roosevelt. Edith and Theodore's first son, Theodore Jr., was two when they arrived. Soon afterward, Edith gave birth to a second son, Kermit, on October 10, 1889. Ethel arrived on August 13, 1891, at Sagamore Hill, and Archibald on April 9, 1894. The sixth and last of the Roosevelt children, Quentin, was born on November 19, 1897, after Roosevelt resigned as commissioner and returned to New York City.

⤸

In the fall of 1878, during his junior year at Harvard, Theodore wrote his sister Corinne that while visiting friends outside Boston he made a "drive home by moonlight after tea" with a Miss Alice Lee.[40] Alice was the daughter of George Cabot Lee, a wealthy Bostonian, Harvard graduate of 1850, and partner in a Boston bank. When they met, Alice was seventeen and Theodore nineteen. Alice was extraordinarily attractive with honey-blond hair, slender in build, and as tall as Theodore. Descriptions consistently flatter her, portraying her personality as bright, cheerful, and high-spirited, and resembling Theodore's beautiful mother, Mittie Bulloch, at that age. During Roosevelt's courtship of Alice in March 1879, Owen Wister, then a freshman at Harvard, sat in the gallery of the gymnasium to watch the annual spring boxing matches.[41] A sparse and wiry Theodore, then weighing 135 pounds, climbed into the ring. Roosevelt won his semifinal bout but lost the final. Across the stands, Wister saw the gorgeous Alice Lee, dressed in the finest furs, sitting with friends and rooting for Theodore.[42]

Captivated with Alice, Theodore called upon her frequently and by the following June proposed. Alice rejected his offer, inciting Theodore to court her more aggressively. He devoted his last two years at Harvard in "eager, restless, passionate pursuit of one all-absorbing object" until she finally relented.[43] During this period Theodore decided against becoming a biologist and now leaned more toward the law and politics, professions more likely to provide a comfortable living for a married couple.

In January 1880 he wrote in his diary that "At last everything is settled." On Theodore's twenty-second birthday, October 27, 1880, they married in Brookline, Massachusetts, on a perfect fall day. Sitting beside Theodore's mother on the front pew of the Unitarian Church were his sister Anna and their childhood friend, Edith Carow. His other sister, Corinne, served as a bridesmaid, and his brother, Elliott, delayed a trip to India to be Theodore's best man. The couple postponed their honeymoon because Theodore had entered Columbia Law School shortly before their marriage. On May 22, 1881, they sailed for Europe on the *Celtic*.[44] Theodore climbed the Matterhorn, worked on his first book, the historical *Naval War of 1812,* and, while in Rome, finished several articles on nature and wildlife for the *Century*. The couple returned to New York City in October on the *Brittanic*.

Theodore and Alice moved into his family's Fifty-seventh Street home, where he took over many of the roles of his late father, including presiding over the newsboys' dinner on Sunday evening and becoming a trustee of the Orthopedic Hospital and the New York Infant Asylum. During this period Theodore purchased a large tract of land at Oyster Bay on which to build a house for Alice, to be called Leeholm. Later, he and Alice moved into their own Manhattan brownstone on West Forty-fifth Street, often whiling away the hours playing backgammon by the fire. By the summer of 1883, Alice was pregnant. About this time

Roosevelt lost interest in the law. He did not return to his classes at Columbia, and in 1882 he abandoned plans of practicing with one of his uncles, Robert Roosevelt. Theodore did not deal well with abstract concepts, and the thought of spending the rest of his life poring over dull law books seemed just as inconceivable as spending it over a microscope in a laboratory. Politics, with its action and the challenge of human contest, rapidly took center stage in Theodore's life.

In November 1881, only a month after returning from his European honeymoon, Theodore campaigned for his first elected office. He ran on the Republican ticket for New York State assemblyman in the city's Twenty-first District, a Republican brownstone bastion. While running for office, Roosevelt learned the ropes of New York machine politics. He joined the Republican Association and attended political meetings in seedy Morton Hall, a large, barnlike room over a saloon on Fifty-ninth Street.[45] Soon he had earned the backing of district leaders and ward heelers, including local political bosses Jake Hess and Joe Murray. When a public hospital scandal tarnished his Democratic opponent, William Straw, Roosevelt's election was guaranteed. Theodore won his seat by 1,501 votes. He wrote a Harvard classmate soon afterward, "Too True! Too True! I have become a political hack."[46]

New Yorkers reelected Theodore to the assembly in 1882 and again in 1883. One of a few energetic young reformers, Roosevelt appeared as "a rather dudish-looking boy with eyeglasses and an Olympian scowlet-for-accent . . . hair parted in the middle . . . and pronounced the word *either* with the *i* sound instead of the *e*."[47] In his third term, Roosevelt led the charge to weaken Tammany control of New York City politics. A controversial Reform Charter Bill eventually stripped city aldermen of their immense power and created a strong-mayor form of government. During the heated debates in the city, New York newspapers began to provide frequent coverage of Theodore's political activities. He began to appreciate the power of the press and the spotlight it offered, although he continued to hate newspapers and would go for days without looking at one.[48]

In early February 1884, Roosevelt labored to build popular support for the Reform Charter Bill, now referred to as the Roosevelt Bill. He spent several days in New York City attending hearings and a rally at Cooper Union. He returned to Albany on the morning of the twelfth, and later that day Alice went into labor. That evening she gave birth to a baby girl. Theodore received a telegram from his sister Anna the next morning saying Alice and the baby were doing fine, but a few hours later a second telegram urgently called him back to the city. On a miserably cold and rainy night, Theodore caught the first train to New York. Hurrying through the fog-shrouded city, he finally arrived at the gaslit door of his Fifty-seventh Street home near midnight.

"There is a curse on this house," spoke Elliott Roosevelt as his brother Theodore entered their home. "Mother is dying and Alice is dying too."[49] The Roosevelt family was in shock. Theodore's sisters and brother told him that the two women most dear to him—his wife and his mother—were desperately ill. Alice had Bright's Disease, a chronic inflammation of the kidneys, and Mittie, typhoid. When he reached Alice, she was delirious. He stayed with her, holding her in his arms until he went to his mother at about three in the morning. Mittie died shortly thereafter, with her four children at her bedside. Returning to Alice, Theodore held his wife for another eleven hours until she died at two in the afternoon.

Theodore was mortified. Then only twenty-five, he already had stared death in the face as a boy with severe asthma attacks and five years before lost his idolized father. He now confronted the loss of the two most beloved women in his life. Clearly, Roosevelt never would be the same. Afterward he rarely talked of the deaths of his mother and father, seldom again mentioned Alice's name, and did not refer to her in his autobiography. In the days after the funeral, Roosevelt erased the record of Alice. He destroyed their letters, cut pages from his scrapbooks, and discarded photographs until he had almost literally removed her from his life.[50] Throughout his life he rarely addressed their child, named for her dead mother, by her given name, Alice. Instead, he called her "Baby Lee" as an infant and "Sister" as a teen.[51]

Shortly after his mother and wife died, on the otherwise blank page of his diary for February 14, Theodore wrote simply, "the light has gone out of my life." Though deeply grieved, he refused to wallow in pity. Never a patient man, his personal tragedies made him less so. He seemed to never have enough time to accomplish the many things he needed to do in what he now saw as an inevitably short and unpredictable lifetime. While devastated, Theodore dealt with his latest personal tragedies just as he did when his father died and as he would during future tragedies in his life. Action served as his remedy. For the remainder of his life, Theodore would run a frantic race with his own mortality, writing later that "black care rarely catches up to a rider whose pace is fast enough."[52] He existed in the present, not wanting to dwell in the melancholy of his past, at least not outwardly. Instead, he threw himself back into his work with unrelenting energy. Three days after the double funeral of his wife and mother, Theodore returned to his desk in Albany and ushered forth a phenomenal tide of bills and speeches. The *New York Times* reported on April 16, 1884, that seven of Roosevelt's reform bills passed the day before.[53] During those frantic days he confessed to Carl Schurz that "indeed I think I should go mad if I were not employed."[54]

After completing his third term in the legislature, Theodore did not run for reelection. His personal tragedy likely provided the significant, if not dominant, reason for his leaving Albany. The sad memories surely were too great and tragic to allow him to return to the New York legislature. Ike Hunt, a fellow assemblyman and Roosevelt's friend, provided a similar explanation when he spoke of the tragedy years later: "[Y]ou could not talk about [the deaths of his wife and mother] . . . you could see at once that it was a grief too deep. . . . There was a sadness about his face that he never had before. . . . He did not want anybody to sympathize with him. . . . He hiked away to the wilderness to get away from the world. . . . He went out there a broken man."[55]

Theodore's lack of interest in his new baby girl, who symbolized a depressing past that he was not yet able to face, offers further evidence of his devastation. Theodore entrusted Alice's care to his sister Anna. Throughout her childhood, the family never celebrated the young girl's birthday, a bitter remembrance always falling two days before the anniversary of her mother's death, February 14, or Valentine's Day.

⌐

In 1891, Roosevelt displayed an increasing interest in protecting the wilderness, conserving natural resources, and establishing a permanent system of national parks. He strengthened his support for environmentalism, an unusual notion in the 1890s when much of the country remained untamed and the nation's natural resources seemed inexhaustible. After his cattle venture in the Badlands failed and shortly before becoming commissioner, Roosevelt and *Forest and Stream* editor George Bird Grinnell formed the Boone and Crockett Club.[56] The club, composed of wealthy and like-minded sportsmen, sought to protect large game animals of the western wilderness from indiscriminate slaughter. Writing the superintendent of Yellowstone, Roosevelt vented his anger over the "recent unfortunate slaughter of buffaloes."[57] With Roosevelt as its first president, the Boone and Crockett Club actively pressed for wildlife preservation and land conservation and supported the creation of a zoo in Washington.[58] The club successfully lobbied Congress for $200,000 to help move animals from cages on the Smithsonian grounds to the new National Zoo being built adjacent to Rock Creek Park.

In March 1891, Roosevelt and the Boone and Crockett Club joined forces with the American Forestry Association to persuade Congress to pass the Forest Reserve Act. The legislation created the national forest reserve and empowered the president to protect forested areas and halt the rapid attrition of western woodlands. The club targeted Yellowstone, a national park since 1872, where developers built resorts unchecked and planned a railroad through the heart of the park. In 1894, spurred by the club's lobbying, Congress passed the Park Protection Act, which saved Yellowstone from further despoliation.[59] Meanwhile, Commissioner Roosevelt joined environmentalist William Hallett Phillips in urging Congress to pass a law professionalizing the administration of Yellowstone.[60] Roosevelt personally lobbied Secretary of the Interior Hoke Smith for a greatly expanded park system. "I am very glad of the position the Interior Department has taken in reference to Yellowstone Park," Roosevelt wrote Smith in April 1894. "I am going to argue against the proposed cutting down of the boundaries of the park and to try to persuade the committee to give you proper police power in the matter. It will be an outrage if this government does not keep the big Sequoia Park, the Yosemite, and such like places under touch."[61]

Breakfast didn't start until well past noon, but for Edith and Theodore Roosevelt the meal invariably was worth the wait. Often on Sundays and soon after Theodore finished his long morning ride along Rock Creek, the young commissioner and his bride headed for Lafayette Square and the home of Henry Adams. The meal was always sumptuous, offering the freshest eggs, bacon, and sausages from local markets, and Adams's two servants treated the guests like royalty. It was not the meal, however, that so fascinated the Roosevelts. The Adams town house, across from the White House at 1603 H Street, was already making Washington legend.[62] Guests entered the rather modernistic three-storied, red brick mansion through a door canopied by a graceful, double-arched entranceway of gray limestone.[63] Inside, a broad staircase led to the second-floor living quarters where polished wood floors glimmered between elegant Kashmir and Kurdistan carpets. Strewn about the high-ceilinged drawing room were lush green potted palms and wine-red leather armchairs, cut unusually low and small to fit their owner. Superb English landscapes—Turners, Constables, and Boningtons—graced the walls, while rare Japanese porcelain and jade bric-a-brac garnished tables and mantelpieces. In the nearby library that held thousands of rare volumes stood a marvelous fireplace carved from translucent, sea-green Mexican onyx.[64]

The town house was legendary not for its opulence, however, but for the brilliant people who passed beneath Adams's arched entrance-way. By the time Theodore Roosevelt arrived in Washington in 1889, Adams's Lafayette Square home was already "the most stimulating intellectual salon in American social history."[65] As a group and as individuals, the callers at 1603 H Street formed a circle of friendship that connected them to the most influential figures of their time. At the center of this circle was, of course, Henry Adams.[66] Short, very bald, and crotchety, Adams was from the Massachusetts blue bloods, great-grandson of John Adams, grandson of John Quincy Adams, and brother of Brooks and Charles Francis Adams. Adams was immensely curious, and his interests swept across the broad spectrum of art, science, philosophy, and history. He was a writer of great prose, suffused with poetry, and a master of irony and contradiction. A vicious wit, Adams had a reputation for "impaling political and social nincompoops on the needles of his conversation." Dressed in somber black suits, he was a recluse who seldom dined outside his home. Adams confessed in his epochal autobiography, *The Education of Henry Adams,* that he had an incongruous "passion for companionship and an antipathy to society."[67] During most summers, however, he embarked on excursions that took him to Europe, the Orient, and the South Seas.

Adams was long acquainted with the Roosevelt family. In 1873, when Theodore was a teen, the Roosevelts spent three months sailing the Nile on a primitive sailboat and exploring the ancient temples and ruins of Egypt. On the upper Nile, near Thebes, they anchored near another *dahabeah* and picnicked with Henry Adams and his wife, Clover, who were honeymooning in Egypt.[68] Three years later, Roosevelt began his first year at Harvard, which was Henry Adams's last year there as a professor of history and politics. When Theodore came down with measles, "Prof Adams" referred him to a doctor.[69] Despite their family connections, Adams showed an initial distaste for young Roosevelt. Two days after Roosevelt arrived in Washington, Adams complained to his beautiful neighbor, Elizabeth Cameron. "Theodore Roosevelt was at Lodge's. You know the poor wretch has consented to be Civil Service Commissioner," wrote Adams. "[He] is to be with us in Washington next winter with his sympathetic little wife. He is searching for a house."[70]

Later, after Roosevelt became president, Adams described Theodore as "an excellent specimen of the genus Americanus egotisticus" and on occasion labeled him insane.[71] Roosevelt also had reservations concerning the often arrogant and intimidating professor, whose intelligence he respected but with whom he often disagreed. Theodore read Adams's novel *Democracy,* which satirized corruption and greed during the presidencies of Grant and Hayes. Published anonymously in 1880, *Democracy* became a best-seller and the object of a national guessing game as to its authorship.[72] Roosevelt felt *Democracy* was "mean and foolish" but concluded that the professor was "a man of infinite research, and his ideas are usually (with some very marked exceptions) excellent."[73]

Although Adams never held public office, he wielded strong intellectual influence over those who did, including Theodore. Like most guests who graced his drawing room, Henry was an ardent reformer. Since editing the *North American Review* in the 1870s, he had fought the rampant spoils and championed civil service reform. He saw the world chiefly as a thing to be bettered, filled with evil forces to be destroyed, and saw no reason to assume that anyone had wholly succeeded in the destruction of evil.[74]

While Adams frequently criticized "Theodore the Talkative,"[75] at least in his private correspondence, he enjoyed Roosevelt's company and found him to be a likable target for his intellectual barbs and colorful descriptions. In one letter, Adams grumbles playfully that "Teddy himself grinds his teeth with such cannibal expression."[76] During a vacation to Asia in September 1891, Adams wrote Elizabeth Cameron shortly after arriving in Ceylon and confessed a lighthearted longing for Roosevelt and Lodge. "After this, if I can only return home contentedly, and help Cabot Lodge and Teddy Roosevelt so save the country. What more has life to offer?" In later years, the astringent Adams appears to have softened when he conceded that Roosevelt's departure from the White House signaled the "last vision of fun and gaiety" and that "never can we replace him."[77]

In the town house next door to Adams lived another frequent guest who forged a lasting and influential friendship with Roosevelt. John Hay stood just over five feet tall, his hair precisely parted in the middle, his beard neatly cropped, and always impeccably dressed. Hay had been a close personal friend of Theodore's father during the Civil War. At the time Hay served as Lincoln's aide, and on occasion he joined Thee Roosevelt in the lobby of Willard's Hotel where the two eavesdropped on generals discussing the next battle.[78]

Theodore admired Hay, a man who blended literary skill with a spirit of public service and possessed "a poet's soul in a diplomat's body."[79] Like Roosevelt, Hay thought America had less to fear from the rich than from the growing political power of immigrants, who in his view were too easily swayed by demagogues. He voiced his apprehensions anonymously in his provocative novel, *The Bread-Winners,* which appeared in 1883.[80]

As secretary of state under McKinley and then Roosevelt, Hay won praise for his open-door policy in China and for the 1901 Hay-Pauncefote Treaty, which led to the eventual building of the Panama Canal by the United States. Over time, however, Theodore became impatient with Hay's more methodical approach to foreign affairs. Four years after Hay died, Roosevelt passed judgment on his former secretary of state. "He had a very easy-loving nature and a moral timidity which made him shrink from all that was rough in life, and therefore from practical affairs," Roosevelt wrote Lodge in January 1909. "He was at his best at a dinner table or in a drawing room . . . [as] Secretary of State under me he accomplished little . . . his usefulness to me was almost exclusively the usefulness of a fine figurehead. He was always afraid of Senators and Congressmen."[81]

Hay and Adams belonged to a small, tight-knit group that called themselves the "Five of Hearts." Using stationery embossed with five small red hearts arranged in the playing-card pattern, the group sent scores of letters back and forth. Beginning in the late 1880s, the five met almost daily for tea. Served promptly at five, tea stretched into supper, and supper became a party that lasted until after midnight, finally ending in the mahogany splendor of Hays's dining room where the five sipped nightcaps of Chatour Latour '64.[82]

The "Hearts" included Hay's wife, Clara, a large, darkly handsome, and docile woman who was the daughter of a Cleveland railway millionaire, and Adams's wife, Clover. Clover Adams was outspoken, rebellious, and pungently clever, and people feared her tongue.[83] Henry James called Clover "Voltaire in petticoats."[84] She was a gifted and passionate photographer, and her portraits of Washington luminaries remain a priceless legacy of the era. In the spring of 1885, Clover's father died and she sank into a depression that never lifted. On December 6, at the age of forty-two, she drank potassium cyanide, one of her photographic chemicals, and committed suicide. Like Theodore, whose first wife died the year before, Henry Adams was devastated and seldom again spoke his wife's name.

The fifth and most notorious member of the "Hearts" was Clarence King. A handsome, muscular bachelor with "blithe blue" eyes who wore his blondish beard and thinning hair cropped close, King was the country's most famous geologist.[85] After graduating from Yale, he began his career surveying the mountains of California and in 1867, at twenty-five, led a ten-year study of the planned route of the first transcontinental railroad. Trekking from the eastern slope of the Sierra Nevada to the Rockies, King's team mapped Yosemite, cataloged flora and fauna, and helped pave the way for settlements that followed. Widely praised, King's work led to the creation of the U.S. Geological Survey, with King as its first chief.[86]

King and Roosevelt often dined together in Adams's town house. The geologist's bubbling energy matched Theodore's, and the two shared a passion for the West and a "love of archaic races, sympathy with the Negro and Indian, and corresponding dislike of their enemies."[87] Roosevelt would not have approved, however, of the dark secret that King kept from his friends. In 1888, posing as a railroad porter named James Todd, the forty-five-year-old King took a common-law wife, a twenty-six-year-old black nursemaid named Ada Copeland. He rented a house on Hudson Street in Brooklyn, where, for the next fourteen years, he and Ada raised their five children. Until he died on Christmas Eve 1901, the restless King shuttled between his one life as a successful, world-famous geologist who would make—and lose—millions in the mining industry and his other life as a blue-collar family man living in a shabby Brooklyn borough.[88]

The truly impressive friends and colleagues surrounding King, Adams, and the "Hearts" would define their age and usher in the twentieth century. Their confidants included Mark Twain, Walt Whitman, Henry James, Edith Wharton, Bret Harte, William Dean Howells, Horace Greeley, Andrew Carnegie, Robert Louis Stevenson, Rudyard Kipling, and every president from Abraham Lincoln to Theodore Roosevelt.[89]

For two decades, Henry Adams's town house served as Washington's intellectual center, where his famous breakfasts, dinners, and teas were governed by only one rule—guests must invite themselves. Adams encouraged his friends to bring new faces, and without being told they understood that their sharp-tongued host would tolerate anyone but a bore. During a Christmas meal at Adams's home in 1892, a startled Theodore discovered that his dinner companion was a four-hundred-pound Polynesian chief. Tati Salmon, the half-English native ruler of the island of Papara, was just another of Henry Adams's fascinating, yet never boring, guests. Roosevelt was delighted, finding the chief to be "a polished gentleman, of easy manners, with an interesting undertone of queer barbarism."[90]

Theodore and Edith were pleased to be among Adams's regular guests. For the young civil service commissioner, being included in Adams's coterie provided a rare opportunity to make lasting friendships, many of which would be essential a decade later when Theodore entered the White House. Along with Henry Cabot Lodge and his wife, Nannie, a violet-eyed beauty and brilliant Wellesley graduate, the Roosevelts spent hours in the Adams's drawing room discussing literature, religion, philosophy, science, art, politics, and the economy with Washington notables.[91] A frequent guest was Adams's neighbor, Elizabeth Cameron. One of Washington's most beautiful women, "Lizzie" was a tall, slim brunette with compelling gray eyes who sometimes was accompanied by her wealthy husband, Pennsylvania senator Donald Cameron. Twenty-four years her senior, the senator "downed a fifth of bourbon a day."[92]

Among the noted artists who frequented Adam's salon was stained-glass master John LaFarge.[93] Six feet tall, dressed in fine silks and linens, balding, with gray-green eyes twinkling through thick spectacles, LaFarge was already famous for his revolutionary use of opalescent glass and his huge murals adorning the home of Cornelius Vanderbilt, the Metropolitan Museum of Art, and Boston's Trinity Church. Another frequenter at the Lafayette Square town house was the sculptor Augustus Saint-Gaudens.[94] Sparsely built, with dark, wavy hair and facial features "as hard and sharp as his sculptor's chisel," Saint-Gaudens was renowned for his distinctive public sculptures.[95] Since unveiling his monument of Admiral David Farragut in Madison Square Garden in 1881, Saint-Gaudens enjoyed international acclaim and a string of impressive commissions. Shortly after Clover Adams's death, Henry Adams turned to his friend Saint-Gaudens to sculpt a memorial for his wife's grave in Washington's Rock Creek Church Cemetery. Completed in the spring of 1891, the bronze masterpiece depicts a beautiful but haunting woman, sitting upon a stone with her eyes closed, with a shawl draped over her head and partially obscuring her mysterious, angular face. Adams was awestruck. "Every detail interested him; every line; every touch of the artist; every change of light and shade," wrote Henry in his *Education*. "As the spring approached, he was apt to stop there often to see what the figure had to tell him that was new; but, in all that it had to say, he never once thought of questioning what it meant."[96] Henry Adams is buried there with Clover.

The Adams salon, as well as other social and official gatherings, gave

Theodore Roosevelt the opportunity to greatly expand his circle of friends during his first six years in Washington. In the capital's small-town atmosphere, most of the intellectual and political elite knew one another. The novelist Henry James, who visited Adams during this period, rightly observed that Washington was a "City of Conversation."[97] On Roosevelt's frequent walks through the city, where "Washington's magical short distances made it easy to keep up with its gay gregariousness," he often encountered senators, congressmen, and cabinet officers whom he would buttonhole and lecture on the latest topic.[98] During this period Roosevelt struck up a friendship with his neighbor, William Howard Taft, when the Ohioan served as solicitor general. The two men often walked to work together, their wives became friends, and their children played together.

Roosevelt dined regularly with Tom Reed of Maine, the Speaker of the House and one of Washington's most sarcastic, crafty, and iron-willed characters. A huge, oddly shaped man with a small, round bald head and "sharp pig eyes," Reed towered above his colleagues in mind as well as body.[99] Other congressional leaders within Roosevelt's circle included the profane, cigar-puffing, and poker-playing Joe Cannon of Illinois, a future speaker, and the more upright William McKinley of Ohio, a future president. Roosevelt forged valuable political friendships over dinner, often at Washington's foremost hotel, the Ebbitt House, a large, ornate six-story hotel dominating the corner of Fourteenth and F Streets. As a sign of progress, the Ebbitt became the first of the city's hotels to stay open all summer.

⌒

Early in the summer of 1891, when Edith and the children left Jefferson Place and returned to Sagamore Hill, Theodore and his close friend Cecil Spring-Rice moved into Henry Cabot Lodge's spacious home at 1721 Connecticut Avenue.[100] At the time, the Lodges vacationed in Europe. Roosevelt met Spring-Rice in November 1886, on the steamship *Etruria* when Roosevelt was on his way to London to marry Edith. After Spring-Rice served as his best man, the two became lifelong friends. With a dark mustache, long face, broad forehead, and hawkish nose, Spring-Rice looked and dressed like the exemplary English gentleman.[101] The same age as Roosevelt, he entered the British Foreign Office after graduating from Oxford and served as a diplomat in the British legation.[102] In 1912 he became British ambassador to the United States.

Spring-Rice was one of the few people who could call his friend

"Teddy" to his face.[103] Roosevelt loved Spring-Rice's highbrow humor and thoroughly British ways. "[Spring-Rice is] a good fellow, and really cultivated," Theodore wrote Anna that summer. "In the evenings he reads Homer and Dante in the originals! I wish I could. At times he has a most querulous feeling towards America, he oughtn't to be a diplomat; he is too serious."[104] Known for his whimsical banter and amusing drawings, Spring-Rice kept up a steady correspondence with Theodore.[105] They often exchanged criticism on the latest literary vogue. "Did you see Joel Chandler Harris's new book *On the Plantation*?" Roosevelt asked Spring-Rice in May 1892. "It is very good. I am also pleased with Kipling's new edition of his poems. . . . I have been reading Chaucer with industry lately, and as I gradually become more used to his language I get to enjoy him more and more; but I must say I think he is altogether needlessly filthy."[106]

In July 1891, Roosevelt recited to Lodge the comedy of living with Spring-Rice:

> When we went to bed last night Springy performed a delicious feat. We went upstairs in the dark, and did not light the gas. I turned into my room; and noticed that, as I got undressed, I did not hear anything of Springy. Soon however I heard my name called from the flight above; and then followed demands to know where *I* was and where *he* was, and where our bedrooms were; and when I answered these questions and lit the light Springy came paddling downstairs a la Lady Godiva, with his clothes, shoes, etc., clasped in his arms. He dreamily walked up one extra flight, undressed and started to get into bed; when it occurred to him as odd that the bed had no sheets. He couldn't find any matches, and began to feel that there was a mystery somewhere; and so he became vocal, and when I answered him from below he at first felt I had gone down to live in the cellar.[107]

Another foreign diplomat Theodore befriended soon after becoming commissioner was Baron Hermann Speck von Sternberg. Then a secretary in the German legation, the short, dapper von Sternberg was a hero of the Franco-Prussian War, a crack rifle shot, an excellent horseman, and an indefatigable walker.[108] Roosevelt enjoyed riding with von Sternberg, making springtime gallops through Rock Creek amidst blooming forsythia and pale bloodroot. At one point Theodore taught the German attaché to play polo. "I am now riding Pickle, a very nice pony, hardy, high spirited, and handy as a jackknife," Roosevelt wrote Anna in May

1891. "Today I rode out with good little Speck. By the way that small Teutonic Baron is quite a companion; he and I took an hour and a half's trot—literally trot—through the woods the other day."[109] Later as president, Roosevelt exerted considerable pressure upon the German government to have his friend von Sternberg appointed ambassador to the United States in 1903. After von Sternberg returned to Washington, the two friends continued their spirited rides together, and Roosevelt often dragged the German onto the White House tennis court.

Another member of the diplomatic corps whom Roosevelt befriended was Sir Michael Herbert, who was "by the way, one of the sweetest and most attractive men I have ever met." Herbert served as secretary of the British legation when Theodore arrived in 1889.[110] Married to an American, "Mungo" Herbert learned the game of baseball from Roosevelt. In 1902, with Theodore in the White House, the British government, again with the urging of the president, chose Herbert as ambassador to the United States. Not surprisingly, the friendships that Roosevelt made with members of the foreign diplomatic corps during the early years became important relationships that may well have influenced the course of world politics.[111] Each of these foreign diplomats whom Roosevelt befriended during his commissionership—Spring-Rice, von Sternberg, and Herbert—would later play a pivotal role in the unfolding world events that eventually climaxed with World War I.

At the same time, Commissioner Roosevelt began to fully appreciate the power of the press and cultivated the friendships of several influential journalists, including the *Century's* Robert Underwood Johnson, *Harper's* William Dean Howells, and *Outlook's* Hamilton Wright Mabie.[112] In December 1892, Theodore first met Richard Harding Davis at a dinner at the British Embassy.[113] Davis managed *Harper's Weekly* and in 1898 climbed San Juan Hill to observe the famous charge of the Rough Riders. Davis's reporting, more than that of any other journalist, created the war hero that the American public desired and propelled Roosevelt onto the highest national stage.

⌒

For Roosevelt the writer, the years at the Civil Service Commission provided an opportunity for intellectual growth. His friends and frequent correspondents included scholars such as historians Frederick Jackson Turner and Francis Parkman, British statesman James Bryce, short story writer Rudyard Kipling, naval strategist Alfred Mahan, literary scholar

Brander Matthews, British historian George M. Trevelyan, paleontologist Henry Fairfield Osborn, aviation pioneer Samuel Langley, and novelist and future Rough Rider John William Fox.[114] Roosevelt never slackened in his steady and often voluminous correspondence to his literary acquaintances. On one occasion he wrote a forty-thousand-word letter to Trevelyan describing his tour of Africa and Europe.[115]

Roosevelt frequently wrote to American historians whom he admired and whose advice he sought. In December 1889 he presented a paper on "Certain Phases of the Westward Movement in the Revolutionary War" at the annual meeting of the American Historical Association. While there he met the association's president, William Frederick Poole, and the two began a scholarly correspondence.[116] Roosevelt also befriended Lyman Copeland Draper, the historian of the early West, who helped him with the research for *The Winning of the West*.[117] Theodore valued the advice of Frederick Jackson Turner, one of the nation's noted historians and then a professor of American history at the University of Wisconsin. Like many aspiring historians of his day, Roosevelt idolized Francis Parkman and dedicated his four volumes of *The Winning of the West* to the premier historian of pioneer America and the scholar who first recognized the closing of the West. Shortly after becoming commissioner, Roosevelt revealed to Parkman his personal tug-of-war between politics and scholarship. "I have always intended to devote myself to essentially American work; and literature must be my mistress perforce, for though I really enjoy politics I appreciate perfectly the exceedingly short nature of my tenure," wrote Theodore. "I much prefer to really accomplish something good in public life, no matter at what cost of enmity from even my political friends than to enjoy a longer term of service, fettered by endless fear, always trying to compromise, and doing nothing in the end."[118]

The Philadelphia lawyer and novelist Owen Wister became another of Roosevelt's favorites. While commissioner, Roosevelt deepened his friendship with Wister and began a correspondence that lasted until Roosevelt's death. Theodore was a junior at Harvard when the freshman Wister, whom he called Dan, arrived. Like Theodore, Wister joined the elite "Dickey." Finishing Harvard in 1885, Wister explored the West and became enchanted with the Wyoming Badlands. He returned to the West many times and wrote of his experiences. The two men shared a love for literature and the wilderness. Roosevelt greatly admired Wister's rugged western fiction, and Wister later dedicated his popular novel *The Virginian* to his friend Theodore.[119]

The varied friendships and acquaintances Roosevelt made during his commissionership served him well in years to come. Prior to his arrival in Washington, Theodore led a sheltered life and made few close friends outside of his family. The commission years thrust him into the bustle of Washington society, and his job forced him to mingle and communicate with people from all walks of life. During those six years, Roosevelt gained a much better understanding of human nature, and although he remained somewhat naive socially, his friends and colleagues brought him down to earth. He recognized the value of his personal relationships, later writing that "the most important single ingredient in the formula of success is knowing how to get along with people."[120]

The friends he made also had long-term consequences for the future president. Many of the same friendships became invaluable both personally and politically and demonstrate how important the civil service years were in providing him the opportunity, at such a young age, to build powerful relationships. In 1905, for example, President Roosevelt turned to several of his old literary friends, including Frederick Jackson Turner, Owen Wister, Alfred Mahan, and Charles Francis Adams, to serve on a presidential commission that studied the use of historical publications and recommended the creation of what is today the National Archives.

Through the friends he admired, Theodore learned to listen to those who were expert in a subject and to value their opinions and advice, a talent he later used well in the White House. Having no patience for fools or dullards, he actively pursued friendships and maintained a robust correspondence with the men he admired and respected. During his thirties he undoubtedly would have made numerous friends wherever he may have lived, for Roosevelt sported a gregarious and vibrant personality. However, the six years at the commission are unique because they took place in Washington, the nation's capital and the nerve center of national politics. When taken collectively, the relationships he cultivated while commissioner became a powerful force in Roosevelt's life and in his trajectory toward the nation's highest office.

⌐

During the summer of 1891, when Roosevelt and Spring-Rice lived together in Lodge's home, Theodore continued to spar with Wanamaker. After each accused the other of lying, the *Washington Star* suggested that "If Mr. R tells the truth there ought to be a new Postmaster-General; if he does not, there ought to be a new Civil Service Commissioner."[121]

On the first of July, Roosevelt visited the White House and tried to persuade the president to side with him against Wanamaker. Harrison was noncommittal, prompting Theodore to quip that the president "is a genial little runt, isn't he." Meanwhile, Theodore's nemesis at the *Washington Post,* Frank Hatton, continued his rabid attacks, describing Roosevelt as "tintinnabulating Ted," "scion of a diluted ancestry," and "Terrapin Teddy" and calling for his ouster.[122]

By the end of the summer, Theodore needed a break. He returned to be with his wife and family to Sagamore Hill, where, on August 13, Edith gave birth to a daughter, Ethel. While his wife and newborn recovered, Theodore frolicked with the other children. On rainy afternoons he played hide-and-seek with the youngsters in the old barn nearby, where hay was stored beneath its giant hand-hewed oak beams. The children delighted in digging narrow tunnels through the hay and watching their stout father trying to squeeze in after them.[123] On sunny afternoons Theodore donned a shiny black one-piece bathing suit buttoned to his neck, lined up his children and the sundry cousins who were always visiting in the summer, including a gangly young Eleanor, and marched them all down the hill to the water's edge. Diving headlong into the bay, Theodore reminded his daughter Alice of a sort of "sea monster who was flailing away in the water, peering nearsightedly at me without glasses and with his mustache glistening wet in the sunlight."[124] During their afternoon plunges, Theodore used a simple but effective method of teaching the younger children to swim. He just threw them into Long Island Sound.

On September 1, Roosevelt caught the train from the little station in Oyster Bay and began another of his trips to the West. Spending six weeks in the Dakotas, he visited the ranches near Medora and hunted for a month in the wilderness. Theodore savored the Badlands, a foreboding yet ruggedly beautiful landscape strewn with dry and sharp buttes, brown grass, water scorings, and small outcrops. Riding alone through the desolate country, he killed nine elks, having the head of a twelve-point stag mounted as a present for Lodge. Roosevelt reappeared from the wilds refreshed and "tough as a hickory knot."[125] His face was tanned and windburned, his hands leathered from the toil of chopping firewood and weeks riding through the wilds. His health was the best of his life, no longer the frail young man who overcame asthma, nor yet exposing the wide girth he flaunted a decade later in the White House. By the end of the summer of 1891, Theodore's body was solid and muscular and his jowls were no longer hollow but filled with a plumpness of life and energy.

Roosevelt returned to Oyster Bay in early October and a week later was back in Washington at his City Hall desk. After arriving at work each morning, his office was soon in shambles. Theodore never blotted his signature on his correspondence but instead scattered documents to dry over his desk and about the room.[126] When he read a magazine article or newspaper, he would tear out each page after it was read and throw it on the floor amidst a growing collection of trash.

Meanwhile, his running battle with Wanamaker continued, although Theodore now showed more confidence that the president would not fire him. "I don't suppose I really shall be turned out," Roosevelt admitted to Lodge. "We'll have two more winters in Washington together."[127] That December Theodore moved his family back to Washington and into the new house he rented on Nineteenth Street. He enjoyed being back at work and settled with his wife and children. Even so, Roosevelt longed for the rugged beauty and peacefulness of the western wilderness. Two nights before 1891 came to an end, he sat at his desk and scribbled a note to his friend Elwood Hofer in Montana. "I am pretty busy at work now and sincerely wish I were out west instead," wrote Theodore, "even in winter I think that teepee would be most comfortable."[128]

4
1892

Making Progress in Civil Service Reform

WITH TUGBOATS STRAINING at her stern, the French liner *La Normandie* slowly backed away from the pier that jutted into the Hudson River from Manhattan's West Side.[1] The huge ship left New York on schedule, just before noon on Saturday, January 9, 1892, and steamed eastward for the weeklong sail across the Atlantic. Passengers standing on the starboard side gazed up at Auguste Bartholdi's awesome Statue of Liberty, erected five years before on Bedloe's Island. As the city's skyline slowly slipped away to sternward, a warm southerly breeze turned falling wet snow into a light rain that glistened on the passengers' ulsters and umbrellas. For one of them, Theodore Roosevelt, the Atlantic voyage offered no vacation. He traveled alone, embarking on an uncomfortable trip to Europe in the midst of winter. He already missed his family, still in Washington, and felt guilty taking a month away from the Civil Service Commission, where he remained embroiled in fights with a hostile Congress, harassing newspapermen, and John Wanamaker.

Roosevelt sailed to France to deal with a family crisis. While his first six years in Washington provided overall happiness to the Roosevelts, sadness and worry lingered within their household. Theodore's brother, Elliott, was their most serious concern. Living in France with his wife and children, Elliott struggled with chronic mental and physical ailments for many years and by the winter of 1892 was in danger. Theodore, despite his taxing work at the commission, felt he had no choice but to sail to Europe to aid his brother.

Theodore was two years older than Elliott. When they were young, Elliott was a strapping boy and often mistaken as the oldest. He stood taller and was stronger and more athletic than Theodore, who for years remained frail and sickly from severe asthma. Elliott was the best-looking and most sociable of the children and in many ways the most endearing and loving of them all. He was neither as aggressive or force-ful as his brother nor as determined and organized as their sister Anna. Elliott appeared more sensitive than most men and, like his father, displayed effortless charm, generosity, and humor; unlike his older brother, he didn't have an enemy in the world.

Elliott never could thrive amid the unrelenting competition that controlled everyday life within the energetic Roosevelt family. This be-came especially true as the two brothers matured, the underachieving Elliott born with natural gifts being compared to the overachieving Theodore, who as a delicate child aggressively overcame his weak-nesses. As a youngster, Elliott lacked confidence in his own abilities. During the family's second trip to Europe in 1873, thirteen-year-old Elliott wrote his father from Liverpool. "What will I become when I am a man?" he asked. "I think Teedie . . . is much quicker and more sure kind of boy, though I will try my best and try to be as good . . . if [it] is in me, but it is hard."[2]

The following year, Elliott fell victim to strange seizures, fainting spells, and fits of delirium that plagued him the rest of his life. "Yester-day during my Latin lesson . . . I had a bad rush of blood to my head," Elliott wrote his father from Oyster Bay. "It hurt me so that I can't re-member what happened."[3] By the time Elliott reached sixteen, his health problems had become so severe that the boy could not concen-trate or study. While the more stable and studious Theodore prepared for Harvard, the family gave up hope for Elliott's formal education. They sent him to the wilds of central Texas to live on an army post at Fort McKavett, where some of his father's Civil War friends were sta-tioned. Elliott seemed to improve, but hope for recovery vanished in February 1878 when his father died. All of the children were devastated, but none as much as Elliott. During his father's agonizing last days, Elliott tried to care for him and attend his needs. Theodore, at Harvard at the time, was spared the worst, but Elliott watched his father die in utter agony. To Elliott, failure to keep his father alive added another example of his inadequacy and shattered his fragile self-confidence.

During this period Elliott worked for an uncle, James Gracie, at a New York City bank. When Elliott's health worsened over the next year, Theodore stepped in to help. After graduating from Harvard in

1880, he accompanied Elliott on a hunting trip into the Midwest.[4] Taking the train to Chicago, the brothers continued west for a month's trek through Iowa and Minnesota. They returned to New York in early October, three weeks before Theodore married Alice Lee. "We have had three days good shooting," Theodore wrote Anna on August 22 while still in the Midwest. "We are dressed about as bad as mortals could be, with our cropped heads, unshaven faces, dirty gray shirts, still dirtier yellow trousers and cowhide boots. . . . I enjoy being with the old boy very much; we care to do exactly the same things."[5] When they reached Chicago on September 12, Theodore wrote his sister Corinne and described what seemed to have been an enjoyable trip for the brothers. In the same letter, he revealed Elliott's increasing taste for alcohol. "We have come back here after a week hunting in Iowa. Elliott revels in the change to civilization—and epicurean pleasures," wrote Theodore. "As soon as we got here, he took some ale to get the dust out of his throat; then a milk punch because he was thirsty; a mint julep because it was hot; a brandy smash 'to keep the cold out of his stomach'; and then sherry and bitters to give him an appetite."[6]

Two months later, after serving as best man in Theodore's wedding to Alice Lee, twenty-year-old Elliott sailed to India by way of London. Crossing the Atlantic on the *Germanic,* he befriended two fellow travelers from New York, James Roosevelt and his wife, Sara Delano, just married and honeymooning in Europe.[7] After he returned to the States, Elliott served as the godfather of James and Sara's new son, Franklin.[8] Elliott never knew that years later the baby Franklin would marry his own daughter, Eleanor.

Elliott returned from India by way of China, then crossed the Pacific in March 1882, having been away a year and four months. He arrived in time to attend his sister Corinne's wedding to Douglas Robinson. After returning from his round-the-world vacation, Elliott began to drink heavily. During that period he met Anna Hall, a tall, stunning belle of New York society. Dazzled with her beauty, Elliott proposed on Memorial Day 1883 and the two married on December 1, 1883, with Theodore as best man. Anna had just turned nineteen, Elliott twenty-three. Theodore hoped that marriage would provide stability for his ailing brother. "I am honestly delighted, however, for I think the dear old boy has won a lovely girl for his wife, and I am greatly mistaken if it does not do him all the good in the world to have something to work for in life," Theodore wrote Corinne after the engagement. "I am very anxious to see her and know her. I am sure I shall like her very much."[9]

The family's optimism, however, soon disappeared. Elliott's wife could not provide the steady influence they hoped. Anna proved to be almost as aimless as her husband, and their life degenerated into an endless blur of parties, polo matches, and vacations. Despite their frivolity, any happiness for Anna and Elliott dissolved as the responsibilities of marriage and the birth of three children—Eleanor in 1884, Elliott Jr. in 1889, and Hall in 1891—increased Elliott's anxiety. No longer a casual drinker, Elliott was now a chronic alcoholic.

From Washington, Theodore watched his brother's dangerous lifestyle with apprehension. In one episode, Elliott broke his collarbone when he rode with the hounds.[10] "Poor, dear old Nell; I suppose it is useless to wish that he would put himself completely under a competent physician," Theodore wrote Corinne in July 1889. "I did my best to get him to."[11] In early 1890, other problems arose. "Ellie has had a real hard illness during this last week," Theodore wrote Anna. "He has had two abscesses on his neck; they prevented him from swallowing, and drove him nearly mad with pain; to complicate matters he got a severe attack of rheumatism. He looks ghastly, can not even sit up in bed, and has been kept much under the influence of anyodynes [sic]."[12]

Elliott's drinking worsened following a riding accident in which he badly broke his leg. Doctors prescribed opiates for the pain, and he apparently became addicted. During this period, Elliott would abandon his wife and children for weeks at a time. The family dreaded scandal. Theodore and his sister Anna recognized Elliott's heavy alcoholism, although Corinne, more tolerant and less willing to judge, remained reluctant to admit the seriousness.[13]

In the summer of 1890, Elliott took his wife and children to Europe, but the change of scenery did nothing to curb his deterioration. In Europe he became violent toward his wife, who was again pregnant. Only weeks after they arrived, the family sent for his sister Anna, who had returned from a summer trip west with Theodore and his family. In early February 1891 Anna sailed to Europe, where she placed her brother in a sanitarium in Austria and rented a nearby room. By April, he improved and his sister escorted him to Paris, where his Anna gave birth to their third child, Hall. That summer, however, Elliott took an American mistress, a Mrs. Evans, and further declined to the point that his sister packed up his wife and children and returned to New York.[14] Even his sister Anna, the most determined, patient, and capable member of the Roosevelt family, had endured enough of Elliott's self-destruction and, now exasperated, left her brother to fend for himself in Paris.

Back in New York, the scandal that the family feared unfolded. Katy

Mann, a pregnant young woman who had been a servant to Elliott and his wife, claimed Elliott to be the father and threatened a lawsuit. Back in Washington, Theodore and Edith dreaded the scandal would ruin the family name, to say nothing of Theodore's political career, as both were well aware that the nation's capital was "the graveyard of reputations as well as the cradle of fame."[15] Roosevelt feared that the pro-spoils newspapers, especially Frank Hatton's *Washington Post,* would have a field day with such juicy gossip. "The last hideous revelation hangs over me like a nightmare," he wrote Anna on January 23, 1891. Theodore anguished over what to do. "I hate the idea of a public scandal; and yet I never believe in yielding a handsbreadth to a case of simple blackmail," he wrote Anna in May. "I am at my wits' end to know what to advise."[16] In June he wrote Elliott saying they should consider paying Katy Mann to keep the scandal out of the headlines. Eventually she dropped the suit when the family provided her a large financial settlement.

To forestall future scandals and the final squandering of Elliott's share of the dwindling family fortune, Theodore and Anna began legal action to have Elliott declared insane. Four days after the birth of Theodore's daughter Ethel and during the period when he sent his scathing Baltimore report to the White House, more scandal surfaced when the press discovered the attempt to have Elliott committed. "Elliott Roosevelt insane," announced the *New York Sun* that summer. "His brother Theodore applies for a writ in lunacy."[17] From Paris, Elliott fought the court action. On January 9, 1892, Theodore sailed to Europe to confront Elliott.[18] When the brothers met in Paris, Elliott resisted his brother's urgings but eventually agreed to separate from his wife, turn over two-thirds of his property to her, and return home for rehabilitation. Theodore and his sister agreed to not declare him insane. Until he could demonstrate his worthiness to the family, Elliott would live apart from his wife and children. Sailing from Le Havre, Theodore returned to New York on February 7, 1892.

↩

Roosevelt was back at his desk at the commission on February 10. The Washington social season was at its peak, with scores of dances, teas, and dinners enlivening the city. Theodore and Edith, however, were now satisfied to stay at home, reading and playing with the "bunnies." When Theodore and Edith did venture out to an evening affair, he often felt awkward. He sometimes encountered cabinet officers and congressmen and felt obliged to socialize pleasantly with them. During the day, his commission duties forced him to battle with many of the same dignitaries he dined with the night before. Theodore, forthright and direct, was uneasy mixing with his adversaries and treating them like friends. To him, an enemy was an enemy and to be treated as such.

While the Congress was predominantly pro-spoils, Roosevelt could count on a few key legislators for support. These included Lodge; Senators Cushman Davis of Minnesota, Orville Platt of Connecticut, and Francis Cockrell of Missouri; and Congressmen William McKinley of Ohio and George Dargan of South Carolina.[19] Even Tom Reed of Maine, who would regain his speakership in 1895, fell behind the reform banner, declaring, "I don't like it [civil service reform] straight, but mixed with a little Theodore Roosevelt, I like it well." Despite the efforts of honest legislators, spoils politicians still controlled both houses of Congress, cabinet members battled the commission, and presidents waffled on crucial occasions. After years of attacks by the more radical reformers, many Washington insiders, especially those whose livelihoods depended on patronage, became "heartily sick of the subject of civil service reform."[20]

Despite a horde of adversaries, by the beginning of 1892 Theodore and his fellow commissioners made some progress in enforcing the Pendleton Act. One small success narrowed the loophole that allowed lame-duck presidents to blanket large numbers of their patronage appointments into the merit service. When Roosevelt arrived, the law provided no restrictions on blanketings, and any patronage appointee with two years in office could be transferred into the merit service by presidential order. Upon the commission's urging, Harrison abolished the grossest abuses and ordered that persons transferred from the unclassified to the classified ranks must first pass the civil service examination. Although widespread blankets continued, the commission curtailed the most blatant abuses and ensured that appointees possessed at least minimal qualifications.[21]

The commission demonstrated its slowly growing power by conducting a number of successful investigations of illegal political removals, assessments, campaigning, and outright fraud. In January 1892, Roosevelt dashed about the commission offices gathering papers and details from a recent investigation into illegal assessments. Based on the evidence he provided, the U.S. district attorney in Owensboro, Kentucky, successfully indicted six federal Internal Revenue officers, including Chief Collector Hancy, for demanding illegal political assessments during the presidential campaign of 1892.[22] Federal courts eventually convicted and fined the Kentucky violators, as well as Postmaster Ickes of Newark, Ohio, accused in a similar assessment case.[23] In other investigations, the commission succeeded in securing the removal of three postal workers in Rochester, two in Buffalo, eight in Omaha, six in Denver, and twenty in Washington, all of whom had been illegally appointed. However, these removals represent a small percentage of the questionable practices investigated. In the majority of cases department heads paid little attention to commission recommendations.[24]

Because of widespread infractions in the civil service law, especially in federal field offices, Roosevelt spent considerable time away from Washington. In April 1892 he inspected federal agencies in New Orleans, followed by a trip to southern Texas where he managed to find time to take a six-day hunting trip near the Nueces River, killing two peccaries. "It was great fun, for we followed them on horseback," Theodore wrote Spring-Rice. "The little beasts fought with the usual stupid courage of pigs when brought to bay."[25] Less than a week after returning from the South, Theodore headed west to Chicago for more inspections.

‿

Back at City Hall, Roosevelt's hunting was not so productive. Despite a few successful indictments, the commission continued to face significant obstacles in investigating wrongdoing. The inability to summon witnesses and to administer oaths especially frustrated the commission, which could gather information only voluntarily or upon presidential order. The commission continued to be hamstrung until December 1901, when President Roosevelt issued an executive order requiring civil servants to testify under oath before the commission.[26]

Once the commission completed an investigation, holding accountable those who broke the law became another difficult task. During the ten years following 1883, the courts convicted few violators of the Pendleton Act, while department heads continually ignored commission recommendations to remove those breaking the law. Nevertheless, even unsuccessful investigations tended to stop abuses by calling attention to them. Roosevelt often turned to pro-reform newspapers such as the *Washington Evening Star, New York Tribune,* and *Philadelphia Press* to decry political shenanigans. As the press began to embarrass the more flagrant wrongdoers, violations decreased and by the mid-1890s the courts had convicted a number of violators.[27]

Roosevelt realized the difficulties of enforcing the Pendleton Act.

"Every case I present to the Department of Justice I have to have worked up so that there can be no possible doubt in the mind of any reasonable man as to the parties' guilt," he wrote Lucius Swift, editor of the *Civil Service Chronicle*. "You will see how careful I am in recommending the prosecution of men even when I have got two witnesses against them. I always feel that I must be ready to defend my action and to show conclusively that I was right in recommending the prosecution."[28] The commissioners, unable to punish or remove most of those who broke the law, only could turn the evidence over to the department heads, who in most cases were spoils advocates who refused to act. Nevertheless, Roosevelt remained determined and investigated violations as aggressively as ever. On occasion he sent circulars to government employees informing them of their rights, the possible penalties for violating the law, and the prohibitions against assessments. When he could not punish violators or coerce action by department heads, Roosevelt turned to the press, who found that his colorful descriptions of political tomfoolery made good copy. Soon, embarrassed party bosses thought twice before they carried out the more flagrant offenses.

The commissioners made progress in improving the examination process. Since 1853, some federal agencies, including the Interior Department under Carl Schurz from 1877 to 1881, required examinations of employee applicants, but standardized exams for the entire civil service did not exist until 1883 and the passage of the Pendleton Act. The Civil Service Commission at first created two different examinations for clerk applicants. A limited examination tested for penmanship, spelling, and arithmetic, and applicants who passed the limited examination qualified for "copyist" positions that paid a maximum salary of $900. Most of the copyist positions were assigned to women. Those applicants competing for higher-paying clerkships took the general examination, which tested skills in grammar, syntax, and more difficult arithmetic problems as well as knowledge of history, geography, and government. Both men and women took the general examination, but since agency heads requested only male candidates for the higher-paying jobs, a high score by a woman was meaningless in most cases.[29] As commissioner, Roosevelt took keen interest in the content of exams. In 1894 he convinced his fellow commissioners to simplify the clerk exams by combining the two categories and offering one clerk/copyist examination that added new test categories, including practical skills such as bookkeeping and letter writing.

The commissioners spent considerable effort overseeing the local boards that administered tests and determined eligibility. During the

Roosevelt years, the number of persons examined nearly tripled from 11,281 in 1888 to 31,036 in 1895. The commission developed, rewrote, and administered over 270 separate kinds of examinations by 1893.[30] The commission also investigated the procedures by which local examining boards operated. In his first week on the job, Roosevelt exposed the illegal sale of exam copies for fifty dollars apiece in the New York Customshouse. As a result of his investigations, Roosevelt helped change the civil service rules so that examining boards no longer kept eligibility lists secret but publicized the examination grade of each applicant. Publicizing the lists lessened the opportunity for manipulation by political bosses. Later, the commission further reduced exam fraud by creating a central board of examiners in Washington under the commission's supervision.[31]

The commission insisted that examinations be practical, not theoretical, and designed to test aptitude for a specific job rather than general knowledge. Local boards used the tests to examine clerks in penmanship, composition, grammar, American history, and geography. Roosevelt wanted to eliminate general aptitude tests, preferring evaluations in useful skills over academic subjects such as arithmetic and spelling, both of which Theodore performed poorly.[32] Ever the erstwhile cowboy, Roosevelt suggested testing horsemanship and marksmanship to select mounted inspectors of the Customs Service on the Mexican border and chafed when he failed to create an exam for cattle inspectors testing brand reading, steer roping, and riding mean horses.[33]

Despite these efforts to keep the examinations practical and job-related, opponents of civil service reform often attacked the commission by arguing examination questions were not realistic. Such an attack led to a prolonged skirmish between Roosevelt and the political boss from Maryland, Senator Arthur Pue Gorman. In 1889, Gorman rose to the floor of the Senate to complain that a "bright young man" from Baltimore had failed the letter carrier examination. "[The examiners] wanted him to tell them what was the most direct route from Baltimore to Japan, and as he said, he never intended to go to Japan," argued Gorman. "He had never looked into that question, and he failed to make the proper answer. They then wanted to know the number of lines of steamers plying between the United States and Liverpool." Roosevelt immediately retaliated, informing the senator that no such questions were on the letter carrier exam. The argument did not end, however, and the same examination controversy flared again two years later, in February 1891, when Gorman chastised Roosevelt on the Senate floor for having "gone beyond bounds of propriety" and acting "outrageous and insolent." Roosevelt struck back a month later, criticizing Gorman for the "untruths you had uttered" and requesting that the senator "give us the name of the 'bright young man,' if he has any name."[34]

Four years later, the "bright young man" had not disappeared. In October 1895, Theodore was no longer at the Civil Service Commission, having become New York City police commissioner. When a Maryland gubernatorial election became hotly contested, Republican politicos invited the colorful Roosevelt to speak.[35] Theodore delighted a Baltimore rally by resurrecting the "bright young man" affair to attack Gorman. "There is an old expression to the effect that a man who is false in one thing will be false in many," Theodore now told his audience. "In the course of my experiences with Senator Gorman in Washington, I caught him in a deliberate falsehood, one so flagrant that it ought to be called by the good, old, simple, direct Anglo-Saxon word of three letters." Then, having told the Baltimoreans how he was purifying New York as police commissioner, Theodore wished them Godspeed and headed for the train station.[36]

⮯

The commissioners fought for authority to investigate illegal removals of government employees. Although the Pendleton Act prohibited firing classified government workers purely for political reasons, the law vested removal power completely in the hands of department heads, who in reality could remove a worker for any cause, including politics. One senator said that omitting removals from the Pendleton Act was like omitting the part of Hamlet from the tragic play.[37]

Roosevelt vigorously battled illegal removals throughout his years at the commission. "I think we ought to be given power to investigate all removals and to report whether or not . . . they were due to political reasons," Roosevelt wrote his reform friend, William Dudley Foulke.[38] "The law is clumsily framed."[39] From the beginning of the Pendleton Act, the arbitrary power to remove employees enabled the patronage system to continue under the guise of removal. Roosevelt's early investigations confirmed the loophole around illegal political removals. His investigation of the Baltimore Post Office in 1889 revealed that 96 percent of the dismissals were for political reasons.[40] Roosevelt campaigned for the law to be strengthened and recommended the commission be given the power to review all dismissals. But neither the president nor Congress took action on Roosevelt's recommendation, and the rule remained unchanged until 1897, when President McKinley issued an order expressly prohibiting dismissals from the classified service "except for just cause and for reasons given in writing."[41] Nevertheless, Roosevelt attacked the more flagrant political dismissals with vigor, sent caustic letters to department heads, and publicized infractions in the press. Over time, he made progress. "Unquestionably a certain number of government employees are still dismissed from the service for purely political reasons," Roosevelt wrote in June 1894. "These cases are rare in Washington but are common in some of the smaller offices outside of Washington."[42]

Besides removals, the question of how promotions should be determined in the classified service remained controversial. Roosevelt believed that a lack of promotional opportunities undermined the morale of the classified service.[43] The commission did not have the ability to investigate numerous incidents when department heads promoted or demoted merit employees simply for political reasons. Roosevelt urged that this practice be curtailed. "Unfortunately promotions and reductions are not touched by the law at all, and we have nothing to do with them," Roosevelt wrote to a former Harvard classmate in December 1894. "The fact that they are made so generally for political reasons affords an excellent reason why the law should be extended to cover them."[44]

Most reformers favored using competitive examinations to determine promotions, while others preferred the traditional method by which supervisors promoted deserving employees. Roosevelt favored a combination of both methods and recommended using a competitive examination in conjunction with a standardized rating given by the applicant's superior. The rating would contain information as to the candidate's efficiency, industry, ability, and morality. He recommended that a weight of about a third be given to the supervisor's efficiency rating and two-thirds to a competitive exam.[45] Roosevelt developed a detailed plan on how his system would operate and presented it to the president. Harrison, however, disregarded Roosevelt's proposal and instead directed his cabinet members to develop their own departmental promotion standards.[46] In December 1891, Harrison ordered Secretary of State Blaine to begin keeping "an efficiency record of all persons within the classified service, with a view to placing promotions wholly upon the basis of merit." Harrison saw no need for competitive promotion tests and rescinded the rule requiring a compulsory, centralized examination. "In my opinion, the examination for promotion . . . should be chiefly, if not wholly, upon their knowledge of the work of the Bureau or Department to which they belong," wrote the president.[47] Harrison also asked all department heads to keep daily accounts of each office worker and give a score from zero (worthless) to seven (perfect) on performance in punctuality, attendance, industry, accuracy, aptitude, conduct, and ability.[48]

Roosevelt resented the "utter silliness and pigheadedness" of Harrison's refusal to put promotions under commission control.[49] Over time, the individual departmental plans proved cumbersome and inadequate because the rules varied considerably among departments. Roosevelt succeeded after Cleveland returned to office when he convinced the new president to order that promotions be determined by voluntary exams in conjunction with supervisor efficiency reports.[50]

Throughout 1892, Roosevelt and his fellow commissioners immersed themselves in the technical drudgery of improving the merit system. They had their setbacks, however. The commission was unsuccessful in closing various loopholes that diminished the effectiveness of the merit system. One problem was that the commission had no control over either temporary workers or those workers designated as "laborers" making less than $720 per year.[51] Although theoretically such employees only performed manual labor, in practice many served as clerks and were hired to circumvent civil service entrance requirements. In 1893, Secretary of the Interior Hoke Smith reported that the civil service system still excluded about one-quarter of the forty-six hundred people employed in his Washington offices.[52] The commissioner of patents also confessed to using the loophole, writing in 1894 that "I found the practice had prevailed under each of my predecessors, since the enactment of the civil service law, of assigning to clerical duty persons employed as messengers and laborers, without any examination under the Civil Service Rules as therein required."[53] By numerous means both fair and foul, spoilsmen continued to sidestep the merit system and place their political cronies into government jobs.

Despite the frustrations of a merit system far from perfect, Theodore did not lose sight of the higher calling of civil service reform. On a cold, gray day in November, while visiting his family at Oyster Bay, he took the train into New York City to speak to a group of city reformers. "People often speak of civil service reform as if it were a matter of mere administrative detail," Roosevelt remarked to his audience. "They do not appreciate that it is not merely a question of changing the methods of administration, but that it is a question of substituting a system of equity and justice for a system of brutal wrong. It is a question of working a great benefit, not merely to the public service, but to our public life. It is a question of making politics purer."[54] Despite attacks from spoils-bent congressmen, cabinet members, and hostile newspapers, Theodore had yet to lose his spirit as a crusader for reform and a battler for good over evil.

⌐

On a sunny Monday afternoon in June, President Harrison took a day off from his presidential chores and, with his new secretary of state, John Watson Foster, left the White House in his carriage and rode up Pennsylvania Avenue, past the Capitol, to a seedy neighborhood called Swampoodle. Known for its street gangs, ramshackle houses, and large number of poor Irish and Italian immigrants, the shantytown also was the site of Washington's baseball stadium, Swampoodle Downs, and home of its professional team, the Senators. From his days watching soldiers playing ball during the Civil War, Harrison enjoyed the sport that quickly was becoming America's pastime. The president was unaware that this day, June 6, 1892, was the first time a sitting president attended a professional baseball game, nor did any of the two thousand fans take special notice of the short, stout, bearded man in a dark suit and top hat. Harrison stayed for the entire game, watching the Cincinnati Reds defeat the lackluster Senators, 7–4, in eleven innings.

Theodore Roosevelt would not have lasted eleven innings. He hated baseball, a game much too slow for his impetuous nature. He preferred more violent sports like boxing, his sport at Harvard, and football. Impatient in action, Roosevelt also was impatient with his fellow man. Spring-Rice once described Roosevelt's impulsiveness: "If you took an impetuous small boy on to a beach strewn with a great many exciting pebbles, you would not expect him to remain interested for long in one pebble."[55] In many ways, Theodore was still an impetuous small boy. He never possessed a refined ability to understand others. Instead of determining whom to trust and whom to mistrust based on their character, he often judged people by their stances on policy issues, jumping to conclusions and branding acquaintances as either close friends or despicable foes, with no one falling in between. The naturalist John Burroughs once complained that Theodore treated people unpredictably, killing "mosquitoes like lions, and lions like mosquitoes."[56]

Roosevelt was quick to judge John Wanamaker, denouncing him as "an ill conditioned creature" and "evasive hypocrite." He did not realize that Wanamaker shared his high moral standards and was eminently trustworthy. Like Roosevelt, Wanamaker firmly believed in equal opportunity. "We never allow religion or nationality or color to enter into the matter of employment of men, women, or children," wrote Wanamaker to one of the customers of his department store.[57]

Standing six feet tall, John Wanamaker was an imposing man whose sturdy build suggested a youth of hard labor and toil. Also like Theodore, Wanamaker had a childhood of perpetually delicate health and turned to physical exercise to strengthen his body.[58] Wanamaker's hands and arms were still powerful from working for his father, a bricklayer. With short brown hair and penetrating gray-blue eyes, the Philadelphia merchant spoke in a deep and resonating voice and captivated his companions with an ingratiating manner that included "the habit of taking the arm of the one with whom he walked."[59] Radiating energy, Wanamaker worked tirelessly on any project he undertook or any cause he championed.

Although Wanamaker yielded to spoils politics as postmaster general, the Philadelphian stood upright and harbored neither dishonesty nor incompetence nor laxity. Commuting each weekend from Washington to Philadelphia to teach Sunday school, Wanamaker pursued lawlessness and immorality as aggressively as Roosevelt. While he was postmaster general, a favorite project was the completion of the new granite Post Office building. One reason for locating the building on its Pennsylvania Avenue site was to help clean up "Hooker's Division," a ten-block zone between Pennsylvania and Ohio Avenues. Named for Civil War general Joe Hooker, whose troops encamped in the area, the zone possessed fifty saloons and more than a hundred houses of prostitution. Of all the major cities, Washington had the highest rate of drunkenness, twice the rate of notoriously besotten New Orleans. The completion of the Post Office, however, had little effect on Washington's seediest area. The "Division" continued to serve Washington's scruffier clientele until 1914, when another moralist, Woodrow Wilson, ordered the area leveled.

Roosevelt and fellow reformers labeled Wanamaker a Republican of the old school and a dyed-in-the-wool spoilsman.[60] Others, however, portrayed him as an effective administrator who balanced the political needs of his party with the efficient management of the Post Office Department. Wanamaker's critics, including Roosevelt, found the Philadelphian difficult to understand because he promoted economy and efficiency in the postal service—the very same benefits that reformers claimed for the merit system—while simultaneously yielding to patronage necessity and practical politics.[61] Wanamaker accepted the theory, often endorsed by Roosevelt himself when criticizing Mugwump independence, that political reform becomes most effective when controlled within the existing party system rather than prompted by idealistic methods outside it.[62] Wanamaker welcomed change and claimed he believed in civil service reform. His business training and success as an innovator suggested a commitment to reform.[63] His colossal Philadelphia department store, employing over two thousand workers, was the first to use electric lights, install telephones, and sell automobiles, airplanes, and Marconi wireless sets.[64] Wanamaker was also ahead of his time in his treatment of workers. He created an employee mutual benefit association, training classes for clerks, paid vacations, a medical clinic, life and pension insurance, and, most radical for the time, profit sharing.[65] In 1889 he dispensed $100,000 to his workers in shared earnings. He fought for Prohibition and permitted female employees to march in suffrage parades during work hours.[66]

Wanamaker brought his skills as a successful businessman to the Post Office, where he achieved a number of modernizations.[67] Always willing to take on thankless tasks, he later remarked that "I always had a broom in my hand."[68] He completely reorganized the department, establishing Rural Free Delivery Service and a commemorative stamp program, integrating the postal service and the merchant marine, and abolishing the lottery. He recommended parcel post, postal savings, and government ownership of the telegraph and telephone. Overall, Wanamaker put the Post Office Department on firm financial footing as the only government bureau to make a substantial profit.

In 1891, Wanamaker created a career structure and a merit promotion system for postal workers administered within the Post Office Department, not from the Civil Service Commission.[69] In creating a Board of Promotions in Washington, Wanamaker endeavored to improve the civil service within the postal service through competitive examinations and equalization of salaries in every post office of fifty or more employees.[70] Meanwhile, a headstrong Roosevelt refused to entertain any positive aspects of Wanamaker's performance as postmaster general, insisting that the commission take control of the hiring and firing of the classified postal workforce.

↬

Until the steamy summer of 1892, the town of Homestead, Pennsylvania, sat peacefully on the left bank of the Monongahela River seven miles east of Pittsburgh. Homestead was a "company town," home of a Carnegie Steel plant that manufactured boiler plate and iron beams. Of the town's more than 10,000 residents, 3,431 worked at the plant. During that spring, the onset of the economic depression of the 1890s caused steel prices to plummet. When the workers' wage agreement expired in June, the company proposed to cut wages between 18 and 26 percent. After the union objected, the company locked out the workers. On July 6 violence erupted, killing seven strikers and three Pinkerton guards hired by the company. At the company's request, 8,000 state militia marched into Homestead and placed the plant and the town under martial law. The company broke the union on July 27 when the plant reopened with a thousand new workers.[71]

Harrison and the federal government took no active role in the strike, but the president monitored the events closely. The strike was yet another signal of a growing unrest in the country that, spurred by economic strife, would reshape the political forces for the rest of the decade. At the same time as the Pinkerton guards faced off against the Homestead strikers, leaders of the Populist movement met in Omaha and inaugurated their first national convention. Calling themselves the People's Party, they resolved "to restore the government of the Republic to the hands of the plain people with whose class it originated."[72]

Roosevelt, braving the summer heat alone in Washington, watched the events in Homestead and Omaha with keen interest. Throughout his life, Theodore feared mob rule and saw labor unrest as a first step to anarchy. To Spring-Rice, he cursed labor unions who "are against the established order and feel bitterly because of wrongs which are really inherent in the nature of things."[73] After the Chicago Haymarket riots in 1886, Roosevelt confessed to his sister Anna that he yearned to lead a band of his Dakota cowboys "with their rifles at one of the mobs."[74]

That summer Roosevelt also recognized the significance of the Populist movement's developing into a full-fledged political party. At the end of 1892 the Populists elected three governors, five U.S. senators, and ten representatives, while their presidential candidate, General Weaver, captured six western states and carried over 8 percent of the total vote.[75] The Populist platform drafted during that summer's convention foreshadowed many of the reforms broached by the Progressives a decade later, including a graduated income tax, direct election of senators, initiative and referendum, and an attack on monopolistic trusts. More fundamentally, the Populists called for government to assume a much greater responsibility in ensuring the economic and social well-being of the nation. In 1892 such a notion of a more active and powerful government was both radical and unpopular. Not until 1901 would the notion become reality under the stewardship of a young and energetic president.

⌇

At about the same time as the Homestead strike, President Harrison began his reelection campaign against his former opponent, Grover Cleveland. Few showed much interest in the presidential race. It was a common saying that one of the candidates had no friends, the other only enemies.[76] For many living on the East Coast, a fierce August heat wave and a cholera epidemic were more worrisome than the presidential race. Meanwhile, Harrison refused to carry his campaign into the country, as his wife was seriously ill with tuberculosis. She died on October 25, near the end of the campaign. Cleveland, in respect for his opponent, also refused to campaign across the country and remained in New York.

The campaign during that summer created another clash between Wanamaker and Roosevelt. Wanamaker refused to believe that Roosevelt had gone west for his health and thought that Roosevelt, like other loyal Republicans, should be on hand to speak in the presidential campaign. To Wanamaker, Roosevelt's departure suggested disloyalty to the president when his friends and political appointees should have rallied round him.[77] Wanamaker was justified somewhat in his criticism, as Roosevelt's letters to Lodge during the period suggest frustration and deteriorating loyalty toward Harrison. In Roosevelt's defense, his trips west each summer were a well-known sabbatical, and Roosevelt had offered his services to campaign the previous October. However, Harrison spurned him. "I broached this at the White House . . . but it was frowned on," Roosevelt wrote Lodge. "If only they would back me up, and then let me act publicly, on the stump, as a Republican! But they won't do either, and seem to regard me with a curious mixture of suspicion and treacherous dislike."[78]

On August 2, 1892, Theodore boarded the *Limited* for his annual trip west. He combined a short hunting trip in the Badlands with campaigning for Harrison and, during September, inspecting Indian reservations in Kansas, Nebraska, and the Dakotas. His support for Harrison was tellingly limited, however, as he stumped for the president only at the opera house in Deadwood, South Dakota.[79] Late that month he published an article in the *Independent* defending the president's foreign policy and his ultimatum to Chile.[80]

Harrison had little chance. He suffered the stigma of the unpopular protective tariff, embarrassments such as the Wanamaker/Roosevelt imbroglio, and an economy slipping quickly into depression. The rising Populist movement also cut into Republican strengths in the West, amassing over a million votes.[81] In November 1892, Cleveland avenged his defeat of four years before and won soundly, capturing 277 electoral votes to Harrison's 145 and Populist James Weaver's 22. The Democrats captured the White House and Congress for the first time since the Civil War, and Cleveland became the only president to serve two nonconsecutive terms. Soon, Harrison returned to Indianapolis to practice law and Wanamaker went back to Philadelphia and his giant department store. Surprisingly, Roosevelt stayed in the capital.

5
1893

Reappointment by the Democrats

A FIERCE, BITTERLY cold northwest wind hurled snowflakes against Grover Cleveland's cheek as he spoke, hatless, to the shivering crowd. The new president stood on an open stage extending out from the east portico of the Capitol and delivered his inaugural address. On the night before, a blizzard struck Washington with late-winter fury and dumped a thick cover of snow at the rate of more than an inch an hour. By the time Cleveland spoke that afternoon, March 4, 1893, the snow had tapered off but the temperature dipped below freezing and the winds blew violently. The weather discouraged many from attending the inaugural parade, and the remaining brave souls filled only half of the stands along Pennsylvania Avenue.[1]

President Cleveland, like Harrison before, campaigned on a mild reform platform and, at least in his rhetoric, favored an attack on the spoils system. He knew Theodore Roosevelt well. The two New Yorkers maintained a guarded friendship, and despite different party loyalties, their politics were not far apart. The journalist Lincoln Steffens once wrote that "Roosevelt was so much of a Democrat and Cleveland so much of a Republican that they meet in the middle."[2] In 1882, Cleveland became governor of New York at the same time Roosevelt ran for his second term in the state legislature. During the next year they worked closely together to pass the first state civil service legislation and other reform measures.

Despite their amiable past, Roosevelt criticized the new president viciously during the 1892 presidential campaign. Derisively described by

Republican critics as a "pig blinking in a cold wind," Cleveland was a three-hundred-pound titan with a walrus mustache, bull neck, and wrestler's shoulders whose stature invited sarcasm.[3] Speaking for Harrison, Roosevelt declared that Cleveland opposed the merit system, that his ruthlessness in discharging faithful government servants "would have done no discredit to Andrew Jackson . . . [and that] he has signally failed to make good his pledges."[4] Behind the scenes, however, communication between Roosevelt and Cleveland suggests at least a much more candid dialogue. On October 15, 1892, a month before the election, Roosevelt sent a cryptic "strictly personal" telegram to Cleveland. "Deeply grateful for your letter," Theodore wired Cleveland from his speechmaking in Princeton, New Jersey. "Propositions that have been made since have totally changed situation so that I will not have to make the demand upon you which three days ago it seemed I would have to for the interest of the Nation. I thank you most deeply and shall write you at length."[5] While the nature of the "demand" remains unknown, the telegram reveals a surprising communication between Cleveland and Roosevelt, who was at the time stumping vigorously for Harrison.

Roosevelt, however, still expected to be dismissed from the commission as soon as Cleveland and the Democrats returned to office, and he predicted his own imminent departure. "When I leave on March 5th I shall at least have the knowledge that I have certainly not flinched from trying to enforce the law during these four years, even if my progress has been at times a little disheartening," Theodore wrote William Dudley Foulke in early December 1892.[6] The press also anticipated Roosevelt's ouster. The *New York Tribune* forecast a complete turnover of the commission members and predicted that Cleveland would remove the "most aggressive Republican" member, Roosevelt. Surely Theodore's overzealousness would not be tolerated by the Democrats.[7] During the next three weeks, however, Roosevelt began to realize that his departure was not certain and that there remained a possibility he could remain at the commission under the new administration. As the chance of a Cleveland reappointment appeared more realistic, Roosevelt turned to an old family friend.

Sixty-four-year-old Carl Schurz was one of the country's most fascinating characters. At first glance, Schurz looked almost insane, with a scraggly dark beard and mad flashing eyes glaring through round spectacles. His tall, spidery frame and long legs were heightened by his dress, which was often threadbare and ill fitting, with coat sleeves and trousers much too short. His appearance, however, belied his intellectual brilliance and the powerful political influence that he brandished for more than four decades. After emigrating from Germany in 1852, at the age of twenty-three, Schurz quickly mastered English and became one of the most prominent public speakers of his time. A fierce abolitionist, he served as Lincoln's minister to Spain, a general in the Civil War, senator from Missouri, secretary of the interior, founder of the *New York Evening Post,* and president of the National Civil Service Reform League.[8]

Schurz was a die-hard civil service reformer. An influential member of the National Civil Service Reform League, he swayed reform politicians in both parties, including Cleveland, and never relented in his fight against the spoils system. Once complaining that office seekers "swarm about me like grasshoppers," Schurz created one of the first effective merit systems while he served as interior secretary from 1877 to 1881. Schurz was a friend of Roosevelt's father and, despite disagreements over many political issues, became an ally of the younger Theodore. Although Schurz opposed Roosevelt during Blaine's candidacy in 1884 and fought Roosevelt's presidential reelection twenty years later, the two men maintained at least a wary friendship. Schurz was one of the few whom Roosevelt forgave for his mugwumpery, although Theodore described the old warhorse as a "pinchbeck."[9]

In December 1892, after learning he was not necessarily persona non grata in Democratic circles, Theodore asked Schurz to see if the new president would allow him to stay. "I am very anxious to see you about civil service matters," Roosevelt wrote Schurz. "I had thought of trying to see Mr. Cleveland but came to the conclusion that this would be an unwarrantable intrusion on my part. I do wish also that you could arrange to have Leupp, the editor of *Good Government,* see Cleveland. He is thoroughly familiar with the situation here and ardently devoted to the reform."[10]

Schurz apparently found Cleveland receptive. "I trust you will not take it as an indiscretion on my part that I communicated to Mr. Cleveland what you had written me about," Schurz wrote Theodore on January 4, 1893. "[I] do not know whether he intends to ask you to remain a member of the Civil Service Commission . . . [but it] seems to suggest that such a thing is possible . . . there is not another man in the country who can do it as well as you can."[11]

Roosevelt remained anxious. "I am greatly touched at the interest you, with your many calls, have taken in the matter," Theodore wrote Schurz the following day. "I should rather communicate with Mr. Cleveland through you; can I not see you first . . . when it is convenient to arrange for my calling on Mr. Cleveland, anywhere he wishes?"[12]

Schurz convinced Cleveland to reappoint Roosevelt, writing the president-elect on January 11, 1893, "You can hardly find a more faithful, courageous and effective aid than Mr. Roosevelt."[13] On January 17, Roosevelt called on Cleveland and the matter was settled. The decision offered a convenient solution to selecting new commissioners, for the Pendleton Act required at least one of the three commissioners to be from the minority party. Roosevelt's record confirmed that he attacked Republican spoilsmongers with as much brazenness as he did Democrats. The outgoing secretary of the navy, Benjamin Tracy, urged Roosevelt to accept Cleveland's offer. "Well my boy, you have been a thorn in our side during four years," Tracy remarked to Roosevelt. "I earnestly hope that you will remain to be a thorn in the side of the next administration."[14]

Theodore saw the irony of being reappointed by the Democrats, for he doubted the same would have been true if Harrison had been re-elected. On March 6 he gave a speech to the Federal Club in New York City and admitted that "had we [the Republicans] been victorious last fall, I would not have been present now."[15] In April, Theodore's place in the Cleveland administration appeared solid. "I saw Cleveland the other day," Theodore wrote Anna. "He asked me to stay for a year or two longer; I shall therefore probably stay at least a year."[16]

⌒

In May 1893, after a vacancy opened at the commission, Roosevelt suggested that the president appoint his friend John R. Proctor. "By the way, I believe I have discovered a first class southern Democrat for Civil Service Commissioner," Theodore wrote Schurz. "He is Proctor, for many years State Geologist of Kentucky, ex-confederate soldier, . . . a strong civil service reformer, and he positively refused, while Geologist, to allow politics to enter into his survey."[17] A dashing-looking gentleman with a shock of white hair, a white handlebar mustache curled up at the ends, and a princely little white goatee, Proctor gained notoriety when the Kentucky governor fired him for refusing to hire the governor's son. Winning widespread praise from civil service reformers, Proctor served on the commission from 1893 until his death in December 1903.[18]

Roosevelt was pleased with his own reappointment to the commission. During the recent election, the Massachusetts legislature elected Henry Cabot Lodge to the U.S. Senate, and Theodore was delighted that they would remain together in Washington. Roosevelt also was pleased that he now became the unofficial chief commissioner, for the minority member customarily supervised commission activities.

While Roosevelt jointly managed the commission with two other commissioners, he never seemed comfortable with divided authority. In all of his public offices, no matter where in the chain of command he resided, Theodore asserted himself as the self-proclaimed and solitary leader. If he had his choice, a single director instead of a cumbersome triumvirate would have supervised the commission. During the absence of his two colleagues, Roosevelt revealed his desire for a single administrator. "My two colleagues are now away and I have all the work of the Civil Service Commission to myself," Theodore wrote to Anna. "I like it; it is more satisfactory than having a divided responsibility; and it enables me to take more decided steps."[19]

Congress also investigated the benefits of having a single commissioner.[20] Roosevelt testified before a House select committee that drafted legislation to replace the three commissioners with a single director. "There is no doubt that . . . a single-headed body is better than a triple-headed one," Theodore claimed. "It is of vital importance now that the President should nominate only men of capacity and with a reputation for scrupulous impartiality, but it would be even more important if only one Commissioner was to be appointed. If the right nomination could be assured, I feel sure that one Commissioner would be an improvement over a board of three."[21]

While arguing the single commissionership was the ideal, Roosevelt nevertheless felt that "the time is not ripe for such a change yet."[22] He recognized that public relations constituted one of the bigger challenges for civil service reform and that the public first must be persuaded of the advantages of having one director. While the select committee recommended a single commissioner, the full House tabled the measure. The triumvirate remained until 1978, when Congress passed the Civil Service Reform Act and put the control of the civil service under a single director.

Edith was relieved when Cleveland asked Theodore to remain at the commission, for she also wished to stay in Washington. She did not want to move that winter, as all of the children were sick with mea-

sles.[23] Despite her natural introversion, she enjoyed the Washington social scene and adjusted well.[24] Edith did not favor any move unless
Theodore first found another job. The civil service salary provided little,
but it provided more than an unemployed husband would. Edith worried constantly over the family's finances. "Theodore feels the poor-
house is pending," she wrote Anna in December 1893.[25] At the time,
Theodore found himself $2,500 in debt. He too bared his financial woes
to Anna three days later and considered selling Sagamore Hill. "The
trouble is that my career has been a very pleasant, honorable and useful
career for a man of means; but not the right career for a man without
the means," Theodore wrote his sister. "If I can I shall hold this position
another winter; about the time I shall publish my next two volumes of
the *Winning of the West;* I am all at sea as to what I shall do afterwards."[26]

While Theodore professed an ambition "to make earning money the
secondary instead of the primary object of my career," he could not
ignore his finances during the first years in Washington.[27] Even before
he moved south, Roosevelt's financial worries made him reluctant to
accept the commissionership. The civil service position provided a
salary of $3,500, barely sufficient for his growing needs.[28] His father's
once-wealthy Roosevelt family suffered during the Panic of 1873, the
worst depression of the century, and sold their glass import business
to a British firm. While Theodore received about $8,000 a year from a
family trust, he was now on his own.[29] Besides his inheritance and writing income, Roosevelt also received funds to raise his oldest daughter,
Alice. Her wealthy Lee grandparents paid Theodore a steady allowance
throughout her childhood.[30] On one occasion, they sent Edith a substantial check for the children and she bought them a pony cart. "It is
like a little nest," wrote Edith to her sister, Emily, "and they go off
chirping like a family of birds."[31]

Roosevelt's losses in the Dakota cattle business during the disastrous
winter of 1886, amounting to half of his $85,000 investment and two-
thirds of his livestock, further depleted his finances.[32] From that time
on he never enjoyed the wealth to which he had been accustomed. In
1892 his financial condition improved somewhat when Edith's uncle,
John Carow, died and left an estate that provided an annual income of
$1,200. Even with Edith's windfall, however, the family struggled to
make ends meet. Theodore was not much help, for he possessed no
talent for economics and business. During the severe depression of
the 1890s he did not grasp the economic and political significance of
the nation's financial woes, nor did he share his wife's concern over the

financial losses the family suffered from their limited investments during the period. In keeping with his financial indifference, Theodore seldom carried money and once had to walk back to the White House for lack of streetcar fare.[33] During his commission years, Edith gave birth to three of their six children, he traveled frequently, and they maintained residences at Sagamore Hill, Washington, and the ranches near Medora, North Dakota. Shortly after arriving in Washington, he wrote Corinne saying he had reluctantly sold his two polo ponies.[34] "This Commissionership, which has prevented my writing, has in consequence cut down my income by seven or eight hundred dollars," Theodore wrote Anna a couple of months later. "Now all my money will be turned over to Edith, and I will draw from her what I need."[35]

While Roosevelt was in the Dakotas in 1890, Edith informed her husband that they owed $1,155.79. "How many of [the bills] do you think you can pay?" she wrote. Coping with Theodore's dues to the Harvard Club, she asked, "could you resign? . . . I am in the depths. I had not allowed myself to think of such a 'damned total.'"[36] As the true financial manager of the family, Edith stretched their income to make ends meet and to maintain their privileged lifestyle in both Washington and Oyster Bay. During the commission years, her Sagamore Hill household budget included the following: clothes, $30 per month; groceries, $35 per month; salaries for a farmer, gardener, coachman, cook, waitress, nurse, maid, chambermaid, laundress, and furnaceman, $210 per month; coal and wood, $300 per year; and doctor bills, $383 in 1890 and $556 a year later.[37] The Roosevelts paid $244 to the town of Oyster Bay for property taxes on Sagamore Hill's eighty acres, assessed at $15,000 in 1894.[38] Although money constantly troubled Theodore and Edith, apparently little of their upper-class lifestyle suffered, for they continued to maintain two residences and a retinue of servants, including Sagamore's superintendent, named Seaman, Hall the coachman, and a crotchety old black gardener named Davis.

While in Washington, Edith skimped on food by shopping at the sprawling Central Market, an immense building covering two blocks along Pennsylvania Avenue between Seventh and Ninth Streets. The market, excellent as well as cheap, provided one of the few Washington locales where the rich and the poor rubbed elbows, where society matrons patronized the market as regularly as boardinghouse keepers. On market day in the 1890s, women with baskets filled the streetcars and the sidewalks and elegant ladies descended from carriages driven by stovepipe-hatted coachmen. They all made the rounds of the stalls to pore over the fresh fruits and vegetables, eggs and chickens, fish and

oysters from the Chesapeake, wild duck, and other specialties in season.[39] To a visiting Henry James the market was "vulgar and vocifer-
ous,"[40] but to the ever-curious Edith the throng of shoppers surely must
have been as fascinating as the bargain-priced foodstuffs.

~

"Such delightful people from all over the world! And then, presto! As
by a swarm of locusts the land is darkened. The office-seekers have
come to town."[41] So it was with every new administration, including
that of President Grover Cleveland, who was back in the White House
in 1893. Although Cleveland was a nominal friend of civil service
reformers, the battle against the spoils system was far from over. At
the center of the battle, of course, was Theodore Roosevelt. As civil service commissioner within the new administration, Roosevelt continued
his reform efforts and attacked the pro-spoils Democrats with the same
tenacity with which he had previously attacked Wanamaker and the
Republicans. Several of Cleveland's cabinet appointments supported
civil service reform. At first the reformers were skeptical of the new ag-
riculture secretary, J. Sterling Morton, who replaced most of the unclassified Republicans with Democrats. However, over the long term
Morton rid his department of its widespread spoils positions, introduced many reforms, and by the end of Cleveland's administration had
the most completely classified department. Likewise, the new navy secretary, Hilary Herbert, won the reformers' praise for continuing the exemplary work of Harrison's secretary, Benjamin Tracy, while the new
secretary of war, Daniel Lamont, made progress in removing undesir-
ables from the War Department.[42]

To Roosevelt's pleasure, Cleveland chose Wilson Bissell as postmaster
general. A former law partner of the president, the portly Bissell was
honest but naive in politics, having never before held public office.[43]
Upon becoming postmaster general, he appeared loyal to civil service
reform and refused to allow widespread pillaging of the Post Office Department. In July 1894, Bissell fired the Troy, New York, postmaster for
making illegal political removals. "The inequities that may exist between the two political parties in the present application of the civil
service law, is a matter which neither you nor I need concern ourselves
about," Bissell explained to the postmaster. "The law is as we know it
to be, and it is your duty and mine to be bound by it."[44]

Roosevelt was optimistic. "Most emphatically, Mr. Bissell [is] more
favorably disposed to the law and far more willing to do what [he]
can to see it legitimately enforced than was the case under the last ad-

ministration," Roosevelt wrote Schurz in June 1893.[45] Two months later, Theodore complained that the press was treating Bissell unjustly. "Doesn't it seem to you that *Harper's Weekly* has been pitching into Postmaster General Bissell too severely recently?" he asked Schurz, then a contributor to *Harper's*. "I do not think it has done him justice, and I feel strongly that inasmuch as Mr. Bissell is the best friend we have got in the Cabinet it is a pity to attack him."[46]

Over the next year, however, Roosevelt turned against Bissell. "We have come almost to a standstill with Mr. Bissell over certain cases of postmasters," Theodore wrote Schurz in June 1894. "I think the President will back him up. He has declined to act on our suggestions. I fear Mr. Bissell is flinching."[47] By February 1895, Theodore had grown "very much disgusted with Bissell,"[48] as the postmaster general ignored the commission's recommendations and refused to punish wrongdoers. "I can't get him to act even upon the clearest cases where it is perfectly evident that the postmaster has turned out men for political reasons."[49] Roosevelt, however, may have acted overly harsh toward Bissell. The postmaster general not only resisted the onslaughts by spoilsmen at the beginning of the Cleveland administration but over the next two years initiated several successful reforms, launched a series of investigations that helped root out corruption, proposed classification of all fourth-class post offices, and improved the overall management of the Post Office Department.

Of all the Cleveland appointments, the reformers objected most loudly to the nomination of James J. Van Alen as minister to Italy. A Rhode Island millionaire, Van Alen contributed $50,000 to Cleveland's campaign fund. To the reformers, Van Alen had purchased a public office in much the way that they accused Wanamaker of doing four years before. E. L. Godkin and other reform editors attacked Van Alen as unqualified, and a bitter debate erupted in the Senate over the millionaire's confirmation. Although the Senate confirmed the appointment, Van Alen resigned soon thereafter. The reformers had won a new victory. The Van Alen case was not only important for showing the power of public criticism in forcing a resignation but also demonstrated a growing public animosity against the influence of wealth in governmental appointments.[50]

Some of Cleveland's cabinet officers fought the commission and civil service reform. Secretary of State Walter Gresham angered Roosevelt and the reformers when he allowed consular positions to fall into the spoilsmen's grasp.[51] Besieged with patronage requests, Gresham chose Josiah Quincy, a civil service reformer from Boston, as assistant secretary to distribute appointments. Quincy's position as the distributor of spoils was much the same as Clarkson's four years earlier. Despite his reputation as a friend of civil service reform, Quincy proved efficient in his new role. By August 1893 he had replaced 117 Republican consular positions with Democrats—more than a third of the foreign service officers. According to Roosevelt, Quincy searched for patronage places like a "pig hunts truffles."[52]

Of Cleveland's cabinet officers, Treasury Secretary John Carlisle became Roosevelt's most notorious adversary. Balding, clean shaven, and glaring sternly with cold eyes, Carlisle previously served as Speaker of the House and remained a popular and important figure of his party.[53] Along with his son Logan, Carlisle "openly sneered at the law" and ruthlessly replaced Republican officeholders with Democrats. "Not even Wanamaker was a meaner, smaller cur than Carlisle," Theodore wrote Anna after the Cleveland appointee took office. "He is dishonest, untruthful, and cowardly."[54] Later, Carlisle angered Roosevelt by shaking up the classified service in the Treasury Department and promoting and demoting clerks not on the basis of ability but to even up promotions between the parties. Carlisle angered the reformers when he removed several long-standing professionals, including Cyrus Stevens, an expert appraiser in New York with twenty years of government experience; A. O. Latham, a veteran Treasury officer; and A. F. McMillan, a deputy first auditor who had served the department for twenty-seven years. The upheaval demoralized career workers. When Roosevelt requested information on the status of classified Treasury employees, Carlisle refused to cooperate and insisted that any correspondence be cleared through his office.[55] A year later, Roosevelt again seethed when Carlisle tore into the Coast Survey. "Carlisle is perpetrating a fresh piece of infamy," Theodore wrote to Carl Schurz. "I quite seriously assert that though perhaps scarcely as repulsive a man as Wanamaker, he is to the full as mean and underhanded a spoilsman and as viciously dangerous to good government. He has just capped the climax by driving one of the most scientific men of the country, Prof. Mendenhall, out of the Coast Survey."[56] Thomas Mendenhall, who set high standards for entrance into his agency, resigned in protest after Logan Carlisle replaced his staff of technical experts with unqualified political appointees.[57]

⌐

Secretary Carlisle infuriated Roosevelt for another reason and one that struck at Theodore's basic sense of morality. To Theodore, firing workers for political reasons broke the law, but firing them for the color of their skin was morally reprehensible. After Cleveland's inauguration, Roosevelt discovered that Carlisle fired a number of black women from the Treasury Department's engraving division. The commission was powerless, as the firings were legal. Roosevelt could do nothing but publicize the facts.[58] Incensed at this practice in other departments, Roosevelt complained to the editor of the *Civil Service Chronicle*. "In making the reductions in the War Department and in the Interior, they have discriminated a great deal because of politics, and still more because of color," wrote Roosevelt. "In the War Department they have turned out about two-thirds of the young colored men who came in through our examinations during the past three or four years."[59]

During the period surrounding his commission years, Roosevelt became increasingly convinced of government's obligation to assist the less fortunate. However, his policies toward race and minorities reveal more contradiction and controversy. The conflict between Roosevelt's racist rhetoric and his often liberal and humane behavior is difficult to resolve. Roosevelt's true feelings toward race relations were muddled because he used the terms "race" and "nation" interchangeably.[60] Nevertheless, Roosevelt's brutal racial statements conformed to those of the majority of his intellectual contemporaries.[61] At Harvard he studied under Nathaniel Shaler, a historian who professed notions of white supremacy, innate black immorality, and the desirability of slavery as a necessary instrument of racial "adjustment." While at Columbia Law School Roosevelt studied under John Burgess, a political scientist who held low opinions of nonwhites and called for the Teuton to eliminate "barbaric populations." Roosevelt also embraced the ideas of Edward Ross, a Lamarckian sociologist who coined the term "race suicide," a belief that entire races face extinction through failure to reproduce in sufficient numbers.[62]

Roosevelt's writings are harshly racist. He saw African Americans, "that most sinned against of races," as a special problem and believed that black inferiority was based on "scientific" evidence. He felt blacks were outcasts, believed that they could not be absorbed into the national bloodstream, and opposed miscegenation.[63] Roosevelt's books written during the commission years, including *The Winning of the West* (1889, 1894, 1895), *New York* (1891), *American Big-Game Hunting* (1893), *The Wilderness Hunter* (1893), *Hero Tales from American History* (1895), and *Hunting in the Bad Lands* (1895), contain references to white racial destiny and supremacy.[64] In *New York*, Roosevelt refers to the English-speaking race as "the mightiest race on which the sun has ever shone," and in *The Winning of the West* he maintains that Anglo-Americans enjoy a biological and cultural supremacy over other stocks.[65]

On the other hand, Theodore's sense of justice consistently overpowered his notions of white male supremacy, and he often acted un-conventionally liberal, tolerant, and above the widespread bigotry of the era. Roosevelt and Lodge courageously endorsed ex-congressman John Lynch, a black Mississippian, for chairman of the 1884 Republi-can convention in Chicago.[66] True to his notions of justice, Roosevelt believed that color should not be considered in punishing criminals, and he deplored lynchings, at the time a common occurrence in the South.[67] He frequently asserted the idea of equal opportunity for all Americans regardless of race, and his later efforts on behalf of blacks earned him an image as a moderating force in an age of high racism.[68] As commissioner he opposed a movement by southern congressmen to segregate the few black workers from their white coworkers.[69] Like most white Americans of the day, he believed that blacks were inferior to whites in terms of education and social attainment but felt that dis-crimination, with its accompanying poverty, was morally wrong.[70]

As civil service commissioner, Roosevelt often adjudicated and some-times provoked racially controversial personnel decisions. During the winter of 1890 he dictated a letter to his overworked stenographer, Orville Swank, and condemned the ability of employers to fire workers based on their race. "I should not think the fact of having red hair a sufficient cause for removal," wrote Roosevelt. "But under the law I could not prevent a man removing a subordinate because he had red hair, having nothing to do with removals unless they are clearly made for political reasons. Personally I think this portion of the law stands in need of change, but at the present all we have to do is administer it."[71]

By late 1894, Roosevelt's sense of racial justice in civil service ap-pointments appears to harden further, as he aggressively challenged powerful southern congressmen who opposed any appointment of blacks. "Congressman [John Sharp] Williams,[72] of Mississippi, attacked the Commission in substance because under the Commission white men and men of color are treated with exact impartiality," Roosevelt charged in a report to Congress. "As to this, I have to say that so long as the present Commissioners continue their official existence they will not make, and, so far as in their power lies, will refuse to allow others to make, any discrimination whatsoever for or against any man because of his color, any more than because of his politics or religion. We do equal and exact justice to all."[73]

⌐

"Hour after hour passed by. A little black woodpecker with a yellow crest ran nimbly up and down the tree trunks for some time and then flitted away with a party of chickadees," wrote Theodore in *The Wilderness Hunter* in the spring of 1893. With his naturalist's eye and vast lore of woodcraft, Roosevelt described a hunting trip near the headwaters of the Madison River in southern Montana.

Flocks of crossbills, with wavy flight and plaintive calls, flew to a small mineral lick near by, where they scraped the clay with their queer little beaks. As the westering sun sank out of sight beyond the mountains these sounds of bird life gradually died away. Under the great pines the evening was still with the silence of primeval desolation. The sense of sadness and loneliness, the melancholy of the wilderness, came over me like a spell. Every slight noise made my pulses throb as I lay motionless on the rock gazing intently into the gathering gloom.

Suddenly, and without warning, the great bear stepped out of the bushes and trod across the pine-needles with such swift and silent footsteps that its bulk seemed unreal. It was very cautious, continually halting to peer around; and once it stood on its hind legs and looked down the valley toward the red west. As it reached the carcass I put a bullet between its shoulders. It rolled over, while the woods resounded with its savage roaring. Immediately it struggled to its feet and staggered off, and fell again to the next shot, squalling and yelling.[74]

Roosevelt wrote his colorful best when he described the life of animals and birds in their natural habitats and other nature subjects with which he was intimately familiar. He described large game vividly, such as the grizzly bear, "a shrewd beast . . . a cover-hunting animal, sly in his ways . . . clinging to the shelter of the deepest forests in the mountains and of the most tangled thickets in the plains."[75] From a literary standpoint the best of Roosevelt's natural history writings was *The Wilderness Hunter,* which suggests that during the commission years he matured as a writer. Theodore continued to do everything in excess, and his writing was no exception. He used the personal pronoun excessively.[76] For the most part, however, he no longer annoyed his reader with repetitions and extravagant generalizations from the limited samples of his own experience.[77] By 1893, Theodore's writings showed more confidence and his storytelling became more natural and at ease, especially when he shared his expansive knowledge of forest and game and his genuine excitement with nature.

Between 1882 and his death in 1919, Roosevelt published at least twenty-four books and countless articles. His serious scholarship began with the *Naval War of 1812,* which he researched while a student at Harvard. Covering a wide range of topics, his books and articles discharge a fusillade of history, criticism, nature writing, political analysis, and moral and patriotic exhortation. He wrote books about the marvels of nature, the wilderness as he encountered it, the conquest of the frontier and the western territories, and three biographies of men he admired: Thomas Hart Benton, Gouverneur Morris, and Oliver Cromwell. His writings provide a valuable impression of Theodore, for in many ways his published works mirror the man, reveal a great deal of his thought and temper, and provide a glimpse into the age in which he lived and which he helped to shape.[78] Roosevelt wrote frequently and abundantly while at the commission. During those six years he composed most of his four-volume *The Winning of the West,* which he regarded as "being of all my axes the one best worth grinding."[79] He also completed *The Wilderness Hunter, Hero Tales from American History, New York,* and over three dozen journal articles, including several arguing the need for civil service reform. His writing interests varied from "Professionalism in Sports" in the *North American Review,* to "What America Means" in the *Forum,* to "Religion in the Public Schools" in the *Boston Herald.* By the time he left the commission, he enjoyed a national reputation as an author.[80]

While Roosevelt always remained dedicated to his writing, his position as commissioner gave him even more incentive to publish. He needed the money, and the journal articles and book advances provided much-needed cash. He also had a vested interest in publishing for his friend and editor George Haven Putnam. While in the New York legislature, Theodore invested $20,000 in G. P. Putnam's Sons, the publisher of his *Naval War of 1812,* and remained a limited partner in the publishing house.[81] Edith, who managed the family finances, recognized Theodore's need to publish. Throughout their marriage he turned to his well-read wife to edit his books and essays, a practice begun on their honeymoon. "I read all [of my essays] to Edith," Theodore wrote his sister Corinne from Europe in 1887, "and her corrections and help were most valuable."[82]

By today's standards of scholarship, Roosevelt's writings appear naive, poorly researched, and filled with the author's personal opinions. In his earlier works, Roosevelt projects himself vigorously into his histories and dogmatically argues his own partisan view of a controversy. His historical *New York* does not qualify as serious history by modern standards, for it uses no primary sources or unpublished manuscripts.[83] One of Roosevelt's earlier biographers dismissed his written work as anti-intellectual, and Henry Adams was not reluctant to attack Roosevelt's writing.[84] In 1889, Adams complained to John Hay shortly after Roosevelt became commissioner. "I see that both Cabot [Lodge] and Teddy Roosevelt are on the shop counters in apparent self-satisfaction, which makes me as sick as Possum to reflect that I too can no longer avoid that disgusting and driveling exhibition of fatuous condescension," wrote Adams. "All books should be posthumous except those which should be buried before death, and they should stay buried."[85]

When measured against the scholarship at the turn of the century, however, Roosevelt compares well with many of the leading historians and political commentators of the time. He also earned their honest respect, and his election to the National Institute of Arts and Letters in 1898 at the age of forty was altogether legitimate. In 1912 he was elected president of the American Historical Association.[86] By the standards of his contemporaries, Roosevelt proved a competent researcher. In 1895, his last year at the commission, he completed a much improved fourth and final volume of *The Winning of the West,* which became a best-seller on both sides of the Atlantic and won the praise of eminent historians Frederick Jackson Turner and William Poole.[87] Living in Washington enriched his scholarship, for he made frequent use of the manuscripts and letters housed in government archives and the Library of Congress. Roosevelt also scoured the major eastern libraries, sought information from several state archives, and begged seldom-used manuscripts from collectors.[88] Described by Brander Matthews as a "severely trained scientific investigator," Roosevelt possessed a researcher's respect for the importance of detail, and his training in biology and the natural sciences provided skills in gathering evidence and empirical observation.[89] Roosevelt always claimed he was "not an impractical theorist; [but] a practical politician" who had little time for abstract "parlor theory."[90] However, his written work reveals a more intellectual Roosevelt who dealt with theory comfortably, criticized it when he disagreed, and created alternative hypotheses to explain complex social, political, and historical phenomena.

Roosevelt demonstrated his penetrating ability to probe theoretical depths in 1894 when Benjamin Kidd's *Social Evolution* was published and quickly became the literary rage on both sides of the Atlantic. Kidd, until then an obscure English government clerk, provided his huge audience with a controversial and peculiar mixture of obscurantism, reformism, Christianity, and social Darwinism. Few works touched more intellectual nerves in Theodore than *Social Evolution.* Immediately after absorbing Kidd's work, Roosevelt wrote a mixed and complex reaction in the *North American Review*. He accepted Kidd's argument that social progress is based upon biological laws; his attack on socialism as regressive; his conclusion that government should equalize the chances of competition but not abolish it; his emphasis on efficiency as the standard for social, political, and economic improvement; and his stress on character as opposed to intellect. He felt, however, that Kidd overstressed the need for competition and understressed the ability of the unfit to survive and grow more fit rather than suffer extinction. Roosevelt argued that Kidd overstated the sufferings of the masses, for in a prosperous society the vast majority of the people are happy and fulfilled and therefore have a rational incentive for contributing to progress. Moreover, he criticized Kidd for condemning all religions as "a succession of lies necessary to make the world go forward," when, according to Roosevelt, Christianity is far superior to other religions in teaching the subordination of the individual to the interests of mankind.[91]

Despite such intellectual excursions as the Kidd review, Roosevelt nevertheless considered himself an amateur in literary and historical circles. He realized his weaknesses as a scholar and seemed quite self-conscious about his writing. While working on his biography of Thomas Hart Benton, he appeared especially self-critical. "I feel a little appalled over the *Benton,* I have not the least idea whether I shall make a flat failure of it or not," Theodore wrote Lodge. "However, I will do my best and trust to luck for the result."[92] Later, from his ranch in Dakota, Roosevelt still struggled with *Benton* and confessed to Lodge, "Writing is horribly hard work for me; and I make slow progress. I have got some good ideas in the first chapter, but I am not sure they are worked up rightly; my style is very rough and I do not like a certain lack of sequitir that I do not seem able to get rid of."[93]

In June 1892 Theodore complained to Brander Matthews, "I struggle and plunge frightfully, and when written, my words don't express my thought."[94] He expressed the same misgivings to Owen Wister. "I wish I could make my writings touch a higher plane, but I don't well see how I can, and I am not sure that I could do much by devoting more time to them," wrote Roosevelt. "I go over them a good deal and recast, supply, or omit sentences and even paragraphs; but I don't make the reconstruction complete in the way that you do."[95]

The commission years provided the opportunity for Roosevelt, already well read, to strengthen his broad academic interests. His thirst for knowledge had always been strong. As a child still in kilts, young Teedie dragged around a huge volume of Dr. Livingstone's *Travels and Researches.*[96] Still intellectually curious, Commissioner Roosevelt expanded his wide-ranging theories on nature, science, society, literature, and government during his first years in Washington. He read critically. "I happen to be devoted to *Macbeth*," he later confessed, "whereas I very seldom read *Hamlet*, though I like parts of it."[97] Often he devoured two or more books in an evening and penned a dozen letters. At Sagamore Hill, books were everywhere, over six thousand of them, in the north room, the parlor, the library, and "the gun room at the top of the house, which . . . contains more books than any of the other rooms, and they are particularly delightful books to browse among."[98]

⌇

Of all of Roosevelt's literary colleagues, Theodore valued none more than his publishing adviser and trusted friend, Brander Matthews.[99] For over three decades the two men promoted a genre of American literature centered on "true Americanism," a virile, rough-and-tumble ideology that contrasted sharply with what Roosevelt termed the "over-civilized, over-sensitive, over-refined" culture of the eastern establishment.[100] For both Matthews and Roosevelt, the toughness of Kipling, Wister, Fenimore Cooper, and similar writers appealed to their sense of rugged individualism. At one point Roosevelt expressed his resolve for a uniquely American body of literature, writing Matthews that "we must strike out for ourselves; we must work according to our own ideas, and must free ourselves from the shackles of conventionality, before we can do anything."[101] Theodore went so far with his nationalism as to halfheartedly suggest that the stone lions in front of the New York City Library be replaced with American bison.[102]

By the time Roosevelt became commissioner, Matthews stood as one of New York City's most impressive men of letters and a wealthy member of Fifth Avenue society. From 1892 to 1924 he taught literature and drama at Columbia University. He befriended Mark Twain, William Dean Howells, and other literary stars of the era and played a significant role in the expansion of realistic American literature at the turn of the twentieth century. To protect American writers, Matthews headed a movement to enact copyright legislation.[103] Roosevelt joined the effort, and Lodge gave a speech on the House floor urging copyright protection.[104] After Matthews sent Roosevelt a copy of an essay proposing copyright legislation, Roosevelt enlisted the help of another friend, House Speaker Tom Reed. According to Matthews, Roosevelt convinced Reed to grant a copyright bill a vote during the end of the 1891 congressional session. Despite strong opposition, the copyright bill became law.[105]

Matthews's role as Roosevelt's literary adviser began when, as an editor for a publishing house, he persuaded Theodore to write a history of New York City.[106] While Theodore was commissioner, his frequent trips to New York City included a lunch with Brander, often at Delmonico's where the steaks were first-rate.[107] Throughout their friendship, Roosevelt and Matthews carried on a lively critique. "By the way, have you seen that London *Yellow Book*?" Theodore wrote Brander. "I think it represents the last stage of degradation. What a miserable little slob Henry James is. His polished, pointless, uninteresting stories about the upper social classes of England make one blush to think that he was once an American. The rest of [his] book is simply diseased."[108]

Roosevelt leaned often on the professor's arm for editorial assistance and literary advice. Over the years the two friends collaborated often, each favorably reviewing the other's works. Like those of Roosevelt, Matthews's literary efforts ran in many directions covering literature, drama, social events, and politics. Brander published three novels, all resonating with Roosevelt's social and political philosophy. *His Father's Son* (1895) attacks the materialist values and corrupt practices of wealthy Wall Street investors; *A Confident Tomorrow* (1899) suggests that radical socialists are as harmful to the national health as the despised plutocrats; and *The Action and the Word* (1900) mocks the New Woman and implies, as Roosevelt insisted, that a woman's true place remained in the home.[109] Matthews, again like Roosevelt, was an imperialist at heart. Matthews's essay "American Character" speaks proudly of the "warlike temper, the aggressiveness, the imperialistic sentiment that is in our blood."[110] One of Brander's short stories reveals his bond with Theodore. Titled "Memories" and written the year Roosevelt arrived at the commission, the story takes place in the rugged Northwest and describes the heroic efforts of U.S. army soldiers who battle Indians and fierce winter weather, climaxing in their enduring a blizzard to search for two lost children. The soldiers occupy a fictitious fort named, interestingly, "Roosevelt." The story electrified Theodore, who wrote to Matthews that "I really think it is one of the best of your stories, and I am very glad to have my name connected with it in no matter how small a way."[111]

↩

By the spring of 1893, Theodore was afraid he might be shot. The pleasant atmosphere at the commission took a turn for the worse after the amiable Governor Hugh Thompson resigned in the summer of 1892 and President Harrison appointed George D. Johnston to fill the vacancy. Johnston and Roosevelt could not have been more different, and from their first meeting "open warfare" began.[112] Twice Theodore's age, Johnston was a crusty Alabama Democrat who despised Republicans and Yankees. He had served in the Confederate army throughout the Civil War, rising from lieutenant to brigadier general, and fought from the Battle of First Manassas until Hood's surrender in Tennessee.[113] Wounded severely in the leg, Johnston carried a limp throughout his life. With his frosty handlebar mustache, panama hat, and white linen suit, he seemed the caricature of an antebellum plantation owner.

From the day he arrived at the commission, Johnston fought civil service reform, balked at any reduction in the number of patronage appointments, and lobbied for a "conservative administration of the law." In November 1893 relations between Johnston and Roosevelt worsened. Early that month, Theodore traveled to New York to attend the Harvard-Cornell football game at Manhattan Stadium, watching his Crimson eleven win handily, 34–0, in cold, rainy weather.[114] Shortly after he returned to Washington, Roosevelt and fellow commissioner Charles Lyman wrote to the president recommending that superintendents of Indian schools be classified. Johnston refused to sign the letter and wrote Cleveland a rambling explanation why the superintendents should remain unclassified.[115] The animosity between Johnston and Roosevelt continued to fester until the end of the month, when the old general complained that the classified service employed too many Republicans. Johnston refused to sign the commission's annual report to Congress and instead issued his own dissenting version. "It is, save for a few cheap phrases, simply a spoils document," Roosevelt wrote Carl Schurz. "The main feature of it is an attack upon the extension of the classified service to the free delivery offices! . . . Altogether it is a rather odd document."[116]

Roosevelt was cautious as he continued to spar with the cantankerous Johnston, wary that the general always arrived at the commission's office with a loaded revolver stuck in his trousers. "I have to be especially careful," Theodore wrote Lucius Swift. "I have to guard at all points against opposition *within* the Commission."[117] Roosevelt saw the president and told him that "he would certainly have to remove either the general or myself. Very possibly he will remove both."[118] Fortunately, Johnston's behavior soon angered Cleveland, and the president offered his fellow Democrat a diplomatic post if he would resign from the commission. When Johnston refused, Cleveland fired the "old fire eater."[119] Johnston returned to Alabama to practice law and served in that state's senate until his death.

A week after Johnston's removal, Cleveland pleased the reformers when he appointed a supporter of civil service reform, John R. Proctor, to the vacant commissionership. When Proctor replaced Johnston, the commission returned to its former relaxing climate and Theodore could breathe easier.

⤶

Shortly after noon on May 1, 1893, more than a hundred thousand spectators crowded in the sunlight along Chicago's lakefront, thankful that an easterly breeze blowing from Lake Michigan helped cool an already tepid day. A heavy rain the night before and into the morning failed to thwart the throngs of visitors, and shortly before noon the skies cleared.[120] Most of the crowd could not hear the short speech given by Grover Cleveland, standing on a rostrum high above, but they could see the huge president, dressed in a dignified dark-gray suit, when he stepped to one side and pressed a golden telegraph key. In a single push, Cleveland set in motion forty-three nearby steam engines powering 127 dynamos that sent electricity coursing through the hundreds of buildings and exhibits of the Chicago World's Fair. At that moment, the fair officially opened. Commemorating the four hundredth anniversary of Columbus's sailing to the New World, the overwhelmingly popular fair provided a six-month feast of sights and thrills for most of its twenty-seven million visitors—nearly a quarter of the nation's population at the time.[121]

A few days after Cleveland opened the fair, Theodore took a week-long break from his work at the Civil Service Commission and, with Edith, his sister Anna, and most of his family trailing behind, boarded one of the *Exposition Flyer* trains that carried thousands of visitors from eastern cities to the fair. The journey westward was exciting, as the *Flyers* pulled a string of luxurious Pullman cars at the amazing speed of eighty miles per hour. After arriving in Chicago, the Roosevelts entered the fairgrounds and quickly were overwhelmed by the impressive architecture of the "White City." Huge, ornate Beaux Arts buildings, each lending a magnificent stuccoed whiteness to the landscape, dominated the fair, while dozens of domed temples added to the majestic spectacle. Amidst this grandeur, gondolas ferried visitors across the lakes and ponds, where dozens of white sculptures rose from the water to enchant the visitors.[122] Theodore's friend Augustus Saint-Gaudens had created one of the fair's most ambitious works. His huge statue of Diana, goddess of the hunt, aimed an arrow at the heavens from her perch atop the agricultural hall designed by McKim, Mead, and White.[123] Edith felt like she was in "fairyland."[124]

The centerpiece of the fair and the engineering highlight was the gigantic Ferris wheel. Created by Pittsburgh bridge builder George Ferris, the huge ride towered twenty-six stories in the air and carried thirty-six wooden cars holding over 2,100 dazzled passengers. The Roosevelts admired the world's first elevated electric railway, a movable sidewalk, and electric boats skimming the lakes and ponds. Food from dozens of countries tempted them, and the fair introduced a variety of new products, including Cracker Jacks, Aunt Jemima syrup, Juicy Fruit gum, Pabst Blue Ribbon beer, the hamburger, and the ragtime music of Scott Joplin.[125] In the Alaskan exhibit, Edith bought a white-furred bunny doll that became her son Kermit's most treasured possession.

A week after the Roosevelts arrived in Chicago, a gondola ferried Theodore to a small artificial island in the middle of the fair's central lagoon. There he dedicated a frontier exhibit built by the Boone and Crockett Club, the sportsmen's group that Theodore and *Forest and Stream* editor George Bird Grinnell formed in 1888. The purpose of the exhibit, somewhat adrift amid the modernistic temples of the "White City," was to depict "a typical and peculiar phase of American national development . . . life on the frontier." The centerpiece of the exhibit was a long, low cabin of rough-hewn logs, rather similar to Theodore's rustic ranch house in Dakota. Inside there was a forlorn table and settles, with bunks in one corner, and a big, open stone fireplace. Elk and deer hides were scattered over the floor or tacked to the walls. In front of the cabin stood a white-capped prairie schooner. Having helped supervise the cabin's construction, Roosevelt was delighted with the exhibit and claimed it to be accurate in every detail.[126]

The fair was a resounding success, for it provided an oasis of fantasy to a nation suffering an economic crisis.[127] Ironically, the fair opened its gates almost at the same time in May 1893 when many bankrupt factories and banks closed their doors. Fantasy prevailed, however, as even the critically observant Henry Adams ignored the economic strife. The reclusive Adams, who seldom dined out of his own house, enjoyed the World's Fair immensely and revisited Chicago for an extra fortnight. To him, the Exposition provided the perfect fin de siècle.[128] Roosevelt agreed. After he returned to Washington, Theodore's excitement still churned when he wrote Brander Matthews.

Indeed Chicago *was* worth while. The buildings make, I verily believe, the most beautiful architectural exhibit the world has ever seen. If they were only permanent! The south lagoon, with the peristyle cutting it off from the lake, the great terraces, the grandeur and the beauty of the huge white buildings, the statue, the fine fountains, the dome of the administration building, the bridges guarded by the colossal animals—well, there is simply nothing to say about it. And the landscape effects are so wonderful. In the fine-arts building, by the way, did you not like the "Death arresting the hand of the sculptor," and the "Peace Sign," the quiet pose of the naked warrior on the naked horse?[129]

6
1894

Building the Merit System

THE COLD, GLOOMY rain that fell upon Washington on Sunday, January 7, 1894, kept the Roosevelt family cooped up in their frame house on Nineteenth Street. Theodore wanted to take the children to nearby Rock Creek for a day of hiking and climbing on the rocks, but the soggy weather kept him and his "bunnies" inside. Instead, he told them Indian stories and pretended he was a bear, crawling about the house on all fours and scaring the little ones.[1] Theodore loved watching his children grow. In another month, Alice, a lovely young girl with flaxen curls cascading down her back, would turn ten. Ted Jr., now in spectacles like his father, was six. Kermit, dressed in Victorian ruffles, was four, and Ethel, a cherubic two. Edith, six months pregnant, tried vainly to ride herd over her unruly children and "the oldest and rather worst child," her husband.[2]

A Sunday romp at home with his children provided a welcome break for Theodore. He worked as busily as ever that winter, kept at his office until after five every day, and felt "very plethoric and lazy in consequence of lack of exercise."[3] Occasionally Edith bundled up the children and, to the delight of Theodore and the clerks, unexpectedly dropped by the commission offices. Alice sat on one side of his desk and Ted Jr. on the other, while the two infants cuddled on their father's lap. On occasion, Ted Jr. dove into the office's wastebaskets in search of canceled postage stamps.[4]

Roosevelt, however, had little time to frolic with his children. Most of his time was spent at the commission, skirmishing with opponents of civil service reform. The work taxed Theodore's energy, but he thrived among challenge and adversity. Political battle had always been in his blood for, as a boy, he received early lessons in raucous New York City politics. Most of New York's wealthy elite rarely served in public office, or the so-called black trade, according to their social kinsmen.[5] The Roosevelt family, however, did not shy away from the political arena. Theodore's uncle Robert Roosevelt became a successful attorney and one of New York's celebrated champions of reform. An outspoken critic of Boss William Tweed and the Tammany machine, "Uncle Bob" served in Congress from 1871 to 1875, as minister to the Hague from 1888 to 1890, and as treasurer of the Democratic National Committee in 1892. Later a trustee for the building of the Brooklyn Bridge, Robert wrote and spoke often for government action to alleviate the sufferings of the poor and authored books on hunting and fishing. Robert lived next door to Thee and his family and, to the delight of the Roosevelt children, kept a menagerie of pets, including a parrot and a rather violent monkey dressed in children's clothes. Although Robert was a Democrat, his colorful public life, love for the outdoors, and success as a writer all served as an inspiration for his nephew.[6]

Theodore's older sister, Anna, also fueled his passion for politics. Anna was the matriarch of the family, the most mature of the children, and the one the family turned to in their many times of need. Only four years older than Theodore, Anna traveled to Cambridge to arrange his lodgings before he entered Harvard. Three months after the deaths of their mother and Theodore's first wife, Alice Lee, Anna moved into a New York brownstone on Madison Avenue and cared for baby Alice until Theodore's marriage to Edith. Indeed, for both of the girls born of her two brothers in 1884, Alice and Eleanor, Anna became their childhood's source of kindness, family stories, humor, and guidance. Only Anna would tell her niece Alice about her mother and openly talk to Eleanor of the tragically short life of her father, Elliott. As Alice later explained, "There is always someone in every family who keeps it together. In ours it was [Anna]."[7]

During Roosevelt's years as commissioner and throughout his life, Anna served as an unfailing source of strength and political advice. She possessed the best mind in the family, was very diplomatic, liked responsibility, and displayed phenomenal energy that rivaled Theodore's. Politics fascinated her. Although she was somewhat homely, her wit and engaging personality more than made up for her drab physical appearance and men naturally became attracted to her. Well read and knowledgeable on the issues of the time, Anna displayed unusual independence in her thinking. Despite Theodore's outspoken support of suffrage, she disapproved of giving women the right to vote, ridiculing the suffragists as "dowdy, overzealous, and misguided" and insisting that giving the vote to women would only multiply the "stupid vote."[8]

Almost every Sunday of his life, Theodore wrote his older sister. Theodore and Anna traded information, political intrigue, gossip, and the latest literary craze.[9] While Theodore proved a shrewd politician, at times he judged people poorly. He gave his trust and affection instantly and without question and, when disappointed or crossed, could just as quickly hate with a vengeance.[10] Anna, on the other hand, had much deeper views of people and understood them better than her brother did. Her advice, plus that of Edith, proved invaluable to Theodore in picking which of his many acquaintances to trust.

Anna persuaded Theodore to return to politics after Alice Lee's death and encouraged his friendship with Henry Cabot Lodge and other prominent politicians. Before Roosevelt married Edith, Anna kept his finances and, during the commission years, arranged his frequent visits to New York City, continued to pay his bills there, and set up his political and social engagements. At ease in literary circles, Anna arranged the breakfasts with his scholarly colleagues, such as in November 1891, when he wrote her, asking, "then, for Thursday morning could I have [essayist and editor] Chas. Dudley Warner, [*Harper's* editor William Dean] Howells, [*Century's* editor Richard Watson] Gilder, [Columbia professor James Brander] Matthews and [military historian Francis Vinton] Green to breakfast, at say, ten? Cabot will be there."[11]

Roosevelt continued to seek Anna's counsel when he moved into the White House. According to his niece Eleanor, he never made an important decision without talking it over first with his older sister.[12] Anna outlived Theodore by twelve years, dying in August 1931, at the age of seventy-six.

⌐

Roosevelt continually skirmished with pro-spoils opponents during the early months of 1894. To Theodore, the attacks came from three sources. First were "those who cannot get office comfort themselves by attacking civil service reform," second were "those whose political power depends upon nothing but their capacity for peddling political patronage, [and who] are of course opposed to it," and the last were those "composed of dull people deluded by the other two."[13] By early 1894 Roosevelt also discovered that his relationship with the new

Cleveland administration was faring no better than that with Harrison's.

From March through August 1894, hostile members of the House constantly attacked the commission, keeping Roosevelt busy fighting several pro-spoils congressmen and their efforts to defeat civil service reform. The attacks included legislation to repeal the Pendleton Act, apportion civil service appointments to congressional districts, increase hiring preferences for Civil War veterans, limit classified employees to four-year terms of office, divide civil service appointments between the two parties that poll the most votes, and other bills and amendments aimed at weakening or destroying civil service reform. Often the attacks of congressmen became personal and nasty. The *Washington Star,* a paper friendly to Roosevelt, demanded that Representative Thomas Stockdale, a Mississippi Democrat, apologize for calling Theodore "corrupt" on the floor of the House. Stockdale refused.[14] Another feisty Democrat, Congressman Benjamin Enloe of Tennessee,[15] accused Roosevelt of having a "meddlesome disposition" and being "as bitter a partisan as there is in the United States." While proposing a bill to abolish the commission, Enloe stood on the House floor and attacked the commission as "unfit and unworthy to supervise an honest civil service based on merit alone. It ought to be swept out of the path of true civil service reform."[16] The House at first passed, 100–71, Enloe's bill canceling the salaries of the commission staff, but William Everett, a Democrat from Massachusetts, argued successfully that the House reverse itself and fund the commission.[17] While the debates raged, Roosevelt frequently rushed the five blocks down Indiana Avenue to the Capitol to defend the commission and testify before committees on various bills. While there, he would twist the arm of any congressman or senator who came within his reach.

During this period, Roosevelt's relationship with Carlisle worsened into "a pretty open break."[18] The Treasury Department frequently promoted or demoted merit employees simply for political reasons. To Roosevelt's dismay, "promotions and reductions are not touched by the law at all, and we have nothing to do with them."[19] In February he wrote Lucius Swift. "Our fight with Carlisle comes on broad grounds, for he has taken the view that it is not a violation of the law to dismiss a man for political reasons," explained Roosevelt. "Even if it is, the remedy must lie in the courts, and that the head of a department need not make his subordinates observe the law."[20]

Because of his conflicts with Carlisle and other members of Cleveland's cabinet, Roosevelt continued to worry about his job. While attending the New Year's Day reception at the White House, he quarreled with bushy-bearded Secretary of the Navy Hilary Herbert over the dismissal of Herbert's friend, the postmaster of Montgomery, Alabama.[21] At the reception, Theodore also tangled with Interior Secretary Hoke Smith in a "rough and tumble argument."[22] Smith was a "big, bluff, and coarse" pro-spoils Democrat from Georgia whose Interior Department demoted 630 employees, mostly Republicans, and promoted 1,341 others, mostly Democrats.[23] By August, Roosevelt's dispute with Smith deteriorated into trivialities. "On July 20th the Commission made requisition for one table . . . instead of the table requested, a worn desk has been sent which cannot be used for the purpose intended," Roosevelt complained to Smith. "The Commission respectfully asks that the desk be removed and the table furnished according to the original requisition."[24]

Despite his amiable relationship with Cleveland, Theodore was unsure of his future within the Democratic administration. "We had a fierce brush in the house over C.S. reform, but won," Theodore wrote Anna during this period. "We'll win right along I think; but I am personally in such a tangle of animosity with Carlisle & Hoke Smith—a pair of scoundrels, especially Carlisle—that I may have to go at any moment."[25]

⌒

Dressed in a stunning gown of black velvet and sable trim that shimmered under the White House's crystal chandeliers, Frances Folsom Cleveland was the darling of Washington society.[26] Tall, graceful, blue-eyed, and chestnut-haired, Frances symbolized beauty and romance to the American people. She was twenty-two and Grover Cleveland forty-nine when they married in the White House Blue Room in 1886 during Cleveland's first term. Now, on a cool February night in 1894, poised next to her standoffish husband, the vivacious First Lady charmed the visitors as they arrived at the White House. Offering a splendid finale to the winter's social season, the formal dinner included several congressmen, Supreme Court justices, the new civil service commissioner John R. Proctor, and Theodore and Edith Roosevelt.[27]

Frances Cleveland enjoyed entertaining and had decorated the White House brilliantly. The mansion no longer resembled a funeral parlor, chastised earlier by Mark Twain as "ugly enough outside, but that is nothing to what it is inside. Dreariness, flimsiness, bad taste."[28] Electric lights, installed in 1891, now illuminated the mansion,[29] allowing brilliant splashes of reds and greens to dazzle the dinner guests when they followed Frances and the president into the East Room. Trays of scarlet tulips amid luscious ferns brightened the length of the vast dining table, clusters of crimson flowers covered the mantelpieces, and red, white, and blue electric lights illuminated large potted plants at each end of the room. As the guests took their seats, Edith was delighted to be placed between the president and his close friend, the prominent writer Richard Watson Gilder. Later that night, while writing a friend from the Lincoln bedroom, Gilder noted the irony of Cleveland's invitation to the Roosevelts. "[Cleveland] invited Commissioners Roosevelt and Proctor to meet us—the first time the Roosevelts had ever been invited to dine at the White House," wrote Gilder. "How is that for Harrison, of Roosevelt's own party."[30]

The irony also did not escape Roosevelt, who was well aware that during the previous four years Harrison, an unsociable "human iceberg," never extended an invitation to his fellow Republican.[31] Cleveland's invitation also gave an indication of the new president's personal support for Theodore and a signal that the commission was on the right track and continuing to make progress. By the middle of 1894, relations with the president eased when Roosevelt convinced Cleveland to classify the Customs Service, one of the many agencies known to be particularly spoils ridden. Work at the commission also improved. "My new colleague, Proctor, is a first rate man; he is congenial in work and play," Theodore wrote Anna. "I feel we are accomplishing something on the Commission. I wish I could say as much for the third volume of my *Winning of the West* which hangs fire badly."[32]

⤻

While at the commission, Roosevelt focused much of his energy on investigating and combating illegal political assessments. Requiring government workers to contribute part of their salary to ward heelers and boodle aldermen was a common and accepted method of party support in American political life. Party machines considered political assessments an indispensable means to finance their campaigns and bribe voters, demanding contributions ranging from 2 to 7 percent of a government employee's annual salary and forcing workers to campaign actively for their candidates.[33] Prior to the act, and indeed afterward, party hacks blatantly demanded assessments, as during Garfield's campaign of 1880 when "a New York City police justice rented a room at the Astor House, took off his coat, sent for all the clerks in the post-office across the street, and levied a tax on each."[34]

Congress attempted to prohibit assessments in 1876, passing legislation that banned government employees from giving or receiving political contributions, but the law was weak, contained no enforcement provisions, and was openly flaunted.[35] The drafters of the Pendleton Act took more extreme measures and inserted detailed provisions banning political assessments. The 1883 act prohibited a government official from soliciting an assessment for political purposes; from firing, promoting, or demoting another government worker for giving or withholding a political assessment; or from contributing a political assessment to another government official. The act also prohibited any person from soliciting an assessment on government property.[36]

Despite these detailed prohibitions, serious loopholes allowed assessments to continue legally. The Pendleton Act did not prohibit private citizens on private property from demanding political assessments from government employees. As soon as he became commissioner, Roosevelt began a running battle with the Old Dominion League, a Virginian Republican club that was notorious for collecting assessments from federal workers.[37] During his early investigation of the New York Customshouse, Roosevelt found assessments to be common practice. When a Democratic Party organization opened a fund-raising office in a Manhattan warehouse, the commission could do little. From the warehouse, the local party boss called in government workers or mailed them cards, telling them exactly how much to contribute. If the government employee refused, party bosses used various means to force compliance. One tactic involved the transfer of the worker from a station near home to another station far distant and inconvenient. The employee received no reason for the transfer, but if the man later paid the assessment, he was transferred back to his old station with no explanation.[38] On other occasions, party bosses disguised assessments as club dues, the cost of a pool table, tickets to a banquet, or the "Widow McGinnis's Pig Raffle."[39]

Roosevelt and his fellow commissioners became especially irritated in the summer of 1894 when Attorney General Richard Olney ruled that soliciting political assessments through the mail was legal. Theodore dictated a five-page letter to the president, describing this new type of assessment as a "peculiarly mean species of blackmail." Black workers in the Treasury Department had received letters "threatening in tone" that demanded they send campaign contributions by mail. A "short,

stout, good-looking and intelligent colored man" spurred the controversy when he was fired as a clerk at the War Department for not contributing to the Democratic campaign fund being conducted through
the mails from his home state of Alabama.[40] One newspaper claimed
that 80 percent of the dismissals of black workers from the War Department were due to a "failure of those whose heads were cut off to contribute funds for democratic campaign purposes."[41]

The commission was powerless in these situations and could not
punish or remove those either levying or contributing political assessments. The commissioners only could turn the evidence over to the
department heads, who were in most cases spoils advocates who refused to follow the commission's recommendations. When department
heads did act, they usually did so against violators who belonged to the
opposite party. This happened in 1892 when Roosevelt called for the
removal of Indianapolis postal workers found making illegal assessments. Wanamaker fired the offenders, conveniently all Democrats.

For the remainder of Roosevelt's tenure at the commission, the party
machines continued to collect assessments from government workers.
However, the practice began to decrease due to the commission's investigations and efforts to publicize it. In a speech before the Boston Civil
Service Reform Association on February 20, 1893, Roosevelt explained
his strategy to combat assessments. "We believe thoroughly that the
American people are at heart sound, and that they have a contempt for
that meanest of blackmailing which consists of robbing government
clerks of a portion of their salaries in the interests of politicians," said
Roosevelt. "If the details of wrong-doing can be made public enough,
this mere publicity will act as the greatest of possible checks."[42]

Over time, Roosevelt's strategy caused party bosses to fear the commission. Spoilsmen who previously had violated the law openly now
resorted to subterfuge and disguises to circumvent the law. Party machines incurred dwindling financial returns from decreasing assessments, prompting further erosion of the influence of the parties upon
career civil service employees.[43] In the case of the Republicans, political
contributions from businesses, perfected into a fine art by Wanamaker,
began to replace assessments as the primary source of party funds.

While frustrated at not being able to curtail all illegal political assessments, Roosevelt, nearing the end of his service at the commission,
nevertheless admitted some success. "Undoubtedly there is some transgression of the law against levying assessments. I am inclined to think
that there is a good deal of transgression," he wrote Henry Melvin in

December 1894. "We haven't succeeded in putting a complete stop . . . but we have very greatly diminished the number of political assessments."[44]

By 1894 the commission had achieved progress in other areas as well. A more aggressive commission and an expanded merit service began to improve the quality of the government workforce, and over time the federal service developed into a career professional service. Before 1883 most government jobs were of short duration and held little hope of advancement, thereby limiting professionalization in the public service. Frequent turnover caused by spoils appointments sapped the bureaucracy of the few talented and experienced personnel. Slowly, however, the federal service became more professional as new employees stayed longer, and it was bolstered by a small core of career employees who survived the tumultuous years of rampant spoils. Among the exceptional careerists were Mrs. S. F. Fitzgerald, a forty-year employee of the Treasury Department who knew "more about National Bank notes than any other living person," and Mrs. Patti Lyle Collins, a longtime postal employee and "the greatest living expert on deciphering illegible and defective letter addresses."[45]

In his last year at the commission, Roosevelt described the need for a professional, nonpolitical workforce. "The civil service is not looked to as a career by anyone. Very few young men come into the service at Washington with any idea of remaining more than a few years," he wrote. "This feeling will continue until . . . promotions are based upon merit, and a check upon unjust removals."[46] As professionalism and tenure improved slowly, there was noticeable progress both in the quality of career personnel and overall government efficiency.[47] A comparison of tenure in the State Department and the Patent Office under the pre-1883 spoils era with tenure in the same offices from 1883 to 1901 reveals a sharp increase after 1883 in the number of individuals who made government service a career. As reformers hoped, the merit system recruited more educated persons of higher caliber than the spoils system attracted. New technologies, notably the typewriter and the telephone, helped to increase the competency of employees, and more college graduates, albeit a small percentage of the workforce, entered government service. During Roosevelt's period as commissioner, the director of the U.S. Mint testified that the quality of federal employees obtained through the civil service examinations proved superior to those hired under the old patronage system.[48] Likewise, Roosevelt argued that the commission's successes improved the image of the public servant. In January 1895, a few months before he resigned from the commission, Roosevelt responded to a citizen critical of the civil service system:

> The confidence has been slowly growing in the public at large. The Washington clerks, however, have gradually come to the belief that the reform is general, and this is shown in a very curious way, namely, by the greatly increased number of real estate purchases in the vicinity of Washington by Government employees. Formerly, under the spoils system, no Government employee would purchase real estate, because he knew that his tenure of office was too frail; and for a number of years after the law went into effect they still felt a little afraid that it might be abolished or evaded, and didn't venture to buy houses. Now they have grown, in the mass, to realize that the new system has come to stay, and in consequence their purchases of real estate has increased four fold.[49]

Roosevelt insisted that the merit system improved government efficiency. In defending the commission's efforts, he offered further evidence of an increasingly effective government workforce and revealed that the Railway Mail Service was at a higher point of efficiency than ever before. When that service came under the civil service law in 1889, the record of correct mail handlings was 2,834 to 1; for the year 1894, it was 7,831 to 1. "The post offices where the law is most faithfully observed are precisely the offices where the best service is rendered to the public and where the employees are most able, courteous, and efficient," Roosevelt wrote to the editor of the *Detroit Evening News* in 1895. He further noted that "the failure to classify the Census Office under the [civil service] law had cost the Government just about two million dollars."[50]

By 1894, Roosevelt claimed that the commission had made substantial progress in increasing the number of merit positions. He boasted that on his watch the number of classified positions had more than doubled and that "in the last six years we have added 25,000 employees to the service."[51] His numbers are correct, but they overstate the role that Roosevelt and the commission played. During the period when he served as commissioner, the number of classified employees did increase significantly. However, the increase in merit employees was due more to political reasons than the efforts of the commission.

A major reason for increases in the numbers of merit employees was the widespread lame-duck blanketing of political employees into the classified service. The phenomenon of lame-duck appointments was not new. A century before, President John Adams appointed several Federalist judges at the last minute to keep the soon-to-be-inaugurated Thomas Jefferson from appointing his own party followers.[52] One of the Adams appointees, William Marbury, sued Secretary of State James Madison after the new administration refused to grant his "midnight" judgeship. Marbury eventually won his case in the Supreme Court in a landmark decision, *Marbury v. Madison* (1803), where Chief Justice John Marshall established the power of the Court to declare acts of Congress, and by implication acts of the president, unconstitutional if they exceeded the powers granted by the Constitution.

Because the Pendleton Act gave a president the power to extend the merit system by executive order, presidents resorted to wide use of lame-duck blanketings to protect their political cronies. As each outgoing president was leaving office, he extended civil service coverage to include the patronage jobs of his supporters and deny the incoming party the opportunity to replace his party loyalists.[53] During the early years of the act, a president could blanket patronage appointees into the merit service without requiring a competitive examination. This made it easy for previously nonmerit patronage positions filled by outgoing party members to be brought into the merit system at the last minute, thus keeping the party members in government jobs and eliminating the opportunity for a new administration to reward its own party members.

Blanketing also contributed to the increase in the merit service because presidents often ordered the classification of high-level positions filled by spoils appointees. After leadership positions became a part of the classified service, efforts to move the rank-and-file positions into the merit system were more successful. Once ensconced in the merit service, high-level political appointees would in turn classify their own party lieutenants. The compensation of classified employees gives evidence to the top-down trend, for as early as 1889, when Roosevelt arrived, the combined salaries of classified employees equaled those of the unclassified employees, even though only a quarter of the service was classified.[54]

Cleveland, normally a supporter of the merit principle, nevertheless yielded to patronage pressures. When Harrison defeated his reelection bid in 1888, Cleveland used the power of the Pendleton Act to blanket over 5,000 Democratic appointees within the Railway Mail Service, increasing the size of the merit service by a third.[55] Harrison followed suit in January 1893 when, two months before leaving office, he blanketed

10,525 Republicans and another three agencies, including 7,660 postal workers and all of the Weather Bureau's 314 workers.[56] Returned to the White House, Cleveland blanketed another 49,179 positions shortly before McKinley's inauguration in 1897. Taft, a lame duck in 1912, blanketed 52,236 jobs.[57] While blanketing for patronage purposes appears as loathsome as traditional spoils appointments, it fortunately was a temporary, one-shot transgression. Once a president blanketed a position into the classified service, future appointments to that position could be made only through merit examinations. In the long run, blanketings, as much as any direct reform effort to expand the merit service, destroyed the spoils system.

⌐

During his last winter at the commission, Theodore Roosevelt sat at his City Hall desk and wrote to Carrie Harrison of Wellesley College to provide his views on women's employment. "No distinction is made in the examinations, or in any proceedings under the commission, between men and women," wrote Roosevelt. "They compete precisely on the same basis."[58] As commissioner, Roosevelt demanded strict fairness and equality in the civil service selections. While he exaggerated the true level of equality of women in the workforce, Roosevelt attempted to place women on the same competitive level with men in many positions and fostered a notable increase in the number of women employed.[59]

Roosevelt was well ahead of his time in his progressive views toward women's equality. His senior thesis at Harvard, titled "The Practicality of Equalizing Men and Women Before the Law," called for true equality for women, including equal rights of inheritance, the vote, and the right to go to law school. In his early writings he even suggested that a woman should not be forced to assume her husband's name when she married.[60]

By the time Roosevelt arrived in Washington, women were beginning to make progress in entering a federal workforce which only a few years before had been exclusively male. In 1862, spurred by the huge expansion of government agencies at the outbreak of the Civil War, U.S. Treasurer Francis Spinner hired the federal government's first female clerks. Responding to the wartime shortage of male clerks, Spinner hired women to sort and package bonds and currency. Although many critics looked upon this "bold experiment" as a scandalous challenge to basic Victorian morality, Spinner found his new women employees to be "cheap and reliable."[61] The number of females employed by the executive departments steadily grew, from 1,773 in 1880 to 5,637 in 1893, when women made up nearly a third of the Washington bureaucracy.[62] However, wide disparities in pay existed between men and women, even if they performed identical clerical jobs.[63] While Roosevelt served as commissioner, most men began their careers in the federal government as first-class clerks averaging $1,200 per year, and those men who worked conscientiously were promoted up the federal ladder to second-, third-, or fourth-class clerkships paying $1,400, $1,600, and $1,800, respectively. Virtually all female clerks, however, began their government service at annual salaries ranging from the minimum $600 to $900. Many women did earn $1,000 or more, but they did so by working their way up a longer, and more rickety, ladder.[64]

Women faced significant obstacles in entering the federal service. Since 1870, federal regulations had allowed department heads to appoint women as clerks "upon the same requisite and conditions, and with the same compensation, as are prescribed for men."[65] Despite such intentions that selections be made with "no distinction on account of sex," actual practice denied female applicants an equal chance at civil service jobs. Women were indeed allowed to compete on all examinations, but they were not ranked with male applicants or appointed to the same positions. The Civil Service Commission had no control over cabinet members and agency heads, who could stipulate the gender of an employee desired for a job. In the vast majority of cases, the agency requested a male. When an agency requested a female, it was most often for a "copyist" position paying $900 a year. Secretary of the Interior John Noble ordered his assistant to discreetly notify officials in his department that "recommendations for promotions of women to places of eighteen hundred dollars will not be approved."[66] As a result of such policies, women did not receive a proportionate share of appointments and promotions. In 1890, out of a total of seventeen thousand clerical positions, Washington offices employed about four thousand women. Between 1884 and 1894, women accounted for between 28 and 43 percent of those passing civil service examinations but received only 7 to 25 percent of the appointments.[67] Women made steady progress, however, in entering the federal workforce, and by 1900 they made up 96 percent of all typists and stenographers and 29 percent of bookkeepers, cashiers, and accountants.[68]

While Roosevelt strove for women's equality in applying for government jobs, his notions of male virility and chauvinism shaped his overall views toward women and may have tempered any dramatic reforms to improve female employment opportunities. He saw women as "equal partner[s]," although his conception seemed romantic and upper class. He opposed the birth control movement of the Progressive Era and did not approve of "modern" women.[69] Victorian in many ways, Roosevelt nevertheless stepped ahead of his colleagues in advocating that women receive equal treatment, including the right to vote. "Much can be done by law towards putting women on a footing of complete and entire equal rights with man," Roosevelt later wrote, "including the right to vote, the right to hold and use property, and the right to enter any profession she desires on the same terms as the man."[70]

Roosevelt was equally tolerant toward religious belief. As commissioner he frequently expressed his determination to appoint men without re-gard for their religion, an unusual stance during a period when anti-Catholic feelings ran high. He strongly opposed the "paranoid nativ-ism" of the American Protective Association (APA), which suggested that a Jesuitic conspiracy threatened the nation. During the economic collapse of the mid-1890s, the APA surged in membership and political clout.[71] In an 1894 letter to Bishop John Keane, rector of Catholic Uni-versity, Roosevelt's sense of overpowering justice is clear. "I don't mean that I will stand up for Protestant against Catholic, any more than for Catholic against Protestant," wrote Roosevelt. "I feel just the same indignation at any discrimination, political or otherwise, against a Catholic, because of his religion, that I feel if a Protestant is discrimi-nated against for similar reasons."[72]

When backed into a corner, Roosevelt came out fighting. In another APA incident, Roosevelt revealed he would act aggressively and bend the rules of the merit system to make his point. In 1894 he planned to appoint a civil service board in Michigan and was in doubt which of two men to select. "The local APA association solved my doubts by en-tering a protest against one of the men on the ground that he was a Catholic," wrote Roosevelt. "The instance they did so I promptly put the Catholic on, just as I would have put on the Protestant if he had been opposed merely because he was a Protestant."[73]

Later that year, Roosevelt again criticized the APA when he argued that his commission decisions were nonsectarian. "[I] recently removed a man from the position of secretary of one of our local boards be-cause he pasted on his desk where applicants could see them slips of paper containing APA and anti-Catholic songs and utterances," wrote

Theodore. "But I could certainly not offhand agree that a man should be removed from the public service merely because he was an APA man any more than I could agree offhand that he should be removed from the public service if he belonged to a similar Catholic Society or order."[74]

Roosevelt believed strongly in the separation of church and state and argued against any involvement of the Catholic Church in the public school system. "I am a straightout adherent of our nonsectarian public school system," Roosevelt wrote Bishop Keane in 1894. "I have always opposed any division of the school fund or any compromise whatever about the school system, and I am against the system of appropriations for sectarian institutions of any kind . . . when I use the words 'nonsectarian' I mean them."[75]

⌐

Roosevelt turned to his family and close friends to unwind. He particularly enjoyed his long rides with Cabot Lodge into Washington's surrounding countryside during springtime, when the "woods are now in full flush of their beauty; the leaves a tender green, the dogwoods and Judas trees in bloom."[76] With a pistol stuck in his belt, Theodore would climb onto "old Dick from the riding school" or borrow Lodge's horse Egypt[77] and together the two friends rode to Georgetown. There they galloped along the towpath where the Chesapeake and Ohio Canal began its westward course and where mules pulled barges slowly along the waterway. A week after Roosevelt first arrived in Washington, the same terrible storm that touched off the Johnstown Flood in Pennsylvania poured torrential rains upon Washington and severely damaged the canal, closing it until September 1891.[78]

Most of all, Theodore enjoyed spending his breaks with Edith and their "bunnies." Wearing his threadbare knickerbockers and hobnail boots, he oftentimes marched his family off on some new weekend adventure. With the "very smallest pairs of feet" piled in a gorgeous red wagon with *Express* painted on its sides in gilt letters, the family trekked about the city, such as to one of Sousa's concerts on the mall where the famous conductor played his "Washington Post March" for the first time.[79] With his family in tow, Theodore especially loved his scrambles along Rock Creek. "Yesterday, Sunday, Edith and I, with Ted, Alice, John Lodge, and various assorted friends took a long scramble up Rock Creek," Theodore wrote Anna in April 1894. "Edith walked so well, and felt so well, that it was a pleasure to see her. Over some of the worst rocks I let down the children with a rope; and did much climbing myself."[80]

On the following Tuesday, just after midnight, Edith gave birth to the fifth Roosevelt child, Archie, in their cozy house on Nineteenth Street. The new child made such little fuss that Mame, the family's crotchety but devoted old Irish nanny, slept upstairs with the other children, unaware of the new arrival. Theodore climbed the stairs to tell Mame, waking Ted and Alice, who sat on the edge of Mame's bed "chattering like parroquets . . . and hugging two darkey ragdollies which they always take to bed." When their father finally allowed them to go downstairs and hold the new baby for a few minutes, Ted and Alice agreed that it was "better than Christmas."[81]

⌐

Grover Cleveland also was busy during the spring of 1894. On the day after Easter, the president and his wife hosted more than a thousand children for the annual Easter egg rolling on the South Lawn. Frolicking about the grounds of the White House, the daintily dressed youngsters provided a holiday magic to the otherwise somber mansion.[82]

At about the same time as the children invaded the White House grounds, a wealthy quarry owner named Jacob Coxey departed Massillon, Ohio, in an open carriage and headed east for Washington. A frail little man with flashing blue eyes behind wire-rimmed glasses and dressed in a dark-gray business suit, Coxey looked more like a college professor heading to class than an idealistic rabble-rouser on a quixotic odyssey. Behind Coxey's carriage trailed a ragtag caravan of unemployed workers, some on horseback, a few walking, and most in wagons pulled by haggard mules. Coxey and his "army," which included an indigent eighteen-year-old named Jack London, headed east to demand that the government launch a half-billion-dollar road-building and public works program to remedy the widespread unemployment that gripped the country. According to Coxey's plan, the government should hire workers for $1.50 per day, thereby creating jobs to reverse the country's economic woes. Coxey was among a growing number of critics who denounced the concentration of wealth in the hands of a few thousand families. The 1890 census revealed that the richest 1 percent of Americans had more total income than the poorest 50 percent. Coxey, like the Populists, labeled both the Democrats and Republicans as tools of business and enemies of farmers, workers, and the jobless.[83]

On May Day, Coxey's army of five hundred jobless workers marched through Washington, past the White House, and up Pennsylvania Avenue. After the protestors reached the Capitol, policemen arrested Coxey for trespassing on the Capitol lawn. In the nearby Senate, legislators ignored Coxey's protest and continued to debate one of Theodore's favorite projects, a bill creating a bird and game preserve within Yellowstone Park.[84] With the loss of its general, Coxey's army disbanded. Coxey's plan, forty years ahead of its time, gathered no support from Cleveland or Congress, and the protest faded away.[85]

The widespread unemployment that spurred Coxey's bedraggled march from Ohio did not disappear, however, for the country was in the throes of a serious depression. The financial crisis had begun in the late 1880s when disaster befell southern cotton-growing regions and the Great Plains bread belt. Goods could not find markets, agricultural exports to Europe crashed, imports soared, and gold poured out of the country.[86] Weeks before Cleveland's second inauguration, a wildly fluctuating stock market forecast the brewing of a financial storm. In late February 1893 the Philadelphia and Reading Railroad declared bankruptcy, followed soon after by the collapse of the National Cordage Company, a great trust so mismanaged that it announced a large cash dividend in the very month it went under. The depression reached Wall Street and touched off a massive worldwide economic crisis.

By the spring of 1894, President Cleveland could no longer ignore the nation's financial calamity. The country had suffered fifteen thousand bankruptcies, a wave of bank failures, and the Erie, Northern Pacific, Union Pacific, and Santa Fe Railroads were in receivership. In the cities and mill towns, four million people were out of work.[87] Cleveland, an otherwise compassionate man, never entertained the unheard-of idea of providing direct federal aid to the unemployed and hungry men. Cleveland and Roosevelt differed in their views on philanthropy. The former showed little interest in either private or governmental charity; the latter, trained by his father to a liberal aristocratic creed of stewardship, had less difficulty accepting the idea that the state sometimes needed to be paternalistic.[88] Ignoring the need to provide relief to an unemployed labor force that would grow increasingly militant, the president instead pressured Congress in August 1893 to repeal the Sherman Silver Purchase Act in an attempt to thwart the depression.[89] Many conservatives claimed the Silver Purchase Act undermined business confidence in the gold standard and was a root cause of the depression. Cleveland's action was futile, however, as the repeal had little effect. Factories continued to shut down and unemployment rose, with jobless industrial workers in some cities exceeding 25 percent.[90] The depression continued through 1896, with the once-popular Cleveland shouldering much of the blame.

To make matters worse for the president, the first national strike in U.S. history erupted near Chicago. The Pullman Palace Car Company, renowned for manufacturing sleeper and luxury railcars, also suffered from the economic depression. After the company drastically cut the wages of its factory workers, the Pullman laborers protested and, on May 10, 1894, walked off the job. The striking workers belonged to the American Railway Union, led by Socialist labor activist Eugene Debs.[91] In support of the Pullman workers, other union members refused to switch trains with Pullman cars. When the railroads fired many of the workers, the strike spread to the entire 150,000 union membership in twenty-seven states. Within days, the strike paralyzed the nation's entire railway system.

On July 2, Cleveland issued an injunction against the leaders of the American Railway Union, and on the following day he ordered federal troops to Illinois to protect the mails. The president vowed that "if it takes the entire army and navy of the United States to deliver a post card in Chicago, that card will be delivered."[92] Riots began on the Fourth of July, and fires consumed seven buildings at the World's Fair. On July 7, National Guard troops fired into a crowd of workers, killing at least twelve people. After police arrested Debs for violating the injunction, the strike began to fail and, on August 2, the Pullman works reopened. Debs fought his arrest in the courts, and in October 1894 the Supreme Court heard his case. A young Clarence Darrow represented Debs, broadly arguing the right of labor unions to form, bargain for rights and benefits, and, if necessary, to legally strike.[93] Debs and Darrow lost their case, but their arguments foreshadowed recognition of union rights during the next century.

The Pullman and Homestead strikes, Coxey's army, and the rise of populism in the West and anarchism in the East were among the seismic events that signaled a growing unrest across the country. The public aimed much of its hostility toward Cleveland and the Democrats. A year earlier the Democrats had captured the Senate, but their elation was short lived. In the 1894 congressional elections they lost 113 House seats to Republicans, beginning an era of GOP power that lasted for the next three decades.[94]

Roosevelt spent most of July with his family in Oyster Bay, busily finishing the third volume of *The Winning of the West*. Nevertheless, he followed the Pullman strike closely, much as he had two summers before during the Homestead strike in Pennsylvania. Theodore still feared anarchy and mob rule and the strike appalled him. To him, one of the most dangerous enemies of America was the "reckless labor agitator who arouses the mob to riot and bloodshed."[95] Roosevelt firmly supported Cleveland's actions in issuing an injunction and sending in federal troops. "We have come out of the strike very well," he wrote Anna after the strike was broken. "Cleavland [*sic*] did excellent."[96]

In August 1894, with few politicians left in Washington to suffer the summer heat, Elihu Root and a group of reformers met with Roosevelt and suggested he run for mayor of New York City. At first, Theodore was enthusiastic. However, Edith, who had recently given birth to their son Archie and was reluctant to leave Washington, convinced him to decline the offer. She also feared that if he lost the election they would forego what little income he brought in as commissioner. Theodore still winced from his third-place finish in the mayoral race of 1886. However, soon after New Yorkers elected Republican William A. Strong as mayor in the fall of 1894, Roosevelt realized that he might have won if he indeed had run. "I made a mistake in not trying my luck in the mayoralty race," Theodore wrote Anna in October 1894 from Washington. "The prize was very great; the expense would have been trivial; and the chances of success were good. I would have run better than Strong. . . . But it is hard to decide when one has the interests of a wife and children to consider first; and now it is over, and it is best to not talk of it; above all, no outsider should know that I think my decision was a mistake."[97]

Theodore was sick with regret. He realized that the mayoralty remained one of his choicest ambitions. "The last four weeks, ever since I decided not to run, have been pretty bitter ones for me. I would literally have given my right arm to make the race, win or lose," Roosevelt wrote Lodge. "It was the one golden chance, which never returns; and I had no illusions about ever having another opportunity; I knew it meant the definite abandonment of any hope of going on in the work and life for which I care more than any other."[98] Edith was distraught when she heard from his sister how Theodore regretted not running. "This is a lesson that will last my life, never to give [my opinion] for it is utterly worthless when given, worse than that in this case for it has

helped to spoil some years of a life which I would have given my own
for," Edith wrote Anna. "He never should have married me and then he
would have been free to make his own course."[99]

⌒

Elliott Roosevelt seemed like "some stricken, hunted creature," Theodore
wrote Anna in August 1894.[100] During that summer, Elliott's health
continued to deteriorate and became a constant worry for his older
brother and sisters. After Theodore's trip to France in 1892, Elliott
agreed to return to the States and enter a five-week rehabilitation program in Dwight, Illinois.[101] He improved somewhat, and Corinne's husband, Douglas Robinson, found Elliott a job in a family coal and timber
business in Abingdon, Virginia, safely away from his wife and children
in New York. In February 1892, Theodore escorted Elliott to Virginia.
The two brothers parted warmly, and Theodore continued on an inspection visit to Owensboro, Kentucky. Several months later and in the
midst of his Baltimore battle, Theodore could only find time to write
his brother. "I had a very good letter from Elliott in answer to one of
mine; it will be out of the question for me to get down to see him,"
Theodore wrote Anna in May 1892. "I am in the final stages of my fight
with Wanamaker, having just sent him my ultimatum, and a copy to
the worried, halting president."[102]

For a time Elliott appeared to be drying out, but tragedies in his life
caused him to relapse. In December 1892, a month after their daughter
Eleanor's eighth birthday, Elliott's wife, Anna, died of diphtheria. Elliott, who failed to reach his wife before she passed away, appeared devastated and drank as heavily as ever. Another crushing blow came five
months later, when his four-year-old son Elliott Jr. died of scarlet fever.
Elliott left Virginia, moved back to New York, took a dingy apartment
on West 102nd Street, and sank deeper into a seedy life of heavy drinking and debauchery. By the time Eleanor reached ten, the letters and
visits from her father stopped.

About this time, Theodore appears to have given up any hope for his
brother's recovery. This is understandable, given Theodore's notions of
rugged individualism and survival of the fittest and his commitment to
social Darwinism. More simply, Theodore abhorred weakness in either
mind or body. Watching his once-strapping brother waste away must
have surely pushed Theodore past the point of brotherly compassion
and into a state of revulsion. His letters convey his anguish. "It is very

sad about Elliott, but there is literally nothing to do," Theodore wrote Corinne on May 3, 1894. "After a certain number of years and trials no one can help another; and his children must of course be saved, and [his wife Anna's mother] Mrs. Hall can best save them."[103]

A distraught Theodore was more direct with his older sister. "Corinne ought to do nothing for [Elliott]. He can't be helped, and he must simply be let go his own gait," Theodore wrote Anna in July 1894. "He is now laid up from a serious fall; while drunk he drove into a lamp post and went out of his head. Poor fellow! If only he could have died instead of Anna."[104]

Elliott's deterioration added to Theodore's other concerns that summer. He remained busy with his commission battles, writing *The Winning of the West,* and trying to decide whether to run for mayor. Ultimately, Roosevelt's workload and personal crises forced him to shorten his September trip west to only two weeks at his Dakota ranch. The trip was a tonic, however, and Theodore reported to Lodge afterward that he felt "as rugged as a bull moose."[105]

As Elliott deteriorated that summer, Edith worried about her husband's career in the face of another possible scandal, fearing that the Roosevelt name would be soiled. "Elliott has sunk to the lowest depths. . . . [He] consorts with the vilest women and Theodore, Anna, and Douglas receive horrid anonymous letters about his life," Edith wrote her mother in August 1894. "I live in constant dread of some scandal of his attaching itself to Theodore."[106]

Elliott continued to worsen. "Elliott is up and about again; and I hear is already drinking heavily; if so he must break down soon," Theodore wrote to Anna, then living in London, on August 12, 1894. "It has been as hideous a tragedy all through as one often sees."[107] Elliott took his final step two days later when, after a severe attack of delirium tremens, he tried to hurl himself from a window, collapsed in a convulsive fit, and died on the floor. He was thirty-four. Theodore hurried to New York to find his dead brother still lying in his squalid apartment. "Theodore was more overcome than I have ever seen him," Corinne later wrote, "and he cried like a child for a long time."[108] Theodore was torn, on one hand devastated by another loss of a dear family member at a premature age while on the other seeing Elliott's death as a blessing in disguise and an end to a life of misery. To his older sister he was blunt. "He would have been in a straight jacket had he lived forty-eight hours longer," Theodore wrote Anna a few days after Elliott's death. "He had been drinking whole bottles of anisette and green mint, besides whole bottles of raw brandy and champagne, some-times half a dozen a morning . . . indeed he was hunted by the most terrible demons that ever entered a man's body and soul."[109]

To the younger Corinne, Theodore showed a more tender side two weeks later:

> My darling little sister. My thoughts keep hovering round you now, and I love you so. There is one great comfort I already feel; I only need to have pleasant thoughts of Elliott now. He is just the gallant, generous, manly boy and young man whom everyone loved. I can think of him when you and I used to go round "ex-ploring" the hotels, the time we were first in Europe; do you re-member how we used to do it? And then in the days of the danc-ing class, when he was the distinctly polished man-of-the-world from the outside, and all the girls . . . used to be so flattered by any attentions from him. Or when we were off on his little sailing boat for a two or three days trip on the Sound; or when he first hunted; and when he visited me at Harvard . . . [110]

7
1895

Returning to New York

THEODORE ROOSEVELT ENJOYED walking from his rented house on Nineteenth Street to his City Hall office at Judiciary Square. At Roosevelt's brisk pace, the jaunt took about thirty minutes. The walk was exhilarating, as the nation's capital was among America's most beautiful and cleanest cities. Unlike the dingy metropolises of Philadelphia, Boston, and New York, Washington endured little factory smoke to mar the sides of the white sandstone government buildings, nor did it suffer the rows of squalid tenements filled with immigrants. No skyscrapers blocked the sun or competed with the Washington Monument, recently completed and no longer resembling, according to Mark Twain, a "factory chimney with the top broken off."[1] Once-unsightly wires for electric light and telephones had been buried underground.[2] The scene of only ten murders in 1895, Washington ranked among the nation's safest cities.[3]

Roosevelt's walks took two general courses. If he chose the more northerly route, he followed tree-lined Massachusetts Avenue, which cut a diagonal swath across other streets to form quaint little parks and circles and passed by some of Washington's most ornate mansions and foreign embassies. If Theodore veered south, he strolled beneath the noble beech trees of Lafayette Park, where pigeons strutted among children playing hopscotch and nursemaids gossiped nearby. In the center of the square he could glance up at an equestrian statue of General Jackson, "as archaic as a Ninevite king, prancing and rocking through the ages."[4] During the springtime he passed straw-hatted men basking on the park's benches reading their newspapers, either the morning's

Post, costing three cents, or the afternoon's *Star,* a penny cheaper. Looking up from their reading, they could glance across the street to admire the reds of tulips blossoming in the huge round bed bordering the White House portico, while open landau carriages drawn by well-groomed horses trotted along Pennsylvania Avenue past the park carrying silk-hatted dignitaries in Prince Albert cutaway coats and striped pants and ladies in sweeping brocades and picture hats.[5]

After skirting the White House grounds, Roosevelt strolled down Pennsylvania Avenue, whose north side was almost Parisian with tall elms shading a wide brick sidewalk that passed theaters, expensive shops, and the finest hotels. Theodore avoided the south side of the thoroughfare, with its gambling dens, brothels, saloons, and flophouses. If he left at an early hour, he might observe the unusual street cleaners that kept the nation's capital as spotless as a parlor floor. City workers rode beastly looking contraptions whose huge rollers were covered with hundreds of stiff little twigs arranged in a spiral. As the horses pulled the machine along, the rollers turned and the broomlike twigs swept the dust and dirt off to the side to be gathered up and carted away.[6]

When the weather was pleasant, Edith would often walk her husband to work. She had tea ready for him when he returned at five.[7] When the weather soured, Theodore turned to Washington's public transportation. In 1895 the city had the most reasonable streetcar fares in the United States. A ride cost two, three, or five cents, depending on its length. A fleet of herdic cabs competed with the streetcars for space on the crowded avenues. The herdics were boxlike little carriages handsomely finished in rich olive green, with glass windows, doors at the back, and comfortably cushioned seats. The drivers sat up front exposed to the weather and handled the horses. Holding up to eight passengers, the herdics offered the chance for a ride with a congressman, a Supreme Court justice, or a simple haberdasher on his way to work. The more expensive two-wheeled hansom cabs also rolled along the Washington streets in large numbers, providing a more dashing conveyance with the driver sitting on a small seat, high in the back, and looking over the roof of the cab.[8]

In his travels about the city, Theodore often stopped at one of his favorite haunts. Located on Lafayette Square at 1525 H Street, the Cosmos Club occupied a square gray town house that had once been the home of Dolley Madison.[9] Organized in 1878 by famed geologist and explorer John Wesley Powell and members of the Philosophical Society, including Henry Adams, the Cosmos Club embraced some of the most interesting men in America. An impressive list of geographers, explorers, teachers, lawyers, cartographers, military officers, and financiers composed the Cosmos membership.[10] A year before Roosevelt arrived, on a January evening in 1888, thirty-three of the members gathered around the club's large mahogany table to discuss forming an organization to foster geographical knowledge. By the end of the meeting they had created the National Geographic Society.

Theodore often relaxed at the Cosmos, which sported a well-supplied wine cellar and a fine billiards room. He spent hours in the club's lounge discussing politics, literature, and world affairs with his fascinating companions or attending one of the frequent scientific meetings held there. Alexander Graham Bell was a member and visited the club when in Washington. Another Cosmos colleague was Professor Samuel Langley, the head of the Smithsonian and an early aviation pioneer and expert in astronomy. To Theodore's daughter Alice, he was simply "Mr. Laggle."[11]

Rudyard Kipling also frequented the Cosmos Club during visits to Washington. Kipling was already the world's most famous living writer and poet when he met Commissioner Roosevelt for the first time.[12] Although Kipling was seven years younger than Theodore, his baldness, dark bushy mustache, bristling eyebrows, and disfiguring thick spectacles made him look the older of the two.[13] The short and wiry Englishman enjoyed dropping by the Cosmos, where "I curled up on the seat opposite and listened and wondered until the universe seemed to be spinning around and Theodore was the spinner."[14] After their first chance encounters, Kipling and Roosevelt forged a rather caustic friendship. Although Roosevelt always admired Kipling's "fresh, healthy, out-of-doors" vision of life, the relationship between the two men began testily. At first Roosevelt disliked the Englishman, whom he described as having a "common little monkey face."[15] Theodore fumed over Kipling's stinging criticisms of American society, especially his portrayal of New York City as "the shiftless outcome of squalid barbarism and reckless extravagance."[16]

"I hope it is true that Kipling is not to be admitted to the Players," Theodore wrote Brander Matthews in May 1892. "There is no earthly reason he should not call New York a pig trough; but there is also no reason why he should be allowed to associate with pigs. I fear he is at bottom a cad."[17] In April 1894 he expressed more disgust. "Kipling is an underbred little fellow, with a tendency to criticize America to which I put a stop by giving him a very rough handling, since which he has not repeated the offense," Theodore wrote to Anna. "But he is a genius, and is very entertaining. His wife is fearful however."[18]

As he came to know Kipling better, Roosevelt's opinions of the Englishman improved. "Kipling's last story was first rate, as indeed all of his animal stories are," Theodore wrote Brander Matthews in March 1893. "I don't myself think he is much of a success when he deals with city life, whether in London or elsewhere. . . . Every now and then he can't resist making a raid on things American."[19] Later, Theodore described Kipling as a genius and wrote to Spring-Rice from Oyster Bay that "the two great fiction writers of today are Tolstoi [sic] and Kipling."[20] Once they became closer, Roosevelt introduced Kipling to his literary and political acquaintances and squired the Englishman around Washington, including to the zoo to see the grizzlies and to the Smithsonian to see Indian relics.[21] Even at the Smithsonian, however, the two friends continued to spar. Kipling infuriated Roosevelt by criticizing America's treatment of the Indian. "I never got over the wonder of a people, who, having extirpated the aboriginals of their continent more completely than any modern race had ever done, honestly believed they were a godly little New England community, setting examples of brutal mankind," Kipling wrote in his autobiography. "This wonder I explained to Theodore Roosevelt, who made the glass cases of Indian relics shake with his rebuttals."[22]

Kipling appears to have been the more patient of the two and generally enjoyed, or at least ignored, Roosevelt's pugnaciousness. "I liked him from the first and largely believed in him," Kipling later wrote. "He would come to our hotel, and thank God in a loud voice that he had not one drop of British blood in him."[23] Early in their relationship, Kipling saw a "big future" in Roosevelt, although he liked to scold Theodore about his political aspirations. "Why don't you leave that sort of skittles [politics] to [William Jennings] Bryan & Co. and go in for being a colonial administrator," wrote Kipling to Theodore when he learned that his friend was nominated for the New York governorship. "P.S. Don't go into politics yet awhile," the Englishman added facetiously.[24] In later years their correspondence warmed, especially after each lost a son in World War I. When Roosevelt died in 1919, Kipling dedicated the poem "Great-Heart" to Theodore and admitted rather sagely that Roosevelt "was a much bigger man than his people understood or, at that time, knew how to use, and that he and they might have been better off had he been born twenty years later."[25]

⁓

Roosevelt and Kipling shared a xenophobic contempt for foreigners.[26] At the time, a tidal wave of immigration was striking against American shores when, during the decade of the eighties, 5,246,613 immigrants arrived.[27] Roosevelt proposed curbing immigration with "more drastic laws than now exist" and in *Forum* in April 1894 suggested that immigrants should change their names and customs to become Americanized. He detested hyphenation, arguing that "once it was true that this country could not endure half free and half slave. Today it is true that it cannot endure half American and half foreign. The hyphen is incompatible with patriotism."[28]

In March 1890 Roosevelt traveled to Chicago to give an address to the Marquette Club. Titled "True Americanism," the speech carried a strikingly xenophobic message.[29] Writing Lodge in September 1892, Roosevelt lamented, "I wish the cholera would result in a permanent quarantine against most immigrants!"[30] He later wrote Kipling that Filipinos were pirates and headhunters and that Colombia was a "corrupt pithecoid community."[31] He disparaged Orientals, suggesting they should be excluded altogether and that Americans and Japanese, the "yellow peril," should not mix racially. In his diary as legislator he described the average Irishman as "a low, venal, corrupt and unintelligent brute."[32] His opinion of Italians was no less harsh. "Monday we dined at the [Senator James and Elizabeth] Camerons; various Dago diplomats were present, all much wrought up by the lynching of the Italians in New Orleans," he wrote to Anna. "Personally, I think it rather a good thing, and said so."[33]

Nevertheless, Roosevelt believed in the melting pot and was optimistic that second- and third-generation Americans would overcome the weaknesses of their immigrant forebears.[34] His tenacious support of assimilation led the British writer Israel Zangwill to dedicate his popular play *The Melting Pot* to Roosevelt in 1908.[35] Theodore's views toward eugenics and assimilation became more tolerant over the years. In a famous lecture given at Oxford on June 7, 1910, the former president must have surprised his ethnocentric British audience when he told them that "a great nation rarely belongs to any one race."[36] By then Roosevelt had accepted completely the melting pot theory, although he remained arbitrary as to who should be allowed in the pot.

⌒

By March 1895, relations between the United States and Spain worsened. Not wanting to miss an opportunity for military action, Theodore sent a handwritten note to Governor Levi Morton of New York. "In the very improbable event of war with Spain I am going to beg you with all my power to do me the greatest favor possible; get me a position in New

York's quota of the force sent out," pleaded Roosevelt. "I was three years captain in the 8th Regiment N.Y. State militia, and I must have a commission in the force that goes to Cuba!"[37]

Roosevelt's craving for conflict influenced his actions and writings. Since his youth, he had yearned for battle. "I have written to Secretary [of War] Endicott offering to try to raise some companies of horse riflemen out here in the event of trouble with Mexico," Theodore wrote Lodge from his Medora ranch in August 1886. "Will you telegraph me at once if war becomes inevitable?"[38] Roosevelt's warrior spirit framed his views of national politics, international relations, and in many respects his family life and the way he raised his four sons. He came of age during the popularity of Tennyson's "Charge of the Light Brigade" when the educated classes romanticized warfare. The warrior spirit intoxicated Roosevelt, but no more so than contemporaries like Kipling, Oliver Wendell Holmes, Brooks Adams, and Alfred Mahan. Quite simply, Roosevelt loved a fight. He became bored when there was not a moral issue he could defend or an immoral person he could attack. "Teddy is consumed with energy as long as he is doing something and fighting somebody," Spring-Rice wrote to Elizabeth Cameron in 1891. "He always finds something to do and somebody to fight . . . [he] is happiest when he conquers but quite happy if he only fights."[39]

Ironically, Roosevelt distrusted career military officers and did not consider himself militaristic, but he clearly argued that the nation should be both prepared and willing to fight.[40] When researching his naval study of the War of 1812, Roosevelt began to lament the historical tendency for the United States to be unprepared for war. While commissioner, Theodore urged his colleagues to build up the navy and to acquire naval bases in Guam, Cuba, Panama, and Puerto Rico, and in October 1894 he suggested to Lodge that the United States "go in avowedly to annex Hawaii and build an oceanic canal with the money of Uncle Sam."[41]

⌐

Hobbling about on two wooden legs, James "Corporal" Tanner symbolized the Civil War veteran who shed his blood on the battlefield and expected the nation to reward him for his sacrifice.[42] After enlisting in the Eighty-seventh New York Infantry, Tanner fought in several early battles and weathered the Peninsula Campaign. At the Battle of Second Bull Run, a Confederate cannonball burst across a Virginia cornfield and smashed into Tanner's body. In the midst of the still raging battle, surgeons barely saved his life by amputating both legs. Studying law after the war, Tanner used his gift for fiery oratory to become a powerful and somewhat unbridled spokesman for the Grand Army of the Republic (GAR). Using his GAR support, Tanner helped to deliver the veteran vote to Harrison in 1888. Shortly before appointing Roosevelt to the Civil Service Commission, Harrison rewarded Tanner for his campaign work by appointing him commissioner of pensions.

While veterans applauded Tanner's selection, reformers railed at Harrison's choice. Labeling the corporal unfit for office, E. L. Godkin called Tanner "a loud-mouthed Grand Army stump-speaker."[43] Immune to criticism and orders from above, the irrepressible Tanner proceeded to overlook legal statutes, administrative procedures, and the pension office's limited budget. He launched a crusade to get the maximum possible pension benefits for "every old comrade that needs it." Earning the wrath of the civil service reformers for vigorously encouraging preference for veterans in government positions, Tanner used his influential position to raise the disability rate of many pensioners, order questionable lump-sum payments to thousands of veterans, and lobbied Harrison to sign a dependent pension bill, previously vetoed by Cleveland, that encouraged a boom in marriages of young ladies to elderly veterans and saddled the government with payments running well beyond the life span of the Union soldiers.[44] To the ire of the reformers, Tanner replaced Democrats with Republicans in the pension office. Two of his replacements were his daughters. Soon, Secretary of the Interior John Noble, himself a popular GAR leader, ordered Tanner to stop the unlawful and enormous flow of money from the Treasury. In September 1899, after Tanner ignored Noble's instructions, Harrison forced the corporal's resignation.

Despite the pension commissioner's notoriety, Roosevelt appears to have gotten "along well with the absurd Tanner."[45] Theodore distrusted career military officers but nevertheless had a soft heart for citizen soldiers like Tanner, a fellow New Yorker. Roosevelt also respected the political power of the GAR, whose membership in 1890 approached a half million, or about a third of the Union survivors of the war.[46] Theodore realized that if the old soldiers voted together, they could "make politicians dance like peas on a hot shovel."[47]

Roosevelt could not agree, however, with Tanner and the GAR in giving hiring preference to veterans. Like most of his reform colleagues, Theodore believed that veteran's preference bogged down administrative efficiency and impaired the integrity of the merit system.[48] Writing the House Committee on Reform in the Civil Service, Roosevelt opposed one of many bills that called for expanding veteran's preference. "Veterans who get into office under this clause are rarely the equal of civilians who stand on the same lists," wrote Roosevelt. "An old soldier who at fifty years of age has to seek employment under the Government is not apt to be able to render as good service as a young man in the prime of his health and strength. . . . It is eminently proper to give to the veteran who needs it and who deserves it a pension, but it is not proper to have him draw money from the Government for doing work which could be performed better by somebody else."[49]

Roosevelt and other civil service reformers had an uphill fight against the veterans and the powerful GAR. Yielding to pressures from veterans, drafters of the Pendleton Act, while creating a merit service, grandfathered previous veteran's preference legislation. The act allowed that "nothing herein contained shall be construed to take from those honorably discharged from the military or naval service any preference conferred."[50] During Cleveland's first administration, the Civil Service Commission succumbed to the inevitable demand for veteran's preference and allowed the grade of eligibility for disabled veterans to remain at 65 percent, compared to 75 percent for nonveterans. When the number of civil servants was reduced, veterans and their widows and orphans who could show equal qualifications with other employees were given preference and retained. Eight bills to secure more preference were introduced during the Forty-ninth and Fiftieth Congresses.[51] Harrison also felt the pressure for rules more favorable to ex-soldiers and ex-sailors.[52] During Harrison's administration, Congress introduced two dozen bills to expand veteran's preference. The Senate passed two of the bills but the House failed to act on them.[53] Interest in veteran's preference proposals remained keen until the end of the Spanish-American War, when more liberal pension policies began to placate the veterans' lobby.[54]

❧

Theodore Roosevelt was a voracious reader. While civil service commissioner, he picked up navy captain Alfred Mahan's classic book, *The Influence of Sea Power upon History*. For the next two days, despite a busy schedule at the commission, Theodore pored through the volume. When he finished, he was greatly moved. "It is a *very* good book—admirable," Roosevelt wrote Mahan a day later. "I am greatly in error if it does not become a naval classic. It shows the faculty of grasping the meaning of events and their relations to one another and of tak-

ing in the whole situation."[55] Over the next two decades, Mahan's theories of naval power would have a significant impact upon Roosevelt
and, indirectly, world history. As assistant secretary of the navy and especially as president, Roosevelt turned to Mahan for much of his geo-
political mantra.

Mahan brandished brilliance, with piercing steel eyes peering from
a hawkish face and neatly trimmed beard. The naval officer became
the most noted naval strategist of his day, the ablest and most effective apostle of imperialism, and Theodore was one of his most devoted
acolytes. Like Kipling, Mahan and Roosevelt distrusted Germany and
feared that the "Furor Teutonicus" would someday overrun Europe.[56] In
Sea Power, Mahan argued that the true great sea-power nations were
those with a productive and healthy domestic economy, vigorous foreign commerce, a strong merchant marine, and a powerful navy capable
of defending its trade routes, colonies, and naval bases. In the *Atlantic
Monthly,* Roosevelt praised Mahan's recognition of the profound effects
of sea power on the development of the great nations of the world. He
commended Mahan's understanding "of the deep underlying causes
and connections between political events and naval battles."[57] Despite
his mistrust of career military officers, Roosevelt maintained a deepen-
ing friendship with Mahan, who was eighteen years his senior, that
lasted until the naval officer's death in 1914. Roosevelt composed the
Outlook obituary applauding Mahan's efforts to educate the public in
the needs for naval power and concluded, "there was no one else in his
class, or anywhere near it."[58]

Brooks Adams became another close friend who influenced Roosevelt's views on foreign affairs.[59] Beginning in the commission years, the
relationship between Theodore and Brooks strengthened, with each
man exerting considerable effect upon the other. Unlike his more passive brother Henry, Brooks cared intensely about social conditions and,
as did Theodore, argued that government should take a more active role
in improving society. In many ways, Theodore and Brooks shared a
common yet complicated social and political ideology. Both men defied
conventional political labels and were at once conservative, liberal, and
progressive. Brooks, and Theodore later, argued that the general function of administration is to facilitate social change, or, paradoxical as it
may appear, to assure social stability by facilitating change.[60] To them,
powerful government must act positively for the common welfare and
work as a unifying force; more specifically, the executive must have full
power to make national policy and direct its administration by means
of an efficient civil service.[61] Adams also resonated with Roosevelt's

militarism. During the 1890s, Brooks seldom missed a chance to praise the purifying virtues of righteous battle and hardened into a philosophical militarist. Brooks believed that the American drive for world supremacy could succeed only if the nation took steps toward becoming a centralized, collectivist state.[62]

While Roosevelt served as commissioner, Adams published his popular but controversial *Law of Civilization and Decay, an Essay in History.* Roosevelt liked the work but found room for criticism. "Have you read Brooks Adams' *Civilization and Decay?*" he asked Anna. "It is from a false standpoint, but is very strong."[63] In a review published in the *Forum,* Roosevelt concluded, "this is not a pleasant theory; it is many respects an entirely false theory; but nevertheless there is in it a very ugly element of truth."[64] Adams's pessimistic predictions, which always seemed to end in catastrophe, revolution, anarchy, or war, disturbed Roosevelt, who saw his friend as "simply reveling in gloom over the appalling social and civic disasters which he sees impending."[65] Adams, unlike Roosevelt, had little faith in the common man. Theodore did not agree that Brooks's theory of social and national decline applied at all times or in all places and could not admit that the United States was militarily weak.[66] Roosevelt was confident that progressive government with self-determined leadership could reverse any decline as suggested by Adams, nor did he agree with Brooks's argument that "government is corrupt from top to bottom."[67] At one point, Theodore wrote to Spring-Rice that Brooks's "mind is a little unhinged," but over the years their friendship blossomed and Roosevelt's regard for Adams improved.[68] As president, Theodore regularly invited his friend to the White House for dinner,[69] and Brooks in turn enthusiastically supported Roosevelt's ill-starred bid for the presidency in 1912.

Roosevelt and Adams shared a disdain for the vulgar rich and the "gold bugs," the masters of finance and industry.[70] Both men recognized the importance of the railroads in American domestic affairs. Roosevelt, like Brooks, feared the huge gap between the rich and poor would provoke social deterioration but, unlike Brooks, remained optimistic that modern civilization could make the necessary political changes to stave off chaos. In his last year at the commission, a confident Roosevelt believed society in good shape when he wrote in the *Sewanee Review* that "at no period of the world's history has there been so much happiness generally diffused among mankind as now."[71] This was ironic, as the nation remained in the throes of one of its worst depressions. Roosevelt, as his letters show, seemed unconcerned with the economic problems of the day. He seems only to have noted the political fallout of economic strife, such as the Republican losses in 1890 over the tariff issue or Cleveland's loss in popularity during the depression that gripped the country. Undeterred by the nation's plight, Roosevelt confidently hoped for the future and displayed a cautious optimism when he wrote in his historical *New York* that "the greedy tyranny of the unscrupulous rich and the anarchic violence of the vicious and ignorant poor are ever-threatening dangers; but though there is every reason why we should realize the gravity of the perils ahead of us, there is none why we should not face them with confident and resolute hope, if only each of us, according to the measure of his capacity, will with manly honesty and good faith do his full share of the all-important duties incident to American citizenship."[72]

By early 1895, Theodore was restless. He neared completion of a much improved fourth and final volume of *The Winning of the West* and saw his *Hero Tales from American History* published. His writing, however, never satisfied his boundless energy and ambition. Likewise, the commissionership no longer provided the challenges upon which he thrived. As he began his sixth year at the commission, Roosevelt felt that the time had come for higher office or at least a post offering more challenge and excitement.

After William Strong won the New York election the previous October, Roosevelt quietly admitted to friends that he might consider an appointment in the new mayor's administration. Roosevelt's political friends approached the new mayor, and by early December, Strong offered Roosevelt an appointment as commissioner of street cleaning. While the job posed a difficult challenge and offered more pay than his civil service position, Theodore turned down the offer before Christmas. "I would have been delighted to smash up the corrupt contractors and to have tried to put the street cleaning commissioner's force absolutely out of the domain of politics," Theodore wrote his journalist friend, Jacob Riis,[73] but with the actual work of cleaning streets, dumping the garbage, etc., I wasn't familiar. . . . I didn't feel that I could leave this work here—in which I believe with all my heart and soul—for at least a year to come, and so I had to refuse."[74] Quite simply, the title of commissioner of street cleaning did not fit Roosevelt's self-image or his ambitions for higher office.

Later, Roosevelt learned that Mayor Strong proposed that Theodore be appointed New York City police commissioner. At first, Roosevelt showed little interest in taking the police commissionership. Edith, however, thought that the New York appointment was a smart move for Theodore's career, and she now wanted to return to the city. Nevertheless, she was reluctant to pressure her husband to accept the new post, for she still regretted persuading him not to run for mayor the year before. Frustrated that Theodore was "much more interested in having Wister and Remington to dinner on Friday" than he was in being appointed police commissioner, she turned to their closest friend, Cabot Lodge, and together they convinced her husband that it was time to leave the Civil Service Commission.[75]

In March 1895, soon after returning from inspecting the Internal Revenue and Post Offices in Cincinnati, Roosevelt began corresponding with the Republican power broker Lemuel Quigg about the police commissioner appointment. At first Roosevelt was coy.[76] "Your letter was a great surprise to me. It had not occurred to me that you would really press my name upon the mayor," Theodore wrote Quigg. "I think I had better not take the position. A year hence I would like to take an active part in the presidential campaign, and I could not well do that as police commissioner; and until a year hence I really ought to be here to complete some work I am now at. I am greatly touched by your thinking of me."[77] A week later, on April 1, Roosevelt telegraphed Quigg to suggest he meet with Lodge in New York to discuss an appointment. Two days later Theodore sent Quigg another confidential telegram that accepted the mayor's offer. The new position was a six-year appointment with an annual salary of $6,000. "Strong first offered me the position of Police Commissioner through a third party and I refused," Theodore wrote Anna on April 14. "He then offered it to me again, directly. . . . I hated to leave Washington, for I love the life."[78]

On April 25, 1895, Roosevelt sat at his City Hall desk and wrote his resignation letter to President Cleveland. "There have been haltings and shortcomings, here and there, but as a whole the improvement in the administration of the law has kept pace steadily with the growth of the classified service," Theodore wrote. "Year by year the law has been better executed, taking the service as a whole, and in spite of occasional exceptions in certain offices and bureaus."[79] While Roosevelt was pleasant to Cleveland, he admitted privately that he found little difference in the Harrison and Cleveland commitments to civil service reform. Writing to Lodge, he confessed that the two presidents were "much of muchness."[80] He later accused Harrison of looting the fourth-class postmasters more rapidly than Cleveland while at the same time he accused Cleveland of looting the consular service more rapidly than Harrison.

"The final result was the same in both cases."[81] Nevertheless, Roosevelt was pleased with his accomplishments at the commission, where for six years he fought "spoils and corruption on every quarter, striking terror into the hearts of contumacious postmasters and collectors of customs."[82] It had been a period of unbridled energy, a time in which he first boasted of feeling "as rugged as a bull moose."[83] After Theodore resigned his civil service commissionership, he returned to New York City to accept the new mayor's offer as New York City police commissioner. On May 8, 1895, he began work in his new office at the Mulberry Street police headquarters, "a gloomy building with subterranean dungeons where rats and vermin assisted the persuasive effectiveness of the third degree."[84]

At his own sprightly pace, Theodore Roosevelt had strolled past the White House many times during his first six years in Washington. He admired the building's classic beauty, disagreeing with Mark Twain's description of the White House as a "fine large white barn, with wide unhandsome grounds about it."[85] Roosevelt admitted that each time he glanced upon the presidential mansion, his heart would beat a little faster.[86] Years later he confessed his earlier presidential ambition, recalling that "in those Harrison years as I passed the White House every day to and from my office, the thought often came to me that possibly some day I would occupy it as President. . . . It thrilled me to think of it as a possibility."[87]

An extremely ambitious man, Roosevelt possessed the confidence, determination, and plain stubbornness to believe that with hard work and a little luck he could reach any goal. "Theodore is never sober," Henry Adams once wrote of Roosevelt's unbridled ambition. "Only he is drunk with himself and not with rum."[88] As he survived successive years at the Civil Service Commission without being dismissed, meanwhile learning more and more about the inner workings of Washington politics, the image of eventually moving into the large white mansion on Pennsylvania Avenue became increasingly distinct and realistic. When Roosevelt arrived at the commission, most agreed his career had ended, but he soon dispelled such a notion. Indeed, he turned the innocuous civil service commissionership into an important stepping-stone toward higher office. He accepted a minor post and took on a seemingly impossible and politically suicidal task and not only survived but increased his political power and visibility while leaving his mark on a greatly improved bureaucracy. Few who knew him well were surprised that when Roosevelt resigned as civil service commissioner he began a period when the momentum of his career as a public servant accelerated at ever increasing speed.

In May 1895, Theodore moved from Washington to New York City, where he served for two years as police commissioner. In April 1897 he returned to Washington, this time as assistant secretary of the navy. A year later the Spanish-American War erupted and Roosevelt left the Navy Department, enlisted in the army, and became a colonel in the First U.S. Volunteer Cavalry, the legendary Rough Riders. Three months later he led the charge up San Juan Hill and two months afterward returned to New York a national hero. "It has been a splendid little war," John Hay crowed in a note of congratulations to his friend Theodore. Three months later, New York voters elected Roosevelt governor. The governorship lasted two years, as the Republicans chose him to run successfully for vice president in 1900. When President William McKinley died of an assassin's bullet in 1901, Roosevelt became president. Six years had passed since he resigned as civil service commissioner.

What was the legacy of the commission years upon Theodore's later career? The influence of the commissionership upon the future president appears profound, for in many respects those six years provided Roosevelt the experiences and skills that he deeply needed at an early stage of his public life. The commission provided an important political education for the future president. Still only in his thirties, he found himself able to become a force in national politics, to make deals, and to learn from his defeats. While the commissionership would have been an obscure posting for most appointees, such was not the case for Theodore. Roosevelt already was fairly well known when he arrived in Washington, for his extensive writings, his previous tenure as a New York legislator, and his father's impressive reputation had made him familiar with the silk-stocking crowd. Moreover, aggressive enforcement of the civil service law catapulted Theodore into the limelight as he became the impetus for an unprecedented attack upon a spoils system that had dominated American politics for over fifty years. The commission previously was a minor player in Washington, but civil service reform remained the biggest and most controversial issue of the time. As such, Theodore arrived in the nation's capital with instant fanfare. On his first day at the commission, the *Washington Star* announced his swearing-in with a lead article at the top of the front page.[89] Cabinet officers did not receive such notoriety.

During Roosevelt's first six years in Washington, he sharpened all the qualities of energy, impatience, courage, pragmatism, political maneuvering, and moral idealism that became well known in the White House.[90] Roosevelt mastered the treacherous political battleground of Washington, and his civil service skirmishes with Wanamaker, Carlisle, and Grosvenor steeled him well for more epic struggles a decade later with the likes of Mark Hanna, William Jennings Bryan, Pitchfork Ben Tillman, William Randolph Hearst, and J. P. Morgan. Maturing into a skilled propagandist, he commanded the attention of the press and recognized not only its value in propelling men to national prominence but also its use as a weapon to be turned against his opponents. Theodore made good copy. Reporters found that his aggressive comments, foppish dress, and unusual candor almost always provided a colorful and controversial story. His physical characteristics, especially the glaring teeth, pince-nez glasses, and constant motion, were a political cartoonist's dream.

Roosevelt matured intellectually during the period. Blessed with a remarkably retentive memory, he applied a scientist's thirst for knowledge and research and mastered a number of policy areas. Reading voraciously, writing prolifically, and socializing with the intellectuals of his day, Roosevelt had the unusual opportunity to exercise his mind, test the theories of others, and develop and refine his own complex views of man and his place in society. By the time he resigned from the Civil Service Commission and departed Washington in 1895, Theodore possessed an extraordinary array of well-honed administrative and communications skills, political acumen, and intellectual capacities.

He learned the value of strong friendships, political allies, and the advice of experts across a diverse array of professions. Many of the friends he made while commissioner became invaluable, both personally and politically, and demonstrated how important the civil service years were in providing him the opportunity, at such a young age, to build relationships that only Washington could provide. For example, as president he often turned to members of his informal "Cowboy Cabinet" for advice, companionship, and the pleasure of swapping tales about the West and American Indians. Owen Wister, George Bird Grinnell, the artist Frederic Remington, explorer Charles Lummis, and Indian rights activist Francis Leupp were all close friends from the commission days who became welcome visitors in the Roosevelt White House.[91]

Theodore also learned to deal with his enemies. Godkin and Hatton were no longer living during Roosevelt's presidency, but he still had to contend with many of his old nemeses, such as Senator Gorman, Congressmen Cannon and Grosvenor, and other legislators who spanned his commission years. While he fought many of these old adversaries on a number of controversial policy matters, Theodore maintained at least a cool cordiality with them that allowed for open communication and, at times, compromise.

Roosevelt also learned, despite his reputation for being headstrong, to listen to others and to value their opinions and advice. Although he was quick to typecast acquaintances as either close friends or bitter enemies, he improved his judgment of human nature. Roosevelt sported a gregarious and energetic personality. During his thirties he undoubtedly would have made numerous friends wherever he lived. However, the six years at the commission are unique for they were in Washington, the center of national politics.

Remarkably, many of the closer friends that Roosevelt cultivated during those first six years in Washington were already either famous or influential, or both, and if not yet, would be so in the future. Spring-Rice, for example, appeared as a minor diplomat during the commission years, but later, as British ambassador during Wilson's presidency, he played a significant role in foreign affairs. Lodge languished as a relatively unknown congressman but would later dominate congressional foreign policy and lead the defeat of Wilson's intent to join the League of Nations. Mahan's naval career was at a standstill, but he soon would rise as the most influential naval theorist of his era. Tom Reed had served a term as Speaker but had not yet amassed the power he later would possess in that office. Owen Wister struggled between a law career and his first novels and would not become a best-selling author until Roosevelt's presidency. Roosevelt attracted energetic, ambitious men like himself, and in turn those were the types to whom he became attracted. Taken as a group, they would join their friend Theodore to make a lasting impression upon the just dawning twentieth century.

How deep was the imprint upon civil service reform that Roosevelt left when he departed Washington in 1895? Over the years, widely differing views have emerged. One view is that Roosevelt championed civil service reform and not only saved the commission from extinction but singlehandedly transformed a corrupt and inefficient bureaucracy into the efficient, effective meritocracy that exists today. The other view is that Roosevelt's tenure at the commission was only bluster, the performance of a rambunctious young politician grabbing headlines and accomplishing little except the alienation of all around him. As is often the case with extremes, the truth likely lurks somewhere in between.

When evaluating his own performance, Roosevelt boasted of his accomplishment of extending the merit system during his watch, claiming that during his six years the commission added twenty-five thousand positions to the merit system and greatly diminished the "vast bribery chest" available to spoils politicians.[92] While a significant accomplishment, this was an area where Roosevelt and the commission made little impact. At least a quarter of the additions to the merit system were due to Harrison's lame-duck blanketing of Republication patronage appointees. Other than his efforts to classify several hundred Indian Service positions, there is little evidence that Commissioner Roosevelt actually caused the transfer of significant numbers of patronage positions into the merit system. In fact, Roosevelt had no power to do so, and his ability to persuade either Harrison or Cleveland to reclassify patronage positions was negligible.

Roosevelt's more direct contributions appear to have been in the areas of acquiring additional funds and personnel for the commission, conducting numerous investigations of illegal political assessments, improving the examination process, extending the enforcement of the Pendleton Act in field offices outside Washington, and ensuring that the merit system was managed with nonpartisan honesty and fairness. In 1890 and 1891, Roosevelt expanded civil service examinations into the Deep South. Until that time, northern Republicans, with the Civil War still a bitter memory, prevented widespread examinations within southern states. The Pendleton Act called for equal selections statewide, and Roosevelt aimed to uphold the law. After gaining the support of southern legislators, he ordered that examinations be given in the South. Northern Republicans raged at Theodore's actions, as many of the southerners who passed the tests turned out to be Democrats, and according to Roosevelt, nearly a fourth were black.[93] The commission later reported that ten times more eligibles had been obtained from the South than in any previous year.[94]

Roosevelt's direct contributions to civil service reform were indeed significant accomplishments. Roosevelt's energy in the day-to-day administration of the commission had long-range consequences, setting higher standards for efficiency, integrity, and initiative. His attention to detail gave the commission and its staff a much deeper appreciation of the legal homework needed to properly enforce the Pendleton Act. As such, Roosevelt can be safely credited with making the commission smoother working, professionally managed, and properly staffed and funded.

While Roosevelt's direct contributions appear noteworthy and numerous, his indirect efforts to civil service reform also made a significant impact. Roosevelt's most important accomplishment appears to be his ability to garner newspaper headlines, to put the commission on the map, and to help ensure its survival during a time when spoils politicians attacked from every quarter. Roosevelt loved the limelight. The newspapers, whether protecting the spoils or bent on reform, gave frequent coverage to his candid comments and bold attacks on political adversaries. Lacing his charges with spirit, intensity, and a flamboyant vocabulary, Roosevelt provided journalistic gems as he ridiculed his opponents. Pro-spoils congressmen may have wanted to repeal the Pendleton Act, but Roosevelt enhanced the visibility of the commission to a degree that opponents began to see an attack on the merit system as too much of a political risk. Even powerful senators knew that if they abused the patronage or attacked reform efforts, they could expect a swift, fierce, and humiliating counterattack from the young commissioner and that the incident would somehow be published in the next morning's newspaper.

As commissioner, Roosevelt delivered countless speeches and lobbied vigorously for increased appropriations and stricter regulations to strengthen the commission.[95] He gave numerous speeches and wrote many magazine articles to publicize and argue the cause for expanding the merit service and abolishing spoils. His articles on civil service reform appeared in the *Atlantic Monthly, Independent, Forum, Boston Herald, Century, Civil Service Reformer, Scribner's,* and the *New York Herald Tribune.*[96] If an opponent denounced Theodore, he answered several-fold. When critics attacked his magazine articles, his wrathful and unrelenting rebuttals often were longer than his original article. He displayed a natural talent for showmanship and "an extraordinary ability to advertise and sell his product and an extreme sensitivity to the realities of political power."[97]

Roosevelt served as a lightning rod for the commission during a vulnerable period. He energized, and in a real sense institutionalized, a commission that had been, until his arrival, a precarious and ill-supported experiment.[98] Consequently, he helped make the commission an accepted and trustworthy player in the Washington bureaucracy and did as much as anyone to assure the long-term future of the civil service reform movement. When he departed, he left the commission firmly established and "stronger in every respect than when he found it."[99] Even some of his former critics recognized Roosevelt's contributions. "What will become of the Civil Service Commission when Mr. Roosevelt leaves it can only be conjectured," the *Baltimore Sun,* a newspaper traditionally unfriendly to Roosevelt, reported on April 23, 1895. "He has been the only vital force in the Commission since it came into existence, and any man who shall take the place after him must show extraordinary enthusiasm, ability, and moral principle, or suffer in comparison."[100] Surprisingly, Roosevelt also had won over Frank Hatton. "Mr. Roosevelt is a sincere and genuine civil service reformer," Hatton wrote in the *Washington Post.* "There have been times in the past when his ideas of reform did not exactly comingle with those of the *Post,* but . . . it will be a sad day for Civil Service Reform when he steps down and out."[101]

Winning over an archenemy such as Frank Hatton was not unusual for Roosevelt. Often, his clashes with a political opponent followed a predictable pattern. At first, Roosevelt infuriated his enemy with a relentless and often personally vicious attack. When his opponent struck back, Theodore counterattacked with increased vigor. Soon, his enemy became exasperated and tired of the battle. Roosevelt simply wore him out. Ultimately, his adversary, while still opposing his policies and methods, began to admire Roosevelt's integrity, determination, and refusal to compromise his values or bend the law. To his opponents, young Theodore was like a feisty terrier, always yapping at their heels, his bite rather harmless and his high-pitched bark irrepressible. Over time, they couldn't help taking a liking to the irritating scamp.

8
1901

Continuing Reform as President

"IT IS ALL THE fault of the Fourth-Class Postmasters," complained President Theodore Roosevelt as he breakfasted with his family doctor at Oyster Bay. "When I can't sleep, and have been struggling all day with intricate problems in all the States of the Union, and the appointments that must be made of the Fourth-Class Postmasters, I go up-stairs, and in order to get to sleep, I sit and study out how the empire of Alexander the Great broke to pieces, and into what other empires it developed. . . . After changing the subject in my mind, I can go to sleep."[1] More than a decade after becoming civil service commissioner, the new president still struggled with the headaches of spoils politics.

Theodore Roosevelt's crusade for reform did not end when he departed Washington in 1895. For the next two years he served as one of New York City's four police commissioners. Earlier, as a New York assemblyman in 1884, Theodore became convinced that police reform was sorely needed in the city, and at that time he unsuccessfully proposed that a single police commissioner replace the four-member bipartisan board.[2] As soon as he became police commissioner, Roosevelt attempted a series of innovations. To the dismay of many of his colleagues, he hired a young woman as secretary to the previously all-male police board. As he had in 1884, he attempted to reorganize the cumbersome four-member board and, again, failed. He was successful in other areas, and during his tenure he helped to build a rigorous system of recruitment, examination, and certification of police personnel as well as a laudable promotion scheme.[3] For the first time, at least a small degree of merit penetrated a police department that was once completely spoils-ridden. Theodore's downfall, however, came when he failed to enforce an almost universally ignored law that prohibited Sunday sale of alcohol. Roosevelt's overzealousness in trying to enforce the unpopular blue law alienated all of his police board colleagues, a majority of the public, and even a previously flattering press. By the end of his two years, Roosevelt could accomplish little as police commissioner.

He remained undaunted, however. As navy secretary, Roosevelt successfully improved the methods for promoting officers, and as governor of New York in 1899 he continued efforts to improve the state's civil service system and to professionalize the government workforce. He also resisted the Platt machine's efforts to control patronage in the state. Although he allowed the Platt organization to select the men for many appointments, as governor he stubbornly insisted that he would have the final say on all selections and that they would be based on fitness and character.[4]

When he became president in 1901, Roosevelt still possessed his dogged determination for civil service reform and would institute numerous and lasting improvements upon the merit system. He had a good memory and did not forget the problems he observed as commissioner. Reformers expected much from the new president, and they were not disappointed.[5] Civil service reform remained an important Washington battleground, although the general public appears to have lost much of the interest of ten years before. As a consequence, spoilsmen were able to gain concessions during the McKinley years. In his first few months in office, Theodore restored to the merit system a large portion of the offices removed under McKinley and ordered the Civil Service Commission to attack the still spoils-ridden smaller post offices. The uncovering of widespread postal frauds showed that administrative discipline had been exceedingly lax in the preceding administration. Six weeks after taking office, Roosevelt issued an executive order transferring six thousand Rural Free Delivery Service employees into the merit system.[6] A new branch of the Post Office Department, Rural Free Delivery would grow to forty thousand postal carriers by 1909.[7]

Besides the Post Office, other important extensions of the classified service included the Forestry Service, Spanish War employees, and Indian agents. In 1906, Roosevelt ordered the classification of deputy collectors of the Internal Revenue Service and in 1908 covered 15,488 fourth-class postmasters north of the Ohio River and east of the Mississippi River.[8]

Roosevelt also issued an executive order bringing the Census Bureau under the merit system. Until then, the bureau was a notorious spoils refuge. While Theodore was commissioner in 1890, its entire staff of 2,150 employees hired to count and tabulate the census was unclassified and appointed by individual congressmen.[9] Cleaning up the Census Bureau had a greater political impact than merely delivering another extension to the classified service. For years, the party in power stacked the bureau with loyal party members who ensured that census counts resulted in desirable redistricting decisions for congressional apportionment, federal judgeships, and allocations of government funds. The stakes were indeed high. Both parties used means both fair and foul and often resorted to "tombstone counting" to ensure favorable tallies. After a bitter fight with congressmen who wanted Roosevelt to blanket their old spoils appointees, Theodore defied the legislature and hired a new merit-based workforce that ensured a much more reliable census count.

The Roosevelt administration made great progress in weakening the patronage link between the Congress and the bureaucracy. While Theodore served at the commission, a congressman of the president's party averaged 250 political appointments within his district, of which 200 were from the postal service. The congressman could expect about 1,700 applications for those positions and spent a third of his time distributing federal offices.[10] Using executive orders to bypass a recalcitrant Congress, President Roosevelt used the rapid expansion of the federal government to build up the merit system. During his presidency, the total number of classified employees surpassed the total number of patronage employees for the first time, with classifieds increasing from 46 percent to 62 percent of the total federal workforce.[11] In 1901 the classified service included 108,967 positions out of 235,766, and by December 1908 it had grown to over 220,000 out of 352,104. During those seven years, Roosevelt moved 34,766 positions into the merit service by executive order.[12]

The Roosevelt administration built a solid foundation that helped to ensure the survival of civil service reform and the commission itself during World War I, for Taft made few significant improvements and Wilson actually strengthened the patronage power in order to expand the wartime federal workforce.[13] While Roosevelt often pushed the Pendleton Act to its legal limits and supplied enormous energy to its enforcement, he also was shrewd enough to know what was not politically feasible. During the first years of his presidency, he made no move to classify fourth-class postmasters. The president agreed with his postmaster general, Henry Payne, who reported that "the transfer of fourth class postmasters to the classified service is such a radical measure that it would be considered revolutionary."[14] Roosevelt wrote Charles Bonaparte that an extension of the fourth-class postmasters could not be made because "in the country districts there is practically no sentiment in favor of such classification."[15] In 1908, during the waning days of his second term when little political risk remained, Roosevelt followed the recommendation of Postmaster General George Meyer and classified a large portion of the fourth-class postmasters.

Soon after taking office, President Roosevelt strengthened the powers of the civil service commissioners. On April 15, 1903, a new, simplified set of civil service rules went into effect that made numerous improvements, including increased investigative powers for the commission, more authority over violations of political neutrality, reduction in the number of temporary appointments, and creation of a formal procedure for expanding the merit system.[16] He appointed two new commissioners—James Garfield, the highly capable son of the martyred president, and his friend William D. Foulke, a prominent Indiana lawyer and civil service reformer. Roosevelt also retained his old Democratic colleague John R. Proctor, who earlier served on the commission with Theodore.[17] Proctor took charge of the examinations, Garfield managed the internal administration, and Foulke conducted investigations and handled publicity. This smooth-working arrangement lasted until Proctor's death in December 1903. Later appointees to the commission included Alford Cooley, an active member of the New York Civil Service Reform Association; Henry Greene, who drafted the Duluth, Minnesota, civil service regulations; and John McIlhenny of Louisiana, a former Rough Rider lieutenant who served capably on the commission until 1919.[18] The only questionable appointment was John C. Black, a former pension commissioner under Cleveland. Despite his excellent character, Black's advancing age and physical infirmities prevented the old veteran from performing credible service to the commission.[19]

Roosevelt appointed the Baltimore reformist Charles J. Bonaparte as secretary of the navy and later as attorney general. With these and other capable assistants, Roosevelt ensured that the Civil Service Commission enforced its regulations much more strictly and consistently. He issued an executive order giving the commission the power to order government employees to provide testimony under oath under penalty of dismissal. In 1902, Roosevelt prompted the commission to fire the collector of customs at El Paso, Texas, and the appraiser of the Port of

New York. He allowed the collectors of internal revenue of Louisville and Nashville to both resign, and he denied the reappointments of the postmaster of Philadelphia and the surveyor-general of Idaho when their terms expired.[20] The commission had previously investigated all of these men under McKinley, who took no action. Roosevelt, once in office, ordered these and other cases reopened and adjudicated. Remarkably, all of the men removed were Republican leaders in their areas. Word spread that the new president would tolerate no abuses in the civil service laws, no matter the party affiliation. Over the next several years the commission reported both a noticeable decrease in the number of violations and a rapid increase in the number of successful prosecutions.[21]

Roosevelt's administration achieved significant improvements in the administrative machinery of the civil service. President Roosevelt convened the first meeting of states and cities with civil service systems.[22] In March 1903 he ordered that the federal civil service rules be entirely revised and systematized.[23] He continued the effort to streamline civil service recruitment by revising the examination process and advocating practical tests. Investigations of wrongdoing took high priority, and it was commonplace for offenders to be "taken by the nape of the neck and ejected from the public service."[24] At the same time, the commission dealt the death blow to political assessments. By the end of the Roosevelt administration, assessments of federal employees had all but disappeared as a source of political funding for candidates.[25]

Roosevelt spurred his energetic Civil Service Commission to set in motion a range of personnel improvements. In 1903 the president persuaded Congress to appropriate additional funds for the commission, allowing it to hire its own adequate workforce of professional personnel and no longer depend on employees detailed from other agencies. The increase of the commission staff was essential, for its duties had expanded severalfold. The civil service system had grown from thirty-eight local examination boards in 1883 to more than a thousand boards in 1900. During the Roosevelt presidency the commission created a permanent field staff, with thirteen federal civil service districts managed by a supervisor responsible only to the commission.[26]

With the added presidential support, finances, and personnel, the commission tackled a number of problems that heretofore had appeared unsolvable due to political or funding obstacles. The lack of an orderly position classification scheme continued to cause needless duplication in examinations and inefficient certification and placement of those employees examined. The commission successfully combined registers and urged departments to be more specific in their personnel needs. Equal pay for equal work remained a more difficult problem because no coordinated pay plan existed. Although the president and the commission had broad powers regulating the civil service, Congress tightly held the purse strings controlling salaries and provided the president with no discretion or flexibility.[27] The commission still operated under the antiquated Classification Act of 1853, which set up the original six-grade pay schedule. Top pay for a chief clerk was $2,200, a figure unchanged for seventy years.[28] Not until 1923 would Congress pass a new Classification Act that mandated a standard wage and salary scale for all federal employees.[29]

Roosevelt opposed widespread political activities by government employees, a practice that he felt was a conflict of interest. As commissioner he had attempted to clarify a confusing circular issued by Cleveland that prohibited partisan activities by all federal employees and warned that public employees "should scrupulously avoid in their political action as well as in the discharge of their official duty, offending by a display of obtrusive partisanship."[30] Over the years the prohibition had remained vague and, consequently, widely ignored. Roosevelt looked upon the Cleveland prohibition as unrealistic and unenforceable, and upon becoming president he took corrective measures. He strengthened the restrictions by requiring that classified personnel, while retaining the right "to vote as they please and to express privately their opinions on all political subjects," could no longer take an active part in "political management or in political campaigns." In June 1902, Roosevelt ordered that political appointees "must not use their offices to control political movements, must not neglect their public duties, must not cause public scandal by their activity."[31] His instructions remained until the passage of the Hatch Act of 1939 under Franklin Roosevelt, and even today there is a distinction between the political activities of classified and unclassified employees.[32] During the 1904 Republican National Convention, Roosevelt gave stern orders to his followers that no classified federal employee would be allowed to take part in the convention and that "no non-classified civil servant, even, shall take part in the convention, where anyone else can be sent who will be equally loyal and intelligent."[33]

Roosevelt served as much more than an ordinary technician in his influence upon the federal service. Overall he can be credited with creating the doctrine whereby the federal government became the model that all organizations, both public and private, should emulate. "The National Government should be a model employer," wrote Theodore near the end of his presidency. "It should demand the highest quality of service from each of its employees and it should care for all of them properly in return."[34] In establishing the government as a model employer, Roosevelt advocated a program of progressive personnel management, including position classification, retirement benefits, workers' compensation, and the maintenance of safe and humane conditions at work. He also took a much more progressive stance toward unionization of government employees. As civil service commissioner, amidst the violent strikes at Homestead and Pullman, Roosevelt employed staunchly anti-union rhetoric, but as president he was much more politic and recognized the need to win over the labor vote. He demonstrated at least a lukewarm sympathy for labor during the summer of 1903. At that time a foreman in the Government Printing Office was fired because he was expelled from the craft union to which he belonged. The foreman appealed his firing to the Civil Service Commission on the grounds that his removal was unlawful. The commission ruled in favor of the foreman and asked that he be reinstated. Roosevelt agreed. "There is no objection to the employees of the Government Printing Office constituting themselves into a union," the president wrote the secretary of commerce and labor on July 13, 1903, "but no rules or resolutions of that union can be permitted to override the laws of the United States, which [it] is my sworn duty to enforce."[35] In effect, Roosevelt's decision allowed the federal service to retain an "open shop." However, his denial of a "closed shop" enraged Samuel Gompers and other labor leaders. At the same time, the perception of Roosevelt's attitude as firmly opposing public service unions provoked criticism among reformers.[36] Nevertheless, Roosevelt's decision still stands, and the federal government has allowed an open shop ever since.

Roosevelt's administrative accomplishments as president also helped to improve the public's opinion of government. "At the close of his administration the public began to feel as it ought always to feel, that the badge of public office is a badge of respect," wrote the editor of *Outlook*. "It began to regard Federal officials as well as Federal clerks as it regards the officers and enlisted men in the Army and the Navy. Certainly this was what Mr. Roosevelt wanted to accomplish." Roosevelt left a legacy of openness and honesty from which the civil service undoubtedly profited and arguably "did more for the practical enforcement of the civil service law than any other single individual."[37]

Roosevelt's interest in reform never ceased.[38] Often he had to put practical politics ahead of his reform ideals, and as president he faced many challenges, especially those in the international arena that were of more immediate importance than civil service reform. Nevertheless, and despite the sad events surrounding his later years, Roosevelt never gave up the fight for reforming the civil service and bettering the conditions of all workers. Shortly before he died and when he planned to run for the presidency again in 1920, Roosevelt penciled a campaign platform arguing continued civil service reform, as well as an eight-hour workday, social security, and old-age pensions—all revolutionary ideas that were well ahead of their time.

⤸

At sixty-three, Marcus Alonzo Hanna walked with an arthritic limp.[39] His health was failing, but the tall, heavy-jowled, and balding Hanna intimidated friends and foes alike with his physical appearance and political power. A wealthy Cleveland industrialist, Hanna was a skillful political kingmaker who launched William McKinley first into the Ohio governorship and then to the presidency. When Roosevelt became president upon McKinley's assassination in 1901, Hanna and other old-guard Republicans worried that a much more progressive-minded president now occupied the White House and gave Roosevelt only lukewarm support. At the time, Hanna served as a senator from Ohio and chairman of the Republican National Committee, and he was the most powerful political boss in the nation. Hanna, always blunt-spoken and businesslike, opposed Roosevelt's nomination for vice president and reportedly complained, "Don't you realize that there's only one life between this madman and the White House?"[40] Hanna almost refused to have supper with Roosevelt on McKinley's funeral train and referred to the new president as "that damned cowboy." Roosevelt would need all of his political savvy to deal with the forceful Hanna, and their running battle demonstrates the spirited power struggle between the presidency and the Congress at the turn of the century.

In dealing with Hanna and the old guard, Roosevelt displayed another of his many contradictions. Although Theodore was a dedicated reformer, he also was a shrewd politician. Expert in not only reforming the civil service but expert at circumventing the merit system, he exploited the valuable knowledge he gained as commissioner and used the loopholes in the Civil Service Act to his political and personal advantage.[41] Roosevelt's commission experience increased his ability as a politician. As president he used both the merit and patronage systems as powerful political tools to placate both the reform and conservative elements of his party. When necessary, he "wielded the long arm of the patronage power to its farthest reach."[42] While Roosevelt still battled the spoilsmen, he had at least unconsciously "absorbed their lore."[43] Despite the efforts of the Pendleton Act and the Civil Service Commission to bring federal employees into the merit system, 130,000 patronage positions remained when Theodore became president. When necessary, Roosevelt yielded to partisan pressures and from time to time accepted the spoils appointees of Senators Platt and Quay, the powerful political bosses who controlled much of the Republican machinery in New York and Pennsylvania.

Soon after becoming president, Theodore dealt quickly and decisively with Hanna. Roosevelt kept peace with the old guards by retaining most of McKinley's cabinet. His first change also suited Hanna, when he appointed Henry C. Payne, a veteran old-guard spoils politician and Hanna ally, to the still-powerful postmaster generalship. Payne's selection shocked the reformers. Carl Schurz, still hardy and irascible at seventy-two, pointed to Payne's appointment as evidence that his former protégé's choice was shamelessly political. Schurz complained that Payne's only ability was as a "not over-nice political pipelayer and wirepuller, whose appointment to control of the great patronage department of the Government, which has the largest field for political dicker, would have fitted the cabinet of a political schemer in the Presidential chair but not the Cabinet of the legendary Roosevelt."[44]

Roosevelt needed Payne. "When President McKinley died I accepted his cabinet in its entirety," Roosevelt explained to William Foulke. "There was not a single politician in it. He did not need any. He was such a skillful politician himself that he did not require the advice of any other, but with me it is different. . . . I want someone who can advise me. . . . That is the reason I have asked Mr. Payne to become Postmaster General."[45] Ironically, Payne turned out to be an excellent choice. He not only served as a key political figure in the cabinet but became surprisingly supportive of an efficient postal service and an expansion of the merit system. Soon after taking office, Payne announced that fourth-class postmasters could not be removed at the end of their terms purely for political reasons.[46]

Roosevelt walked a tightrope with Hanna and the old guard. During the first months of his presidency he cleared an enormous quantity of minor patronage through the Ohio senator.[47] Over time, however, Roosevelt's strategy was to use Payne's skill as a spoilsman to undermine Hanna. When warned of Hanna's opposition, Theodore remarked, "What can I do about it? Give him complete control of the patronage?"[48] While he allowed the old guard to share in the patronage, he refused to compromise the merit principles of honesty and competency that he forged during his commission years. One month after taking office, Roosevelt described his intention to balance politics and merit appointments. "In the appointments I shall go on exactly as I did while I was Governor of New York," he wrote Lodge. "The Senators and Congressmen shall ordinarily name the men, but I shall name the standard, and the men have got to come up to it."[49] The president usually held firm. If an appointee proposed by a senator or congressman did not meet Roosevelt's standards or in some way stirred up public wrath, the president did not hesitate to either request another name or reject the legislator's recommendation outright.[50] "I was on the whole successful," Roosevelt wrote to his son Kermit years later. "I utilized the reformers without letting them grow perfectly wild-eyed, and I yet kept in some kind of relations with the machine men, so as to be on a living basis with them, although I had to thwart them at every turn."[51]

Over time, Roosevelt used patronage to erode Hanna's power. The president's strategy was to divide and conquer. Using political appointments as a wedge, he split the political power between Hanna and his opponents and eventually weakened both sides while increasing his own political strength. Hanna continued to lose power, and by the time of the senator's death in 1904, Roosevelt had reduced the Ohioan to almost a figurehead and took firm control of the Republican Party organization.[52]

Roosevelt made other appointments that appeased the old guard and angered the reformers. Besides naming Payne as postmaster general, he selected Leslie Shaw, the standpat governor of Iowa, as secretary of the treasury.[53] He also appointed Richmond Pearson as consul to Genoa. While serving as a North Carolina congressman in 1897, Pearson introduced a bill to abolish the Pendleton Act. In 1904, just before the Republican convention, Roosevelt angered reformers when he appointed the spoilsman James Clarkson as surveyor of customs in New York. Clarkson previously served as Wanamaker's assistant postmaster and spoils hatchet man and had been an irritating thorn in then-commissioner Roosevelt's side. When confronted by the press on Clarkson's controversial selection, the president confessed privately that "in politics we have to do a great many things that we ought not to do."[54] After William Foulke, then a civil service commissioner, complained of the appointment, the president cautioned Clarkson. "Be particularly careful not to get into any conflict with the Civil Service Commission," Roosevelt wrote Clarkson. "As you know, I am rather a crank on the civil service law. In view of the attacks upon you I am exceedingly anxious that there should be no possibility of the people who have made these attacks saying that any action of yours toward the Civil Service law has justified them."[55] Looking to the ideal but acting in terms of the feasible, Roosevelt attempted to balance his commitment to civil service reform and his role as a practical politician. As commissioner, Roosevelt was foremost a reformer and attacked both parties indiscriminately, but as president he was ultimately a politician. Roosevelt the politician needed the shrewd Clarkson to help him reunite a splintered Republican Party and to establish control over wavering factions in the South and groups loyal to Hanna. By the time Clarkson and other handpicked Roosevelt operatives finished, the president firmly controlled his party organization and was guaranteed his 1904 nomination.

Political pressures in the White House caused Roosevelt to alter some of his previous reform policies. When he was commissioner, the nature of his job caused him to be primarily *a*political, but as president he could not shun politics and more than often put political goals before reform. While commissioner he opposed giving ex-soldiers and ex-sailors preference in hiring and strictly adhered to the merit principle, but a combination of Roosevelt's experience in the Spanish-American War and the political necessity of GAR votes appears to have caused him to surrender to the veterans' cause. As New York governor, Roosevelt recommended that the Civil War veteran be guaranteed preference in appointment and retention, and as president he reaffirmed that "preference shall be given . . . to honorably discharged veterans of the Civil War who are fit and well qualified."[56] As Roosevelt's reelection of 1904 approached, he appears to have courted veterans' votes even more aggressively. An executive order of July 8, 1903, provided that veterans be excluded from age limits placed on civil service tests.[57] Further pursuing the GAR, President Roosevelt chose John C. Black as a civil service commissioner upon the death of John Proctor. Black was a former pension commissioner under Cleveland and commander of the GAR. Black was a "physical wreck," and his allegiance to the GAR was hardly in harmony with the merit system. Later, Roosevelt ignored the ire of civil service reformers and appointed the notorious Corporal Tanner, fired earlier by Harrison as pension commissioner, as register of wills for the District of Columbia. Again, Tanner was rewarded for delivering the veteran vote.[58]

Another example of President Roosevelt's diminished reform zeal was a shift in his support for equal treatment of African Americans. Soon after North Carolina's George White, the last Reconstruction-era black congressman, left office in 1901, Roosevelt appears to have lost much of his enthusiasm for finding jobs for black Republicans. More often he yielded to the wishes of southern congressmen who fervently fought integration of the federal workforce at every opportunity. In 1893, 2,393 blacks were employed by the federal government in Washington, but by 1908 that number had dropped to 1,450, about 4 percent of the workforce.[59]

Yet another example of a lessening zeal for reform was Theodore's use of patronage. Although President Roosevelt vocally opposed the spoils system, he skillfully dealt out patronage to keep errant legislators in line. By tradition, congressmen nominated the men for appointments within their own districts. However, if a congressman opposed Roosevelt on an issue, he soon would find his nominations ignored or held up. Once Theodore wrote the postmaster general, "[Colorado Republican congressman Warren] Haggott voted against us on ship subsidy and about everything else last year, and is entitled to no favors."[60] Roosevelt also resorted to patronage for personal reasons. He appointed friends from his Badlands days to several federal posts, including William Merrifield as marshal of Montana, Sylvane Ferris as land officer in North Dakota, and Joe Ferris as Medora postmaster.[61] On another occasion, he gave his writer friend Hamlin Garland a position in the office of the commissioner of Indian affairs.[62] In 1902, Roosevelt used a loophole in the civil service law to appoint Joe Murray as an assistant immigration commissioner. An old friend, Murray had nominated Theodore as New York assemblyman twenty years before.[63] Theodore also had a fondness for his old Rough Rider companions and appointed several of them to government positions in the West.[64] Roosevelt rewarded Major W. H. Llewellyn's battlefield valor with an appointment as U.S. attorney in New Mexico.[65] Roosevelt's personal appointments prompted Elihu Root to chide, "Well, Mr. President, there is a rumor going around . . . that every Rough Rider who isn't dead holds a federal office. Is that right?"[66]

In one of his more flagrant, but fortuitous, acts of presidential intervention, Roosevelt rewarded an army officer who had impressed him during his Spanish-American War service in Cuba. In 1906, Roosevelt promoted John J. "Blackjack" Pershing from captain to brigadier general, jumping over 257 captains, 364 majors, 131 lieutenant colonels, and 110 colonels. The unprecedented promotion angered the army rank and file but proved to be a brilliant decision years later when Pershing ably commanded U.S. troops in World War I.[67]

In 1905, the poetry of Edwin Arlington Robinson captivated the president, who later praised the poet's work as "an undoubted touch of genius . . . a curious simplicity and good faith." After inviting the reclusive Robinson to the White House and finding him destitute, Roosevelt secretly ignored civil service rules and arranged a political appointment for the poet.[68] Theodore sounded like a die-hard spoilsman when he wrote Robinson that "I think I can appoint you after July 1st to a $2,000 position as a special agent of the Treasury, say in New York, although possibly in Boston. It will give you plenty of time to do your outside work."[69] A few weeks later, Robinson took a post at the New York Customshouse. There is no evidence that Roosevelt saw either the irony of using his political power to give Robinson a job at the once-notorious customshouse or the contradiction of a staunchly reform president turning to patronage to bestow a personal favor.

↢

Whenever he visited the nation's capital, Owen Wister liked to drop by the White House and visit his friend the president. The two men spent many hours discussing the latest literary craze, their Harvard days, their love of the rugged West, or "cliff swallows, or cliff dwellers, or anything whatever." In the midst of these rambling conversations, Theodore often would receive a telephone call or an unexpected official visitor. Without hesitation, Roosevelt would turn immediately to the issue at hand, grasp the essentials, ask the caller pertinent questions, rise from his massive mahogany desk, and dictate a memo to a stenographer always within earshot. With the caller dispatched and the issue resolved forthwith, Theodore would return to his conversation with Wister as if there had never been an interruption, picking up exactly where they had left off.[70]

As commissioner and as president, Roosevelt exhibited an extraordinary ability to focus on an array of complex issues simultaneously. According to Wister, Roosevelt was one of those rare men who "have the power to organize and concentrate themselves wholly upon a given matter, in an instant, leaving nothing of themselves out; and then, when this is despatched, drop it as if it had never existed, and go on to the next matter. This does not mean that they are not carrying a multitude of other matters in their heads, turning these over, studying them, getting ready for conclusions that some day will seem to leap out like improvisations, it means merely that they are men with a capacity of the first rank."[71]

An able politician, Roosevelt also became an extraordinary administrator and arguably would not have been so without his experience as commissioner. Those six years were essential in his progress, for they allowed him to sharpen his exceptional administrative talent to a fine edge. Among the reasons for his success as an administrator were his continuous attention to detail, his occasional readiness to compromise constructively, and his capacity for growth.[72] He managed his duties efficiently and overcame the inertia of a three-person commission that was a cumbersome piece of administrative machinery. He learned that most of the work of government is not legislation but administration and recognized that research and committee work are essentials for modern decision making.[73] Observing thousands of civil service appointments as commissioner, Roosevelt cultivated an ability to make decisions rapidly, to choose able and first-rate men for important administrative posts, to give them both authority and support, and to centralize responsibility and clarify chains of command.[74] He valued lines of authority and the importance of efficiently designed organizational structures, realizing that efficient government depends upon the delegation of authority as well as responsibility.[75] He gained experience carrying out investigations, interpreting a vague and controversial Pendleton Act, operating with scarce funds, and dealing with a large number of personnel at all levels of government. He liked being around people, judged them carefully, if not always impartially, and consistently used character as the defining value of his fellow man.

Theodore's love of the limelight increased during his commissionership, a period when he fine-tuned his skills in managing the press. As such, Roosevelt was the first modern president to show a sophisticated appreciation of the power—and pitfalls—of public relations. He was the first president to allow a press room in the White House. His wife also appears to have learned these lessons, and her influence upon her husband-president in dealing with the media was low-key but profound. Edith was the first presidential spouse to employ a social secretary, and she brought a level of efficiency and management to the White House unseen prior to 1901.[76]

Roosevelt won his battles with powerful political wheelhorses and party bosses partly because he exhaustively researched the issues. Often he knew the administrative workings of government departments as well as, or better than, the cabinet secretaries. The commission posting provided an invaluable opportunity to observe dozens of federal agencies, to grasp what worked and what did not, and to observe how his colleagues exercised leadership. His fights with Wanamaker and Carlisle forced him to acquire a deep understanding of how the large Post Office and Treasury Departments operated. At the same time, he became familiar with the administrative workings of a variety of smaller agencies, such as the Indian Service, the Census Bureau, and the Lighthouse Board.

Roosevelt became an authority of his day on national security, immigration, women's rights, Indian affairs, conservation of natural resources, naval warfare, and, of course, civil service reform. He gained valuable lessons watching Harrison and Cleveland deal with the economic depression of the 1890s, as well as their response to strikes and labor unrest. Roosevelt turned to his strikebreaking observations in dealing with the nationwide coal strike during the fall of 1902. He skillfully used J. P. Morgan to negotiate a settlement between John Mitchell, president of the United Mine Workers, and coal mine owners, averting what would have been a crippling coal shortage that winter.

As a political realist, Roosevelt admitted that administration cannot be completely isolated from partisan politics. However, he recognized the value, whenever feasible, of separating politics and efficient administration and therefore proposed the creation of commissions of experts empowered to make recommendations that Congress could accept or reject but not amend.[77] Congress fought Roosevelt on this reform and passed legislation in 1905 forbidding the federal government from employing personnel without compensation, as Roosevelt apparently used volunteer committees to bypass the legislature.[78] Roosevelt appreciated the advantages of creating more efficient administrative commissions, staffed by nonpartisan experts and free from the political interference of legislatures. He recognized the need to separate politics and administration when, as New York governor, he reorganized the state's canal system, correction institutions, and the factory inspector's office by restructuring agencies to greatly reduce political influence from the legislature and party bosses. By identifying and isolating key administrative functions, the new structures provided a more clear chain of command and improved line managers' accountability to the executive.[79] Roosevelt's attitude toward democratic representation and delegated power created another of his many contradictions. On one hand, he believed strongly that the people should have a powerful voice in government and accordingly favored direct primaries and the recall of state judicial decisions. On the other, he believed that congressmen responded too readily to the special interest of their constituents and interfered with the day-to-day administration of government.

While Roosevelt clearly possessed extraordinary administrative talents, he was not without his faults. He never understood or showed much interest in economics and was often fiscally irresponsible. He was prone to rash impulses, egocentrism, and self-advertisement. Even as president he could be overly absorbed with details and fall into the trap of micromanagement. "Theodore is devoured by small personal details; appointments or removals of fourth-rate officials in remote mountains under cowboy influence," Henry Adams observed cynically in 1902. "I wonder whether he will ever grow up out of Civil Service Commissioner statesmanship."[80]

Roosevelt exhibited a strain of ruthlessness often associated with his competitiveness. He at times broke his own rules of justice and fairness and later admitted that, when dealing with adversaries, he seldom "used a feather duster."[81] He condemned individuals without first giving them a hearing, rarely conceded the possibility of error, and used the dangerous tactic of guilt by association. When opponents refused to agree with him, he labeled them liars or crooks or traitors.[82] In so many ways, Theodore was a bundle of tensions. Within his perplexing personality, progressive reform collided with old-guard conservatism, humanism and philanthropy clashed with chauvinism and xenophobia, and his love of nature coexisted paradoxically with his love of war. Because Roosevelt was so complex and held such contradictory views, his behavior often appeared inconsistent and even irrational, but those who knew him well saw a man who was much more shrewd and calculating and who never made a decision, despite its apparent impulsiveness, without serious thought.

Roosevelt displayed all of these characteristics, including his refusal to "use a feather duster," when he dealt with a racial incident during the summer of 1906. Amid the stifling heat of August, tensions in steamy Brownsville, Texas, erupted into a gunfight between white citizens of the town and a dozen black soldiers stationed at a nearby army fort. Several townsmen were shot and one died. During an investigation of the riot, all of the black soldiers at the fort refused to testify against their comrades. Outraged, the president ordered the dishonorable discharge of three entire companies of black soldiers. Among the 160 soldiers discharged were men who had served in the army for fifteen years and six Medal of Honor recipients. Northern newspapers attacked Roosevelt as racist, while the southern press applauded his actions. Roosevelt's extreme punishment of the black soldiers may have resulted from his racial prejudices, but it is likely that his response stemmed more from his horror of any situation bordering upon anarchy. Likewise, Roosevelt's decision in Brownsville underscores his ruthlessness, stubbornness, and tendency to abandon his sense of justice and fairness when order is threatened with chaos.

President Theodore Roosevelt accomplished a range of awesome administrative tasks that remains unparalleled. He managed the administrative process as well as or better than any other modern president, and his administrative exploits are conspicuous throughout his two terms as chief executive. Roosevelt arbitrated labor disputes, pushed through a pure food and drug law, reformed the consular service into a professional diplomatic corps, created the Meat Inspection Service, and reoriented the navy toward modern warfare. He established the Department of Commerce and Labor as a cabinet post and snatched 148 million acres of forestland from under the noses of lumbermen to expand the national park system severalfold. He skillfully orchestrated control over railroad rates through the passage of the Elkins Act of 1903 and the Hepburn Act of 1906, two landmark laws that gave teeth to the Interstate Commerce Act of 1887. These statutes allowed the first substantial regulation of the railroads and established a precedent for an expanded federal role in the general regulation of business.[83] He was the first president to attack the powerful trusts of J. P. Morgan, James J. Hill, Edward H. Harriman, and other financial giants.

Along with Governor-General William Taft, Roosevelt developed civil government in the Philippines.[84] He appointed the capable Gifford Pinchot, a future governor of Pennsylvania, as head of the Forestry Service. A tall, sparse, and dashing man whose angular face was framed by a dark handlebar mustache, Pinchot not only made great strides in the conservation of natural resources but reorganized the Forestry Service into an outstanding component of the civil service and a model agency for successful implementation of the merit system.

Displaying remarkable administrative perception, Roosevelt personally redesigned the organization for the building of the Panama Canal and centralized authority from an unworkable seven-man commission into a single directorship.[85] He disliked divided authority. His prior experience with the inefficient three-man Civil Service Commission served as a lesson Roosevelt put to use. In 1904 he extended the classified service to include the majority of the Isthmian Canal Commission employees.

During his year as secretary of the navy, Roosevelt had the opportunity to apply some of the administrative lessons learned at the Civil Service Commission. He took steps to alter one of the sacred traditions of the navy, that of promotion only through strict seniority. Inspired by his progressive crusade for meritocracy, Roosevelt urged that officers be promoted to command positions on their record and merit, based on their skill and bravery, and not on their years of service. The navy needed younger men in command because they were creative and energetic. His friend Alfred Mahan argued these points and Roosevelt acted upon them, authoring the Naval Personnel Act of 1898, which Congress passed. The act increased the opportunity for the best officers to advance rapidly, while the less fit were encouraged to retire after twenty years of service. Roosevelt's impetus also helped merge naval line and engineering officers in the reorganization of 1899.[86] The combined efforts of Roosevelt and Mahan produced positive and far-reaching consequences on the navy, especially when compared to the army and its antiquated organization and personnel policies.

In 1903, Roosevelt began a major reorganization of the U.S. Army, which until that time remained structured much the same as during the Revolutionary War. As civil service commissioner, Roosevelt had criticized army organization and leadership. He deplored the massacre of the Indians at Wounded Knee in December 1890 and blamed the carnage on General Nelson Miles, who then commanded the western troops and later, by nature of his seniority, served as army general in chief during Roosevelt's presidency. Roosevelt labeled Miles a "perfect curse" and a "detriment to the army."[87] Roosevelt also faulted the regular army based on his experiences as colonel of the Rough Riders during the Spanish-American War, when he observed military organization in chaos. He wrote Lodge from a troop transport on June 12, 1898, that "this mismanagement here is frightful."[88] He criticized the army's weak and confusing chain of command, recording in his diary that "there is no head, no energy, no intelligence in the War Department."[89]

President Roosevelt relied heavily on the advice of Secretary of War Elihu Root to achieve major changes in the army. Despite strong opposition from General Miles, other senior army officers, and members of Congress, Roosevelt abolished the position of general-in-chief, who in peacetime was a powerless figurehead, and created a new army head, the chief of staff, to whom the once-autonomous bureau chiefs would now report. Roosevelt's reform, the General Staff Act of 1903, created a unified chain of command where authority flowed clearly from the president, through the secretary of war, to the chief of staff and the army commands.[90] In effect, the reorganization simplified decision making and strengthened civilian control of the military, a concept that Roosevelt vigorously supported. Roosevelt agreed with former general in chief General William T. Sherman, who believed that civilian control of the military essential, objected to the use of the army as a domestic police force, and strongly advocated a separation of the military from politics.[91]

Roosevelt also objected to the army's slow, conservative promotion policies, which relied totally on seniority. However, he failed to change the antiquated system. The army refused to adopt merit-based promotions of military officers until General Pershing's reforms during World War I. Roosevelt did succeed in requiring a systematic rotation of military officers between Washington and field commands. No longer could officers remain in Washington staff positions for more than four years. Known colloquially as the "Manchu Act," this new rotation policy broke the tradition of a few select officers homesteading in Washington and gaining political influence for promotions and the choicest assignments.

After gaining some success with the army, Roosevelt attempted to reorganize the navy into a naval general staff. Since 1842 the navy had been divided into eight separate and autonomous bureaus. The divided authority in the navy created jurisdictional conflict, duplication, overall inefficiency, and powerful political fiefdoms for the bureau chiefs. During his presidency Roosevelt drafted several proposals for naval reorganization that show an acute understanding of administrative theory, including the relationship between line and staff, centralized authority, a clear chain of command, and ultimate civilian control of the navy. Congress, however, refused to act on any of Roosevelt's proposals. In retrospect, much of the success of the army reorganization was due to the superb legal and political skills of Secretary of War Root. On the other hand, Roosevelt led the fight personally for naval reorganization, most often without competent advice from the men who served as his secretary of the navy.

⤺

During his second term as president, Theodore Roosevelt expanded his reform efforts into more general administrative functions. He shifted from a focus on particularistic improvements, such as improving the examination process or increasing the merit service within a specific agency, to a focus upon improving and reforming overall government administration. Once elected on his own in 1904, he appears to have gained the confidence to attack major administrative problems rather than make marginal improvements.

As civil service commissioner, Roosevelt observed numerous and significant problems in the federal bureaucracy. He detested the widespread inefficiency, incompetence, and frequent corruption within the federal service and criticized presidents reluctant to tackle obvious administrative problems. Observing widespread organizational inefficiencies, he recognized the need to separate administrative functions into their most definitive and efficient components and to pinpoint responsibilities. By the time he became president, Roosevelt clearly saw that reorganization of the government was necessary. He also recognized that the process of major administrative reform remained slow, resistant, relatively unrewarding, and always difficult.

During his first six years in Washington, Theodore observed attempts by Congress to make much-needed bureaucratic reforms. From 1887 to 1889, a Senate committee began an investigation "to inquire into and examine the methods of business and work in the Executive Departments."[92] Francis M. Cockrell, a popular Missourian who served in the Senate from 1875 to 1905 and later on the Interstate Commerce Commission under President Roosevelt, chaired the committee. Amassing huge amounts of information on the bureaucracy, Cockrell's report identified numerous examples of unnecessary forms and duplication, arrearages, accumulation of useless documents, archaic office methods, and general laxness in operations. While the report provided well-justified criticism, it suggested no true remedies.

In 1893, as complaints of government inefficiency, incompetence, and corruption continued, Congress established a joint effort known as the Dockery Commission to search for remedies to the bureaucratic chaos. The commission was made up of three members from the House and three from the Senate, including Cockrell, and was chaired by Democratic congressman Alexander Dockery, a future governor of Missouri. Although the commission had wide investigative powers, most of its examination focused on accounting procedures. Completed in 1895, the Dockery report provided valuable statistical data on bureaucratic activities, reorganized accounting procedures in the Treasury Department, cut some minor clerks from Washington departments, and reduced paperwork in routine matters.[93] However, like Cockrell's earlier effort, the Dockery Commission made few significant recommendations and added little to the art of administration.[94]

From his seat at the Civil Service Commission, Roosevelt observed the futile congressional attempts at administrative reform and came to realize that reform resided more appropriately in the executive rather than the legislative branch. A decade later, President Roosevelt revisited many of those administrative problems and aggressively took steps to correct them. In 1905, soon after the inauguration of his second term, he established the Keep Commission, formally known as the Committee on Departmental Methods, to examine government administration and improve efficiency. He charged the commission to carry out a systematic effort to "place the conduct of the executive business of the Government . . . on the most economical and effective basis in the light of the best modern business practice" and to assume that "the President ought to be responsible for the condition of administration."[95] The deliberations of the Keep Commission provide an excellent example of Roosevelt's keen administrative vision. Described as the "first of the orderly examinations into [federal] administrative problems" and as a "landmark of executive introspection,"[96] the commission forecast an eventual and clear shift of administrative leadership from congressional to presidential dominance.

Roosevelt appointed Assistant Treasury Secretary Charles H. Keep to chair the commission. Two dominant members were Gifford Pinchot, chief of the Forestry Service, and James Garfield, whom Roosevelt appointed as civil service commissioner, commissioner of corporations in 1905, and secretary of commerce and labor in 1907. Pinchot and Garfield belonged to Roosevelt's informal but influential "Tennis Cabinet."[97]

Roosevelt's detailed instructions to the commission reveal a sophisticated awareness of administrative theory and practice that goes beyond the specifics of individual agencies. The president divulged his own strikingly modern convictions about administration when he charged the Keep Commission to ensure that salaries should be commensurate with the character and market value of the service performed and uniform across departmental lines; that government supplies should be standardized and purchased through a central purchasing office; that fiscal restrictions should not interfere with executive discretion; that comparative costs should be ascertained; and that there should be interdepartmental cooperation in the use of expert or technical knowledge.[98] At the time and to this day, such administrative depth and awareness remains especially rare in the White House.

Although the Keep Commission focused primarily on departmental methods and organization, it did not ignore questions involving the civil service. The commission pointed out the Pendleton Act's failure to provide a uniform pay plan for civil servants and noted that the last general salary legislation dated back more than fifty years. The commission recommended a complete revision of the job classification system, increased pay for all employees that would make government service competitive with private business, and the creation of a pension plan supported by a combination of employee and government contributions. A report on hours of work, equal pay for equal work, and sick and annual leave recommended more uniform practices. Unfortunately, most of these Keep Commission proposals fell on deaf ears, as Congress failed to make meaningful changes in personnel policy or to provide additional funding for employee pay and pensions. Roosevelt sent two messages to Congress urging action, but to no avail.[99] Congress did not accept the Rooseveltian view that overhauling the executive machinery was essentially an executive responsibility. Many in Congress resisted Roosevelt's efforts, such as Senator Thomas Carter, a Montana Republican, who saw the reforms as "executive encroachment on the sphere of congressional action."[100] Led by tough, leather-faced Joe Cannon in the House and Nelson Aldrich in the Senate, Congress rejected every one of the Keep Commission's long-term recommendations for administrative reform.[101]

As civil service commissioner, Roosevelt opposed creating a retirement system for federal employees, writing that he saw "no reason why a man who gets well paid as a Government clerk should expect when he grows old to have a pension rather than a man who has been poorer paid as an ordinary clerk outside."[102] Years before, as a state assemblyman, he had opposed giving pensions to New York City schoolteachers.[103] On becoming president, however, Roosevelt's attitude changed. Two years before establishing the Keep Commission, he requested that the Civil Service Commission investigate the feasibility of a retirement system. Roosevelt's commissioners recommended that a retirement system be implemented based on the estimate that the loss of efficiency from superannuation resulted in an annual cost of over $400,000.[104]

The Keep Commission recognized the problem of superannuation of the government workforce and recommended a comprehensive retirement plan. The commission proposed to pay every classified federal employee, upon reaching the retirement age, an annuity equal to 1.5 percent of his or her pay for each year of service. Under the proposed retirement plan, each employee would contribute to the retirement fund an amount essential to create his own annuity, with the government only funding the cost of administration. In February 1908, Roosevelt transmitted the retirement plan to Congress. Although Congress failed to pass the controversial proposal, the legislature eventually enacted the Civil Service Retirement Act of 1920.[105]

Based on another Keep Commission recommendation, Roosevelt created a General Supply Committee to centralize and standardize government procurement of supplies, thereby laying the groundwork for the eventual creation of the General Service Administration. The commission suggested that the federal government publish an official gazette containing executive orders, advertisements of contracts, legal notices, and other official announcements. Although this suggestion was not acted upon at the time, Congress created the *Federal Register* in 1935. Similarly, the commission recommended that important official records no longer in use be preserved in a "National Archives House." Although Roosevelt transmitted this recommendation to Congress in February 1909, Congress would not pass the National Archives Act for another quarter of a century.[106] Remarkably, a number of Roosevelt's recommendations would only become reality during later administrations, including that of his distant cousin Franklin.

⌐

There is little doubt that Theodore Roosevelt became an extraordinary administrator who made a lasting and profound imprint on the presidency and the federal bureaucracy. In many ways, the Roosevelt years created and reoriented new presidential powers that were previously legislative prerogatives. With Roosevelt's ascendancy, the president became involved deeply in managing administration, a radical change from the nineteenth-century design he inherited upon McKinley's assassination. To transform the presidency and American governance in such a dramatic manner required a president of immense administrative ability. In many ways, Roosevelt displayed his unusual abilities in his childhood and teens when, despite his frail health, he revealed an intense ability to focus and an unquenchable thirst for knowledge. Whether making poignant observations in his diary as a young boy, pursuing ornithology with a deep scholarly passion, or joining a score of Harvard clubs of wide interests, he displayed unfailing energy and a keen attention to detail, and he organized his life and complex interests in such a way that he appears to have always produced results in any endeavor pursued. With these early talents recognized, Roosevelt certainly would have developed his natural aptitudes into mature administrative competencies and likely would have made a success in any vocation. In later years, however, his true administrative skills thrived. He showed bursts of administrative talent while a New York legislator, especially after his first wife's death when he threw himself into his work and pushed through an unprecedented number of bills. His years as assistant secretary of the navy and, especially, as New York governor provided important experiences in the development of his administrative ability which would be so prominent in the White House. His term as governor of the nation's most populous state was the final, and perhaps the most important, phase of his preparation for national leadership.[107]

During his years at the Civil Service Commission, Roosevelt formed, tested, and honed his administrative abilities, and without those formative years his dominance as an administrative president may not have been so complete. The commission years provided Roosevelt with a powerful combination of experiences. He matured in many ways, not just as an administrator, but also as a politician, writer, husband, and father, and as a man much more confident about his place in society. He served at the commission for six years, a period long enough to provide stability, if such a term can be used in describing Roosevelt's energetic public and private lives. The only period of his public service that lasted longer was his seven years in the White House. Roosevelt spent his years on the commission in Washington, the epicenter of American politics, and not even New York City could have provided him the political and administrative experiences that the nation's capital offered. The commissionership, despite being a minor political appointment, allowed Roosevelt to "get his nose under the tent" and see how Washington worked. He absorbed the legislative process, learned firsthand how to overcome the bureaucratic red tape that could hamstring reform, and determined who really possessed power and who merely served as figurehead. It is doubtful that Roosevelt could have undertaken so successfully many of his administrative reforms without the detailed bureaucratic knowledge he gained as civil service commissioner.

Epilogue
1916

Rapprochement

FOR A CENTURY and a half, New York City's Cooper Union has served as one of the country's most distinguished institutions of learning and free speech. Covering an entire triangular plaza at the corner of Seventh Street and Third Avenue, the Union's grand Italianate building has been the setting for a flow of American history and ideas, where audiences celebrate a pageant of famous Americans and hear rebels and reformers, poets and presidents, and a score of notables at historic events. The Red Cross and the National Association for the Advancement of Colored People were organized at Cooper Union, and Thomas Edison and Felix Frankfurter studied there. Cooper Union has been the highlight of many presidential campaigns, none more so than in October 1859 when Abraham Lincoln assured his election as president by giving his "Right Makes Might" speech from the great hall podium.

A half century after Lincoln's speech, shortly after eight on a crisp evening in November 1916, two men strode across the polished oak stage of the Union's great hall and stood before an overflow crowd of over a thousand spectators. Theodore Roosevelt and John Wanamaker, both tempered with age since their days skirmishing over civil service more than two decades before, stood together in another epic occasion for Cooper Union.

⌐

Roosevelt's conflict with Wanamaker did not end when the wealthy retail merchant left Washington in March 1893 and returned to Philadelphia. Eight years later the two men again collided when Roosevelt entered the White House, and they continued to battle throughout the Roosevelt presidency and beyond. Wanamaker helped McKinley in 1896 and again in 1900, when he deposited $50,000 in a New York bank to fund the prosecution of Democratic election frauds. From 1888 to 1900, Wanamaker's "moderation and common sense" helped to strengthen Republican Party organization, ensuring the victories for McKinley, and, ironically, provided a solid party foundation that made possible then–vice president Roosevelt's rise to the presidency upon McKinley's death in 1901. During Roosevelt's reelection in 1904, however, Wanamaker appears to have done little except make the campaign contributions expected of a prominent Republican. Wanamaker again became active in 1908, campaigning energetically for Taft, a close Wanamaker friend for more than twenty years.[1] In 1911, President Taft dedicated Wanamaker's newest Philadelphia store, the largest in the world with forty acres of floor space and sixty-eight elevators.[2]

In 1912, however, the animosity between Wanamaker and Roosevelt again boiled to the surface. Wanamaker supported his friend Taft for reelection and seconded his nomination at the Republican convention. The Philadelphian became incensed when Roosevelt bolted the party after being denied the nomination and chose to run on a third-party ticket. The disloyalty of Roosevelt and other progressive Republicans disturbed Wanamaker deeply. "Theodore Roosevelt should prefer to have his right hand cut off rather than to have penned the things he has written against Republicanism," Wanamaker wrote at the time. As the split between the old guard and the Progressives widened, Wanamaker foresaw the Republican disaster with the departure of Roosevelt and the creation of the Progressive Party. "I do not believe Roosevelt can be elected," Wanamaker correctly predicted in his diary. "By dividing the party he will prevent the election of Taft and open the way for a Democrat [Wilson]." He added later that the country wanted no "whirligig administration of an unbalanced president," describing Roosevelt as "a madman trying to wrest the presidency from [Taft] who, in all fairness, should have Roosevelt's support."[3]

After the election, with Wilson victorious over Roosevelt and Taft, Wanamaker agonized over the defeat. "Well, the stormy war is settled," Wanamaker wrote in his diary. "How hateful to many states to drive them off from their old party of glorious history, and rather than trust themselves to Nero Roosevelt, thrown in their lot with the untariffsafe Democrats. Pity of Pities."[4]

To the loyal old-guard Republican John Wanamaker, having the Democrat Woodrow Wilson in the White House felt gut-wrenching.

The Philadelphian hoped that a Republican would capture the presidency again when Charles Evans Hughes challenged Wilson's reelection in 1916. He believed extreme measures were necessary for Hughes to defeat Wilson. Wanamaker, ever the innovator, conceived of inviting his old enemy but still-popular ex-president, Theodore Roosevelt, to make a keynote campaign speech for Hughes in the final week of the campaign. Wanamaker sent a telegram a month before the election,

> Dear Colonel Roosevelt: There is still much to be done to make sure the election of Mr. Hughes . . . it seems as though you might crown your splendid work for Mr. Hughes by the soul cry of a true patriot from Cooper Union [in New York City] Friday night, November 3rd, awakening the people to the crisis of the hour, like unto the speech of Abraham Lincoln, delivered on the same spot, which roused the people of the United States to put their seal upon him for the presidency. The fight is becoming more intense daily and next Friday would be the psychological moment for your supreme effort for Hughes and the Republican and Progressive parties, for which every loyal American will rise up and call you blessed. Please wire. Your friend, John Wanamaker.[5]

Three days later, from Toledo, Roosevelt accepted. The Cooper Union meeting sealed the return of Roosevelt to the Republican Party and the remarriage of the Republican old guard and the Progressives.[6] The meeting also marked the rapprochement of Roosevelt and Wanamaker. To Wanamaker, who presided over the meeting seated at the same desk and chair that Lincoln used, bringing Roosevelt back into the Republican fold was a most satisfying political and personal achievement.[7] Standing proudly at the podium, Wanamaker warmly introduced Roosevelt and compared his former nemesis to none other than the Great Emancipator himself. Stepping briskly to the rostrum, a crimson-faced Theodore gave one of his most intoxicating speeches. Pounding his clenched fists angrily, Roosevelt waged a relentless attack on Wilson and the president's "too proud to fight" policy of neutrality. On the night before, Wilson had spoken to fifteen thousand spectators at Madison Square Garden, and as Roosevelt attacked the president's speech point by point, Wilson rested on the presidential yacht *Mayflower* anchored in the harbor only a couple of miles away. Roosevelt waved a bloody shirt symbolic of the 1,198 persons, including 128 Americans, who died when a German submarine sank the *Lusitania* on May 7, 1915. Interestingly, Theodore's speech made little mention of the Republican candidate, Charles Evans Hughes, who lost the election a week later to Wilson.

There is no evidence that Wanamaker continued to hold any animosity toward Roosevelt after the speech, and if there had been, the Cooper Union meeting replaced it with the Philadelphian's gratitude. Age probably helped create their new harmony, as Wanamaker approached eighty and Roosevelt sixty.

~

Theodore Roosevelt never recovered from his son Quentin's death. When the United States entered World War I in 1917, all four of Roosevelt's boys were eager to get into the fight. So too, of course, was their bellicose father, but President Wilson denied Theodore's request to put his uniform back on and form a volunteer regiment like the Rough Riders of nineteen years before. For the remainder of his life, a bitter Roosevelt never forgave Wilson for what he saw as a politically motivated decision.

Wanamaker appears to have agreed with Roosevelt. "Washington, the Capitol City, looked at the United States through the little end of the telescope when it ignored your patriotism, pluck and perseverance, and went on knitting in trying to get America to move on immediately," Wanamaker wired Roosevelt soon after Wilson's decision became public. "The effect of your being on horseback, as Chief of Command of an Army of half a million of men would have hastened the ending of the War as much as another Liberty Loan."[8]

Roosevelt had to settle for watching his four sons march off to war without him. Nevertheless, he was the proudest of fathers, bragging that "never did four falcons fly with such daring speed at such formidable quarry."[9] His oldest son, Ted, served as an army officer in France. Gassed severely near Cantigny, France, he was later shot in the left knee.[10] Kermit also saw considerable combat, but escaped the war with only malaria. He first served as an officer in the British army and fought against the Turks in the Middle East, where he received the British War Cross for gallantry. Kermit later transferred to the U.S. Army as an artillery captain and distinguished himself in the Battle of the Argonne. Archie also saw bitter combat in France, where German shrapnel shattered his kneecap and broke an arm.

The youngest of the Roosevelt boys was Quentin, who in many ways appears a blond miniature of his father. While his brothers were frail and serious, Quentin was more cherubic and by far the most personable and outgoing. Adventurous and carefree, he joined the air corps and trained to be a pilot. In July 1918, in a dogfight with a formation of German fighters, Quentin died when an enemy pilot shot his plane down behind German lines.[11]

In public, Roosevelt bravely controlled his emotions and put up a stern front. Inside, of course, he was in agony. Those close to him said that he seemed to age years when Quentin died, and he never again showed his boundless vitality.

In his sixty years, the seemingly inexhaustible Theodore Roosevelt packed several lifetimes into a mortal body that inevitably and finally wore down. Blind in one eye, still carrying the bullet in his chest from an attempted assassination six years before, ravaged with malaria from a South American expedition, and heartstruck with the memory of a dead son, Roosevelt lost his frantic race with mortality. On January 6, 1919, his heart gave out and he died in his sleep in the house he built on Sagamore Hill.

John Wanamaker was shaken when he learned that Roosevelt had died. "Not since Abraham Lincoln fell asleep has there been in this country such a sorrow as on Monday when the messages came from Theodore Roosevelt's silent home," Wanamaker recorded in his diary. "Like a flash of lightning, it touched the whole world. The immeasure-ableness of the loss to America and the world at this time is beyond human thought. It were well worthwhile to seek for the real secret of Theodore Roosevelt's masterful greatness. Was it in the fact that no in-sincerity lurked behind his ever-welcoming smile?"[12]

Throughout his life, Roosevelt either conquered his enemies or won them over with his irrepressible energy and engaging personality. Wanamaker, one of Roosevelt's more capable adversaries, became an-other of Roosevelt's converts, albeit after three decades of conflict. John Wanamaker outlived Theodore Roosevelt for two more years and died in Philadelphia at the age of eighty-four, leaving a fortune estimated at thirty-five million dollars.

Appendix

The Civil Service Act and Revised Statutes

An act to regulate and improve the civil service of the United States.

Be it enacted by the Senate and House of Representatives of the United States of America in Congress assembled, That the President is authorized to appoint, by and with the advice and consent of the Senate, three persons, not more than two of whom shall be adherents of the same party, as Civil Service Commissioners, and said three commissioners shall constitute the United States Civil Service Commission. Said commissioners shall hold no other official place under the United States.

That President may remove any commissioner; and any vacancy in the position of commissioner shall be so filled by the President, by and with the advice and consent of the Senate, as to conform to said conditions for the first selection of commissioners.

The commissioners shall each receive a salary of three thousand five hundred dollars a year. And each of said commissioners shall be paid his necessary traveling expenses incurred in the discharge of his duty as a commissioner.

Sec. 2. That it shall be the duty of said commissioners:

First. To aid the President, as he may request, in preparing suitable rules for carrying this act into effect, and when said rules shall have been promulgated it shall be the duty of all officers of the United States in the departments and offices to which any such rules may relate to aid, in all proper ways, in carrying said rules, and any modifications thereof, into effect.

Second. And, among other things, said rules shall provide and declare, as nearly as the conditions of good administration will warrant, as follows:

First, for open, competitive examinations for testing the fitness of applicants for the public service now classified or to be classified hereunder. Such examinations shall be practical in their character, and so far as may be shall relate to those matters which will fairly test the relative capacity and fitness of the persons examined to discharge the duties of the service into which they seek to be appointed.

Second, that all the offices, places, and employments so arranged or to be arranged in classes shall be filled by selections according to grade from among those graded highest as the results of such competitive examinations.

Third, appointments to the public service aforesaid in the departments at Washington shall be apportioned among the several States and Territories and the District of Columbia upon the basis of population as ascertained at the last preceding census. Every application for an examination shall contain, among other things, a statement, under oath, setting forth his or her actual bona fide residence at the time of making the application, as well as how long he or she had been a resident of such place.

Fourth, that there shall be a period of probation before any absolute appointment or employment aforesaid.

Fifth, that no person in the public service is for that reason under any obligations to contribute to any political fund, or to render any political service, and that he will not be removed or otherwise prejudiced for refusing to do so.

Sixth, that no person in said service has any right to use his official authority or influence to coerce the political action of any person or body.

Seventh, there shall be non-competitive examinations in all proper cases before the commission, when competent persons do not compete, after notice has been given of the existence of the vacancy, under such rules as may be prescribed by the commissioners as to the manner of giving notice.

Eighth, that the notice shall be given in writing by the appointing power to said commission of the persons selected for appointment of employment from among those who have been examined, of the place of residence of such persons, of the rejection of any such persons after probation, of transfers, resignations, and removals, and of the date thereof, and a record of the same shall be kept by said commission. And any necessary exceptions from said eight fundamental provisions of the rules shall be set forth in connection with such rules, and the reasons therefor shall be stated in the annual reports of the commission.

Third. Said commission shall, subject to the rules that may be made by the President, make regulations for, and have control of, such examinations, and, through its members of the examiners, it shall supervise and preserve the records of the same; and said commission shall keep minutes of its own proceedings.

Fourth. Said commission may make investigations concerning the facts and may report upon all matters touching the enforcement and effects of said rules and regulations, and concerning the action of any examiner or board of examiners hereinafter provided for, and its own subordinates, and those in public service, in respect to the execution of this act.

Fifth. Said commission shall make an annual report to the President for transmission to Congress, showing its own action, the rules and regulations and the exceptions thereto in force, the practical effects thereof, and any suggestions it may approve for the more effectual accomplishment of the purposes of this act.

Sec. 3. That said commission is authorized to employ a chief examiner, a part of whose duty it shall be, under its direction, to an act with examining boards, so far as practicable, whether at Washington or elsewhere, and to secure accuracy, uniformity, and justice in all their proceedings, which shall be at all times open to him. The chief examiner shall be entitled to receive a salary at a rate of three thousand dollars a year, and he shall be paid his necessary traveling expenses incurred in the discharge of his duty. The commission shall have a secretary, to be appointed by the President, who shall receive a salary of one thousand six hundred dollars per annum. It may, when necessary, employ a stenographer and a messenger, who shall be paid, when employed, the former at the rate of one thousand six hundred dollars a year, and the latter at the rate of six hundred dollars a year. The commission shall, at Washington, and in one or more places in each State and Territory where examinations are to take place, designate and select a suitable number of persons, not less than three, in the official service of the United States, residing in said State or Territory, after consulting the head of the department or office in which such persons serve, to be members of boards of examiners, and may at any time substitute any other person in said service living in such State or Territory in the place of any one so selected. Such boards of examiners shall be so located as to make it reasonably convenient and inexpensive for applicants to attend before them; and where there are persons to be examined in any State or Territory, examinations shall be held therein at least twice in each year. It shall be the duty of the collector, postmaster, and other officers of the United States, at any place outside the District of Columbia where examinations are directed by the President or by said board to be held, to allow the reasonable use of the public buildings for holding such examinations, and in all proper ways to facilitate the same.

Sec. 4. That it shall be the duty of the Secretary of the Interior to cause suitable and convenient rooms and accommodations to be assigned or provided, and to be furnished, heated, and lighted, at the city of Washington, for carrying on the work of said commission and said examinations, and to cause necessary stationery and other articles to be supplied, and the necessary printing to be done for said commission.

Sec. 5. That any said commissioner, examiner, copyist, or messenger, or any person in the public service, who shall willfully and corruptly, by himself or in cooperation with one or more other persons, defeat, deceive, or obstruct any person in respect of his or her right to examination according to any such rules or regulations, or who shall willfully, corruptly, and falsely mark, grade, estimate, or report upon the examination or proper standing of any person examined hereunder, or aid in so doing, or who shall willfully and corruptly make false

representations concerning the same or concerning the person examined, or who shall willfully and corruptly furnish to any person
any special or secret information for the purpose of either improving or injuring the prospects or chances of any person so examined,
being appointed, employed, or promoted, shall for each such offense
be deemed guilty of misdemeanor, and upon conviction thereof,
shall be punished by a fine of not less than one hundred dollars,
nor more than one thousand dollars, or by imprisonment not less
than ten days, nor more than one year, or by both such fine and
imprisonment.

Sec. 6. That within sixty days after the passage of this act it shall be
the duty of the Secretary of the Treasury, in as near conformity as
may be to the classification of certain clerks now existing under the
one hundred and sixty-third section of the Revised Statutes, to arrange in classes the several clerks and persons employed by the collector, naval officer, surveyor, and appraisers, or either of them, or being
in the public service, at their respective offices in each customs district where the whole number of said clerks and persons shall be
all together as many as fifty. And thereafter, from time to time, on
the direction of the President, said Secretary shall make the like
classification or arrangement of clerks and persons so employed, in
connection with any said office or offices, in any other customs district. And, upon like request, and for the purposes of this act, said
Secretary shall arrange in one or more of said classes, or of existing
classes, any other clerks, agents, or persons employed under his department in any said district not now classified; and every such arrangement and classification upon being made shall be reported to
the President.

Second. Within said sixty days it shall be the duty of the Postmaster-
General, in general conformity to said one hundred and sixty-third
section, to separately arrange in classes the several clerks and persons
employed, or in the public service, at each post-office, or under any
postmaster of the United States, where the whole number of said
clerks and persons shall together amount to as many as fifty. And
thereafter, from time to time, on the direction of the President, it
shall be the duty of the Postmaster-General to arrange in like classes
the clerks and persons so employed in the postal service in connection with any other post-office; and every such arrangement and
classification upon being made shall be reported to the President.

Third. That from time to time said Secretary, the Postmaster-General, and each of the heads of departments mentioned in the one hundred and fifty-eighth section of the Revised Statutes, and each head of an office, shall, on the direction of the President, and for facilitating the execution of this act, respectively revise any then existing classification or arrangement of those in their respective departments and offices, and shall, for the purposes of the examination herein provided for, include in one or more of such classes, so far as practicable, subordinate places, clerks, and officers in the public service pertaining to their respective departments not before classified for examination.

Sec. 7. That after the expiration of six months from the passage of this act no officer or clerk shall be appointed, and no person shall be employed to enter or be promoted in either of the said classes now existing, or that may be arranged hereunder pursuant to said rules, until he has passed an examination, or is shown to be specially exempted from such examination in conformity herewith. But nothing herein contained shall be construed to take from those honorably discharged from the military or naval service any preference conferred by the seventeen hundred and fifty-fourth section of the Revised Statutes, nor to take from the President any authority not inconsistent with this act conferred by the seventeen hundred and fifty-third section of said statutes; nor shall any officer not in the executive branch of the government, or any person merely employed as a laborer or workman, be required to be classified hereunder; nor, unless by direction of the Senate, shall any person who has been nominated for confirmation by the Senate be required to be classified or to pass an examination.

Sec. 8. That no person habitually using intoxicating beverages to excess shall be appointed to, or retained in, any office, appointment, or employment to which the provisions of this act are applicable.

Sec. 9. That whenever there are already two or more members of a family in the public service in the grades covered by this act, no other member of such family shall be eligible to appointment to grades.

Sec. 10. That no recommendation of any person who shall apply for office or place under the provisions of this act which may be given by any Senator or member of the House of Representatives, except as to the character or residence of the applicant, shall be received or considered by any person concerned in making any examination or appointment under this act.

Sec. 11. That no Senator, or Representative, or Territorial Delegate of the Congress, or Senator, Representative, or Delegate elect, or any officer or employee of either of said houses, and no executive, judicial, military, or naval officer of the United States, and no clerk or employee of any department, branch or bureau of the executive, judicial, or military or naval service of the United States, shall, directly or indirectly, solicit or receive, or be in any manner concerned in soliciting or receiving, any assessment, subscription, or contribution for any political purpose whatever, from any officer, clerk, or employee of the United States, or any department, branch, or bureau thereof, or from any person receiving any salary or compensation from moneys derived from the Treasury of the United States.

Sec. 12. That no person shall, in any room or building occupied under the discharge of official duties by any officer or employee of the United States mentioned in this act, or any navy-yard, fort, or arsenal, solicit in any manner whatever, or receive any contribution of money or any other thing of value for any political purpose whatever.

Sec. 13. No officer or employee of the United States mentioned in this act shall discharge, promote, or degrade, or in any matter change the official rank or compensation of any other officer or employee, or promise or threaten so to do, for giving or withholding or neglecting to make any contribution of money or other valuable thing for any political purpose.

Sec. 14. That no officer, clerk, or other person in the service of the United States shall, directly or indirectly, give or hand over to any other officer, clerk, or person in the service of the United States, or to any Senator or Member of the House of Representatives, or Territorial Delegate, any money or other valuable thing on account of or to be applied to the promotion of any political object whatever.

Sec. 15. That any person who shall be guilty of violating any provision of the four foregoing sections shall be deemed guilty of a misdemeanor, and shall, on conviction thereof, be punished by a fine not exceeding five thousand dollars, or by imprisonment for a term not exceeding three years, or by such fine and imprisonment both, in the discretion of the court.

Approved, January sixteenth, 1883.
Source: *U.S. Statutes at Large* 22 (1883): 403.

United States Civil Service Commissioners

Dorman B. Eaton	New York	Mar. 9, 1883	Resigned Apr. 17, 1886
John M. Gregory	Illinois	Mar. 9, 1883	Resigned Nov. 9, 1885
Leroy D. Thoman	Ohio	Mar. 9, 1883	Resigned Nov. 9, 1885
William Trenholm	South Carolina	Nov. 9, 1885	Resigned Apr. 17, 1886
Alfred Edgerton	Indiana	Nov. 9, 1885	Removed Feb. 9, 1889
John H. Oberly	Illinois	Apr. 17, 1886	Resigned Oct. 10, 1888
Charles Lyman	Connecticut	Apr. 17, 1886	Resigned Mar. 24, 1895
Hugh Thompson	South Carolina	May 9, 1889	Resigned June 23, 1892
Theodore Roosevelt	New York	May 13, 1889	Resigned May 5, 1895
George D. Johnston	Louisiana	July 14, 1892	Removed Nov. 28,1893
John R. Proctor	Kentucky	Dec. 2, 1893	Died Dec. 2, 1903
William G. Rice	New York	May 16, 1895	Resigned Jan. 19, 1898
John B. Harlow	Missouri	May 25, 1895	Resigned Nov. 14, 1901
Mark S. Brewer	Michigan	Jan. 19, 1898	Died Mar. 18, 1901
William Rodenberg	Illinois	Mar. 25, 1901	Resigned Mar. 31, 1902
William D. Foulke	Indiana	Nov. 15, 1901	Resigned Apr. 30, 1903
James R. Garfield	Ohio	Apr. 24, 1902	Resigned Feb. 25, 1903
Alford W. Cooley	New York	June 18, 1903	Resigned Nov. 6, 1906

Continued on the next page

Henry F. Greene	Minnesota	June 20, 1903	Resigned Apr. 30, 1909
John C. Black	Illinois	Jan. 16, 1904	Resigned June 10, 1913
John A. McIlhenny	Louisiana	Nov. 30, 1906	Resigned Feb. 28, 1919

Source: U.S. Civil Service Commission Annual Reports.

Growth of the Merit Service
(Compiled from U.S. Civil Service Commission Annual Reports)

President Chester Arthur
January 16, 1883, to March 3, 1885

	DATE	POSITIONS	TOTAL
First classification	Jan. 16, 1883	Customs, Post Office	13,924
Extension	Sept. 1883– Feb. 1885	Departmental	1,449
Growth of service		Post Office	200
Total classified	As of Mar. 3, 1885		15,573

President Grover Cleveland
March 4, 1885, to March 3, 1889

	DATE	POSITIONS	TOTAL
Executive order	Mar. 1, 1888	Civil Service Commission	8
Revision of statute	June 29, 1888	Departmental	1,931
Executive order	Dec. 5, 1888	Railway Mail Service	5,320
Growth of service		Post Office	800
Miscellaneous growth		Departmental	3,698
Total increases			11,757
Total classified	As of Mar. 3, 1889		27,330

President Benjamin Harrison
March 4, 1889, to March 3, 1893

	DATE	POSITIONS	TOTAL
Executive order	Apr. 13, 1891	Indian Service	626
Executive order	May 5, 1892	Fish Commission	140
Executive order	Jan. 5, 1893	Weather Bureau	314
Executive order	Jan. 5, 1893	Free Delivery Post Offices	7,610
Growth of service		Post Office	500
Miscellaneous growth		Departmental	1,345
Total increases			10,535
Total classified	As of Mar. 3, 1893		37,865

President Grover Cleveland
March 4, 1893, to March 3, 1897

	DATE	POSITIONS	TOTAL
Executive order	May 11, 1894	Indian Service	89
Executive orders	May 1894– May 1895	Department of Agriculture	787
Executive order	July 25, 1894	Department of Interior	2
Executive order	Nov. 2, 1894	Messengers and Watchmen	868
Executive order	Nov. 2, 1894	Customs Service	1,527
Executive orders	Nov.–Dec. 1895	Post Office	43
Executive order	Dec. 12, 1894	Internal Revenue Service	2,939
Executive order	Mar. 4, 1895	Census Bureau	90

Executive order	June 13, 1895	Government Printing Office	2,709
Executive order	June 15, 1895	Departmental Firemen	94
Executive order	June 15, 1895	Pension Agencies	505
Executive order	Mar. 20, 1896	Indian Agency	743
Revision of rules	May 6, 1896	All branches of service	27,045
Growth of service		Customs and Post Office	119
Miscellaneous growth		Departmental	6,549
Executive order	Nov. 2, 1896	Laborers in navy yards	5,063
Total increases			49,172
Total classified	As of Mar. 3, 1897		87,044

President William McKinley
March 4, 1897, to September 13, 1901

	DATE	POSITIONS	TOTAL
Executive orders	July 1897– June 1900	Customs, Coast Survey	302
Executive orders	Jan. 1899– May 1900	Naval personnel	192
Executive order	May 29, 1899	Temporaries made permanent	1,221
Growth of service		War, Treasury, Puerto Rico	258
Growth of service		Post Office and Free Delivery	1,673
Miscellaneous growth			15,900
Withdrawals	1897–1901	Departmental	−385
Withdrawals	Nov. 1, 1901	War Department Field Service	−1,888

Total increases			17,273
Total classified	As of Sept. 13, 1901		104,317

President Theodore Roosevelt
September 14, 1901, to June 30, 1903

(After June 1903, the Civil Service Commission began to estimate the growth of the classified service)

	DATE	POSITIONS	TOTAL
Executive order	Nov. 27, 1901	Rural Free Delivery Service	6,351
Executive order	Feb. 1, 1902	Insular and naval	34
Revision of rules	Feb. 11, 1903	Departmental	118
Act of Congress	Apr. 15, 1903	Census Bureau	837
Act of Congress	Mar. 6, 1902	Emergency war employees	850
Growth of service	Apr. 28, 1902	Free Delivery Post Offices	538
Growth of service	Estimated	Departmental	22,409
Total increases			31,137
Total classified	As of June 30, 1903		135,454

Examinations and Appointments for Classified Civil Service
Clerk Positions, Washington, D.C., 1883–1894

Year	Number Passing Examination	Number Appointed	Percentage of Those Passing Appointed
1884	459	53	12
1885	1,338	438	33
1886	826	234	28
1887	2,598	547	21
1888	1,551	352	23
1889	1,630	338	21
1890	1,521	416	27
1891	2,634	986	3
1892	1,997	356	18
1893	1,212	296	24
1894	1,388	73	20

Year	Percentage Women Passed	Percentage Men Passed	Number Passed	Percentage Women Appointed	Percentage Men Appointed	Number Appointed
1884	28	72	1,338	11	89	438
1885	28	72	826	13	87	234
1886	33	67	2,598	17	83	547
1887	40	60	1,551	14	86	352
1888	42	58	1,630	22	78	338
1889	42	58	1,521	13	87	416
1890	41	59	2,634	16	84	986
1891	43	57	1,997	25	75	356
1892	38	62	1,212	24	76	296
1893	31	69	1,388	7	93	273

Sources: U.S. Civil Service Commission Annual Reports, 1884–94.

Notes on Sources

ANY RESEARCHER who dares to probe the fascinating life of Theodore Roosevelt faces both the blessing and curse of a man who has spawned a wealth of material not only from a score of historians and biographers but from Theodore's own prolific pen. Exhaustively researched works, both on Roosevelt's entire lifetime and on important episodes of his life, provide an incisive and often controversial biographia that is surpassed in volume by writings on only a few other public personages. The vast Roosevelt lore notwithstanding, several sources stand out as critical to any research. In his life, Roosevelt wrote more than 150,000 letters, of which about 10 percent are published. *The Letters of Theodore Roosevelt,* an eight-volume set edited by Elting Morison, offers the most priceless glimpse into Roosevelt's correspondence and provides the backbone of Rooseveltian research. Henry Cabot Lodge and Roosevelt's sister Anna Roosevelt Cowles each published other volumes of his letters, and Lawrence Oliver edited the letters between Roosevelt and Brander Matthews. Unfortunately, Roosevelt's second wife, Edith, destroyed much of their personal correspondence after his death in 1919.

The Theodore Roosevelt Collection at Harvard remains the dominant research source. The collection houses a vast store of Roosevelt's personal and professional letters, records, pictures, scrapbooks, and assorted correspondence. Far from static, the collection continues to expand as additional Roosevelt material is bequeathed to Harvard by heirs and collectors. The Theodore Roosevelt Historical Site at Sagamore

Hill contains many of the housekeeping records maintained by Edith Roosevelt.

Record Group 146 of the National Archives, College Park, Maryland, contains the files of the U.S. Civil Service Commission. Important holdings include the commission's *Annual Reports* and official minutes, which provide valuable insight into the day-to-day workings of the commission and the numerous decisions being made. The Library of Congress houses many rare and obscure works, including those involving the civil service reform movement and the presidential papers of Grover Cleveland, Benjamin Harrison, William McKinley, and Roosevelt, as well as the newspaper archives of the *Washington Post, Washington Star,* and other journals. The Washingtoniana Room of the Washington, D.C., Public Library contains a variety of rare books, maps, pictures, and archives of the nation's capital during the 1890s. The files of the National Civil Service Reform League, housed at the University of Wyoming, provided valuable information on the league's activities.

Numerous secondary works are essential in understanding Theodore Roosevelt. Cindy Aron's doctoral study of civil service workers during the Victorian era provides a fascinating view into the lives of middle-class clerks working in Washington. Hermann Hagedorn's early research into Roosevelt's personal life remains fundamental in viewing Theodore as a living, breathing man of boundless energy and ambition. Edmund Morris's first volume, *The Rise of Theodore Roosevelt,* is outstanding in scholarship and masterfully written. William Harbaugh's biography of Roosevelt remains the best single volume, and more recent biographies by Nathan Miller and H. W. Brands provide valuable new material and glimpses that contribute to the overall Roosevelt biographia. Especially noteworthy is Kathleen Dalton's *Theodore Roosevelt: A Strenuous Life,* the first biography in several decades to present substantial new research. It provides a much deeper and warmer understanding of the relationship of Theodore and Edith Roosevelt. Betty Caroli's biography of the Roosevelt women and Sylvia Morris's work on Edith provide important insights of their family life. David McCullough's *Mornings on Horseback* is a poignant saga of Roosevelt's early years, capturing the heart and life of Theodore's family. To understand the complicated civil service reform movement of the mid– and late nineteenth century, the collective works of Paul Van Riper, Ari Hoogenboom, and A. Bower Sageser are essential.

Finally, the scholar and researcher to whom I turned to the most was, of course, Theodore Roosevelt himself. His phenomenal outpouring of correspondence provides a fascinating glimpse into his mind and spirit, and the dozens of volumes of his formal publications offer a huge challenge to even the most dogged researcher. The challenge is worth the effort, however, for in most cases any Rooseveltian researcher falls prey to Theodore's charm and cunning much like his friends, colleagues, and adversaries who knew him personally. Generations after his death, Roosevelt continues to beguile scholars with his complex, controversial personality and, if nothing else, wins over or at least wears out his biographers with his relentless energy and overpowering written legacy.

Notes

ABBREVIATIONS

AHC   American Heritage Center, University of Wyoming, Laramie
ARC   Anna Roosevelt Cowles
BHP   Benjamin Harrison Papers, Library of Congress, Washington, D.C.
EKR   Edith Kermit Roosevelt
GCP   Grover Cleveland Papers, Library of Congress, Washington, D.C.
HCL   Henry Cabot Lodge
TR   Theodore Roosevelt
TRC   Theodore Roosevelt Collection, Harvard University
TRP   Theodore Roosevelt Papers, Library of Congress, Washington, D.C.

INTRODUCTION

1. TR to John Strachey, Mar. 8, 1901, TRC; Roosevelt, *Letters,* ed. Elting E. Morison, 3:1942.
2. Adams, *Letters* (1930), 2:417.
3. Sageser, *First Two Decades,* 234.
4. Hoogenboom, *Outlawing the Spoils,* vii.
5. Adams, *Letters* (1930), 2:295.
6. Low, "Washington," 771.
7. Roosevelt, *Works,* 20:163.
8. Teplin, "Theodore Roosevelt," 5.
9. Roosevelt, *An Autobiography,* 14.
10. Hagedorn, *Boy's Life of Theodore Roosevelt,* 3.

CHAPTER 1

1. *Washington Star,* May 13, 1889.
2. Latimer, *Your Washington and Mine,* 224.

3. Adams, *Letters* (1930), 2:253.

4. Logan, *Thirty Years in Washington,* 463.

5. In 1883 Congress attempted to standardize the workday for all agencies and specified that departments open at nine and close at four, six days a week, with clerks lunching from noon to 12:30. Most agencies, however, ignored the legislation and continued to operate under their own more flexible and liberal work standards (Aron, *Ladies and Gentlemen of the Civil Service,* 94).

6. Logan, *Thirty Years in Washington,* 526. In this thick volume, Mrs. John A. Logan, wife of a Union general and stalwart Republican senator from Illinois, describes Washington during the Gilded Age. She devotes chapter after chapter to describing the inner workings of government bureaus.

7. James, *American Scene,* 339.

8. Adams, *Education,* 253.

9. Reps, *Monumental Washington,* 66.

10. *Washington Star,* Mar. 5, 1889.

11. Green, *Washington, Capitol City,* 4; Latimer, *Your Washington and Mine,* 315.

12. Jeffers, *An Honest President,* 2.

13. Halloran, "Theodore Roosevelt," 60; *Washington Evening Star,* May 13, 1889.

14. John Ireland (1838–1918). Roman Catholic archbishop of the diocese of St. Paul. Emigrated from Ireland, educated in France, served as chaplain to the Fifth Minnesota Regiment during the Civil War, rector of the Cathedral of St. Paul. Strong supporter of temperance among Catholics and initiator of colonization campaign to bring northern European Catholic immigrants to Minnesota. Promoter of "Americanism," the rapid acculturation of the European immigrant church in America.

15. Halloran, *Romance of the Merit System,* 56; Busch, *T.R.,* 88. This often-quoted remark is attributed to Matthew Halloran, the Civil Service Commission's executive secretary and an employee there for forty-five years. Halloran began service at the commission as its first messenger in 1883.

16. Josephson, *Politicos,* 422.

17. Roosevelt, *Letters,* 1:69.

18. Ibid., 142.

19. Malin, "Roosevelt and the Elections of 1884 and 1888," 37; E. Morris, *Rise of Theodore Roosevelt,* 390.

20. Nov. 18, 1888, Roosevelt, *Letters,* 1:149.

21. *Washington Star,* May 5, 1889; Green, *Washington, Capitol City,* 82.

22. On Dec. 2, 1889, Roosevelt and Lodge threw their support for Speaker of the House behind Reed, who was elected to the post on that day.

23. James G. Blaine (1830–93). American politician, born in West Brownsville, Pennsylvania, graduated from Washington College in 1847. In 1854 moved to Maine and edited the *Portland Advertiser* and *Kennebec Journal.* Elected to Congress in 1863 and Speaker in 1868. Unsuccessful candidate for presidential nomination in 1876 and 1880. Appointed secretary of state by Garfield but refused to serve under Arthur after Garfield was assassinated. Won Republican Party presidential nomination in 1884. Campaign not helped by notorious cartoon in the magazine *The Judge* which depicted Blaine's body tattooed with

charges of corruption from his checkered political past. Narrowly defeated by Cleveland. In 1888 appointed secretary of state by Harrison.

24. Garraty, *Henry Cabot Lodge,* 104; Volwiler, *Correspondence between Harrison and Blaine,* 1940; Muzzey, *James G. Blaine.* Although Harrison did not approve Walker Blaine as assistant secretary, he served as his father's private secretary and in many ways de facto secretary of state until his untimely death in January 1890.

25. Hagedorn, *Boy's Life of Theodore Roosevelt,* 23.

26. Pringle, *A Biography,* 166.

27. Williams, "Theodore Roosevelt," 9.

28. Bishop, *Theodore Roosevelt and His Time,* 1:44.

29. Roosevelt, *Works,* 20:77.

30. Harrison, *Speeches,* 200.

31. Sageser, *First Two Decades,* 127.

32. TR to Harrison, Jan. 13, 1889, BHP.

33. Stewart, *National Civil Service Reform League,* 53; Hoogenboom, *Outlawing the Spoils,* 262.

34. TR to Harrison, Jan. 1, 13, Mar. 28, 1889, BHP.

35. Mar. 30, 1889, Roosevelt, *Letters,* 1:156.

36. Halford, "Roosevelt's Introduction," 293.

37. Harrison, *Views of an Ex-President,* 507; Harrison quoted from a speech given at Carnegie Hall, New York, Apr. 19, 1900.

38. Socolofsky and Spetter, *Presidency of Benjamin Harrison,* 40–41; Busch, *T.R.,* 89.

39. Charles Bonaparte (1851–1921). U.S. cabinet official, lawyer, and political leader identified with reform causes. Appointed by President Roosevelt to investigate conditions in the Indian Territory. Secretary of the navy, 1905; attorney general, 1906. Active in suits against the trusts. Largely responsible for breaking up the tobacco monopoly. Founder, president of the National Municipal League.

40. May 14, 1889, Roosevelt, *Letters,* 1:161.

41. Henry Cabot Lodge (1850–1924). Staunch Republican, served in the Massachusetts House in 1880 and 1881, U.S. House from 1887 to 1893, and U.S. Senate from 1893 until his death. After World War I, vigorously opposed Woodrow Wilson and fought membership in the League of Nations. Graduated from Harvard in 1871 and earned a doctorate there five years later after studying political science under Henry Adams. From 1876 to 1878, taught American history at Harvard. Editor of the *North American Review* 1873 to 1876 and author of *A Short History of the English Colonies in America* (1881) and *Alexander Hamilton* (1882).

42. Roosevelt, *Works,* 20:74.

43. O'Toole, *Five of Hearts,* 208.

44. Adams, *Letters* (1930), 2:420.

45. The civil service appointment was not the only position Lodge obtained for Roosevelt. On Apr. 19, 1897, Theodore became assistant secretary of the navy, an appointment due largely to the intervention of then-senator Lodge.

46. TR to HCL, May 5, 1884, Roosevelt, *Letters,* 1:68.

47. Foraker, *Notes of a Busy Life,* 1:168.

48. Lodge, *Correspondence,* 25.
49. Harbaugh, *Power and Responsibility,* 71.
50. McCullough, *Mornings on Horseback,* 312.
51. L. D. White, *Republican Era,* 300.
52. Oct. 30, 1889, Lodge, *Correspondence,* 97.
53. *Washington Post,* May 15, 1889.
54. Klein, "Gospel of Wanamaker," 28.
55. *Washington Post,* May 3, 1889.
56. *New York Times,* May 10, 1889; *Nation,* May 9, 1889, 375.
57. *Washington Star,* June 19, 1889.
58. Harvey, *Civil Service Commission,* 224.
59. "Theodore Roosevelt as Civil Service Commissioner," typescript, Collection A5.2, Box 1, National Civil Service Reform League Archives, AHC; Harvey, *Civil Service Commission,* 224.
60. Pringle, *A Biography,* 121.
61. Sept. 27, 1889, Roosevelt, *Letters,* 1:192.
62. Oct. 19, 1889, ibid., 199.
63. L. D. White, *Jacksonians,* 279.
64. Roosevelt, *Letters,* 1:161n. 1.
65. Hoogenboom, *Outlawing the Spoils,* 6.
66. Pearson, *Theodore Roosevelt,* 48.
67. Jefferson was the first president to yield to pressure from his party and resort to spoils politics. After his election in 1800 he replaced a number of Federal employees with his own Republicans. Ostensibly he dismissed some of the Federalists because they showed no zeal for carrying out his policies. See Morstein Marx, *Elements of Public Administration,* 18. Clay quote from Hoogenboom, *Outlawing the Spoils,* 8.
68. Wheeler, "Rise and Progress of the Merit System," 487.
69. *Civil Service Record,* July 1889, 116.
70. Humes, *Wit and Wisdom of Abraham Lincoln,* 31.
71. L. D. White, *Jacksonians,* 394.
72. Van Riper, *United States Civil Service,* 201.
73. In 1892 the U.S. Civil Service Commission reported that 164 men and 209 women had taken the examination for typewriting (*Ninth Annual Report,* 120).
74. Painter, *Standing at Armageddon,* xxxi.
75. Josephson, *Politicos,* 412.
76. Hoogenboom, "Thomas A. Jenckes," 644.
77. Hoogenboom, *Outlawing the Spoils,* vii.
78. T. C. Smith, *Life and Letters,* 1152.
79. "Civil Service Chronology" (1956), typescript, National Civil Service Reform League Archives, Box 224, AHC.
80. Sproat, *Best Men,* 259.
81. Thomas Allen Jenckes (1818–75). Born in Cumberland, Rhode Island. Republican. Member of Rhode Island state legislature; U.S. representative from Rhode Island First District, 1863–71. Graduated from Brown University, studied law; admitted to the bar in 1840 and commenced practice in Providence. Clerk

in the state legislature, 1840–44; member of the state house of representatives, 1854–57; unsuccessful candidate for reelection, 1870.

82. Hoogenboom, "Thomas A. Jenckes," 636.

83. Lyman Trumball (1813–96). Born in Colchester, Connecticut. Taught school in Connecticut, 1829–33; studied law; admitted to the bar and commenced practice in Greenville, Georgia. Moved to Belleville, Illinois, 1837. Member, state house of representatives 1840–41; secretary of state of Illinois in 1841 and 1843; justice of the supreme court of Illinois, 1848–53; elected to U.S. Congress in 1854, but before the beginning of the Congress elected to the U.S. Senate; reelected in 1861 and again in 1867, serving from Mar. 4, 1855, to Mar. 3, 1873. Was at various times a Democrat, then Republican, then Liberal Republican, then Democrat. Resumed law practice in Chicago. Unsuccessful candidate for governor of Illinois, 1880.

84. "That the President of the United States be, and he is hereby, authorized to prescribe such rules and regulations for the admission of persons into the civil service of the United States as will best promote the efficiency thereof, and ascertain the fitness of each candidate in respect to age, health, character, knowledge, and ability for the branch of service into which he seeks to enter; and for this purpose the President is authorized to employ suitable persons to conduct said inquiries, to prescribe their duties, and to establish regulations for the conduct of persons who may receive appointments in the civil service" (16 U.S.C. 514, 1871).

85. George William Curtis (1824–92). Essayist, moralist, orator, idealist, and foremost leader of reform. Born into a prosperous family in Providence, Rhode Island. Private education included tutelage under Emerson, Hawthorne, and Thoreau. Author, editor of *Harper's Weekly,* influential advocate of civil service reform, president of the National Civil Service Reform League.

86. L. D. White, *Republican Era,* 283.

87. Hansen, "Theodore Roosevelt and Civil Service Reform," 10.

88. L. D. White, *Republican Era;* Van Riper, *United States Civil Service.* For a more detailed history of the Grant commission see Murphy, "First Federal Civil Service Commission." The "rule of three," still in use by many governments, requires officials to select a new employee from the top three names on a competitive list of applicants.

89. Sproat, *Best Men,* 260.

90. Pendleton Act, *U.S. Statutes at Large* 22 (1883).

91. The other two commissioners were John M. Gregory of Illinois and Leroy D. Thoman of Ohio.

92. Van Riper, *United States Civil Service,* 98–100.

93. Hoogenboom, *Outlawing the Spoils,* 253.

94. Ingraham, *Foundation of Merit,* 32.

95. Roosevelt, *Administration,* 6.

96. 51st Cong., 1st sess., *Hearings before Subcommittee on the Legislative, Executive, and Judicial Appropriations Bill* (Washington, D.C.: Government Printing Office, 1890), 3.

97. L. D. White, *Republican Era,* 310.

98. Hoogenboom, "Pendleton Act," 306.

99. Wiebe, *Search for Order,* 61.

100. Van Riper, *United States Civil Service,* 203.

101. U.S. Senate, *Report on the Conditions of the General Land Office,* 47th Cong., 1st sess., 1884, S. Rpt. 362, p. 84; Aron, *Ladies and Gentlemen of the Civil Service,* 163, 225n. 6.

102. Emily Neyland to John Noble, Aug. 3, 1890, no. 1322, Appointments Files, Record Group 48, Interior Department, National Archives, College Park, Maryland; Aron, *Ladies and Gentlemen of the Civil Service,* 146, 151, 222n. 24.

103. Emily Neyland to John Noble, Aug. 3, 1890.

104. Several popular 1890s novels fictionalized the plight of women workers like Emily Neyland. In James Edwards's *The Court Circle: A Tale of Washington Life* (Washington, D.C., 1895), the central character is Bertha Raymond, a twenty-year-old woman who moves from New York to Washington to support an ailing mother after the family fortunes fail. She becomes a clerk in a federal bureau, suffers harassment by an autocratic boss named Mr. Clack, loses her job because she lacks patronage, and regains it through connections with a sympathetic congressman.

105. U.S. Civil Service Commission, *Seventh Annual Report,* 9–12.

106. *Washington Star,* June 5, 1889.

107. Foulke, *Fighting the Spoilsman,* 13.

108. Bishop, *Theodore Roosevelt and His Time,* 1:46; Foulke, *Roosevelt and the Spoilsmen,* 13.

109. Adams, *Letters* (1930), 2:256.

110. Crichton, *America 1900,* 150.

111. Bishop, *Theodore Roosevelt and His Time,* 1:47.

112. Busch, *T.R.,* 90; Sievers, *Hoosier President,* 77.

113. TR to HCL, June 24, 1889, Roosevelt, *Letters,* 1:166.

114. Sievers, *Hoosier President,* 79; Socolofsky and Spetter, *Presidency of Benjamin Harrison,* 41.

115. U.S. Civil Service Commission, *Eleventh Annual Report,* 270.

116. Socolofsky and Spetter, *Presidency of Benjamin Harrison,* 41.

117. Stewart, *National Civil Service Reform League,* 57.

118. June 29, 1889, Roosevelt, *Letters,* 1:167.

119. June 24, 1889, ibid., 166.

120. TR to Halford, July 24, 28, 30, 1889, BHP.

121. Aug. 1, 1889, Lodge, *Correspondence,* 87.

122. Sievers, *Hoosier President,* 86.

123. Lodge, *Correspondence,* 89; Aug. 8, 1889, Roosevelt, *Letters,* 1:185.

124. Teplin, "Theodore Roosevelt," 17.

125. Shaw, *A Cartoon History,* 23.

126. Herbert Welsh. Wealthy Philadelphia reformer, organizer of the Indian Rights Association, and publisher of *City and State,* a weekly newspaper devoted to good government. Helped the civil service reform movement by mobilizing various religious denominations. During the 1880s and 1890s, prompted numerous sermons supporting civil service reform.

127. July 1, 1889, Roosevelt, *Letters,* 1:169.

128. August 7, 1889, ibid., 185.

129. Muzzey, *James G. Blaine*, 469n. The "marble statue" description of Harrison was attributed to New York political boss Thomas Platt.

130. July 11, 1889, Roosevelt, *Letters*, 1:171.

131. Gibbons, *John Wanamaker*, 254.

132. Ibid., 259; Skowronek, *Building a New American State*, 75; Fowler, *Cabinet Politician*, 209.

133. Josephson, *Politicos*, 425.

134. Ibid., 440; Appel, *Business Biography of John Wanamaker*.

135. Fowler, *Cabinet Politician*, 210.

136. Josephson, *Politicos*, 407.

137. Gibbons, *John Wanamaker*, 260; Sievers, *Hoosier President*, 15.

138. Sievers, *Hoosier President*, 23.

139. Gibbons, *John Wanamaker*, 266.

140. Williams, "Theodore Roosevelt," 27; Gibbons, *John Wanamaker*, 266.

141. Fowler, *Cabinet Politician*, 212.

142. Gibbons, *John Wanamaker*, 299.

143. U.S. Civil Service Commission, *Ninth Annual Report*.

144. Hoogenboom, *Outlawing the Spoils*, 2.

145. Gibbons, *John Wanamaker*, 327.

146. Skowronek, *Building a New American State*, 69.

147. Hoogenboom, "Pendleton Act," 305.

148. *Nation*, May 22, 1890, 403; Fowler, *Cabinet Politician*, 214.

149. Foulke, *Fighting the Spoilsman*; Pringle, *A Biography*, 123; Fowler, *Cabinet Politician*, 214.

150. *Civil Service Chronicle*, Sept. 1889, 52.

151. Busch, *T.R.*, 90, 208; Foulke, *Fighting the Spoilsman*.

152. Fowler, *Cabinet Politician*, 214.

153. Foulke, *Fighting the Spoilsman*, 60.

154. *Harper's Weekly*, Dec. 20, 1890, 987; Fowler, *Cabinet Politician*, 215.

155. Williams, "Theodore Roosevelt," 28; Sievers, *Hoosier President*, 74.

156. Gibbons, *John Wanamaker*, 327.

157. August 23, 1890, Roosevelt, *Letters*, 1:230.

158. Hagedorn, *Roosevelt Family of Sagamore Hill*, 4–5.

159. Aug. 28, 1889, Roosevelt, *Letters*, 1:253.

160. Minutes of the U.S. Civil Service Commission, May 13, 1889, Record Group 146, National Archives, College Park, Maryland.

161. Edward Lawrence Godkin (1831–1902). Journalist, born in Ireland. Covered the Crimean War for the *London Daily News*. In 1856 immigrated to New York. During Civil War served as war correspondent for the *Daily News*. In 1865 founded the *Nation*, a weekly journal of political opinion that supported free trade, railed against political corruption, and advocated liberal reforms. In 1881 sold the financially ailing magazine to the *New York Evening Post* but stayed on as editor until 1899. In 1883 became editor-in-chief of the *Evening Post*, expanding both its readership and influence as an opinion-maker.

162. Hoogenboom, *Outlawing the Spoils*, 19; Muzzey, *James G. Blaine*, 269.

163. *Nation*, Mar. 22, 1866, 355.

164. Sproat, *Best Men*, 137.

165. Nov. 16, 1892, Roosevelt, *Letters,* 1:297.

166. *Washington Post,* Aug. 27, 1889.

167. *Civil Service Chronicle,* Sept. 1889, 52. Clipping in TRC.

168. *New York Sun* clipping in scrapbook, TRC.

169. John James Ingalls (1833–1900). U.S. lawyer and political leader, leader in Kansas free-state movement; senator from Kansas, 1873–91; eloquent speaker, Kansas secretary of state, rose to the rank of lieutenant colonel in the Civil War.

170. Sproat, *Best Men,* 67.

171. Josephson, *Politicos,* 443.

172. Roosevelt, *Works,* 14:89.

173. Arthur Pue Gorman (1839–1906). As a young man, served as secretary to Senator Stephen A. Douglas. Maryland legislator, 1869–79, elected to U.S. Senate, 1880. Gorman, who had become one of his party's leaders in the Senate, was defeated in 1898 but reelected in 1903 and served as minority leader until his death. Gorman's enmity for Roosevelt continued over the years. He opposed Roosevelt's treaty with Panama and was a leading Democratic candidate to run against Roosevelt in 1904.

174. J. R. Lambert, *Arthur Pue Gorman,* 85.

175. *Congressional Record,* 50th Cong., 2nd sess., 1889, 20, pt. 2, 1606–7.

176. Mar. 1, 1891, Roosevelt, *Letters,* 1:239–40.

177. *Civil Service Chronicle,* Sept. 1889, 49.

178. TR to Wister, Feb. 12, 1894, Wister, *Roosevelt,* 46.

179. Roosevelt's handwritten speech notes, TRC.

CHAPTER 2

1. *Washington Evening Star,* Dec. 31, 1889. Samuel Pierpont Langley (1834–1906). American scientist. Professor of physics at the University of Pittsburgh, 1866. In 1887 became secretary of the Smithsonian Institution and established the Astrophysical Observatory and the National Zoological Park. Constructed power-driven model aircraft that flew successfully.

2. John Philip Sousa (1854–1932). Enlisted in the marines as apprentice musician, 1867. In 1872 published his first composition, "Moonlight on the Potomac Waltzes." In 1875 left marines and began conducting theater orchestras. In 1880 assumed leadership of Marine Band. Conducted "The President's Own" under Presidents Hayes, Garfield, Cleveland, Arthur, and Harrison. After two tours with the Marine Band in 1891 and 1892, resigned and organized a civilian concert band that made nationwide and worldwide tours. In 1896 composed "The Stars and Stripes Forever," the last piece he conducted before his death.

3. S. J. Morris, *Edith Kermit Roosevelt,* 123.

4. *Washington Post,* Jan. 2, 1890.

5. *New York Times,* Jan. 2, 1890; *Washington Evening Star,* Jan. 1, 1890. In 1894, Great Britain and France acknowledged the growing importance of the United States in world affairs by upgrading their legations in Washington to the rank of embassy.

6. *Cleveland Leader,* Sept. 30, 1882; Green, *Washington, Capitol City,* 12.

7. S. J. Morris, *Edith Kermit Roosevelt,* 124.

8. Roosevelt, *An Autobiography,* from *Works,* 20:329; Jusserand, *What Me Befell,* 336; Pinchot, *Breaking New Ground,* 314.

9. Jan. 4, 1890, Roosevelt, *Letters,* 1:208.

10. Renehan, *Lion's Pride,* 42.

11. Harbaugh, *Power and Responsibility,* 69.

12. Lansford, *"Bully" First Lady,* xiv; Hagedorn, *Roosevelt Family of Sagamore Hill,* 30.

13. Caroli, *Roosevelt Women,* 206.

14. Hagedorn, *Roosevelt Family of Sagamore Hill,* 9.

15. Renehan, *Lion's Pride,* 42.

16. Roosevelt, *Diaries of Boyhood and Youth,* 103; June 3, 1877, Roosevelt, *Letters,* 1:28.

17. McCullough, *Mornings on Horseback,* 164.

18. Roosevelt, *An Autobiography,* from *Works,* 20:328.

19. Nov. 10, 1878, Roosevelt, *Letters,* 1:36; McCullough, *Mornings on Horseback,* 190.

20. Lorant, *Life and Times of Theodore Roosevelt,* 240.

21. Lansford, *"Bully" First Lady,* 21.

22. Caroli, *Roosevelt Women,* 83.

23. Lansford, *"Bully" First Lady,* 24; E. Morris, *Rise of Theodore Roosevelt,* 368. Robert Browning (1812–89). Great English Victorian poet, noted for his mastery of dramatic monologue. Received scant formal education but had access to his father's large library. Influenced by Shelley, who inspired him to adopt atheistic principles for a time. In 1846 married the poet Elizabeth Barrett (1806–61) and settled with her in Florence. In 1869 wrote his greatest work, *The Ring and the Book,* based on the proceedings in a murder trial in Rome in 1698. It consisted of ten verse narratives, all dealing with the same crime, each from a distinct viewpoint. Died in Venice, and his body was returned to England for interment in Westminster Abbey.

24. Renehan, *Lion's Pride,* 10.

25. Roosevelt, *An Autobiography,* from *Works,* 20:322. Roosevelt originally named his new Oyster Bay home Leeholm after his first wife, Alice Lee, but after her death he renamed it Sagamore Hill in honor of the Indian chief Sagamore Mohannis, who originally signed over the area to white settlers.

26. TR to ARC, Sept. 13, 1887, Roosevelt, *Letters,* 1:132.

27. Sageser, *First Two Decades,* 72.

28. E. Morris, *Rise of Theodore Roosevelt,* 406.

29. Fowler, *Cabinet Politician,* 181.

30. *Washington Post,* July 29, 1889; *Baltimore Sun,* undated clipping in file CR-1, TRC.

31. TR to Lucius Swift, Feb. 26, 1894, Roosevelt, *Letters,* 1:365. Hamilton G. Ewart (1849–1918). Born in Columbia, South Carolina. Republican. Member of North Carolina state house of representatives, 1887–89, 1895–97, 1911–13; U.S. representative from North Carolina Ninth District, 1889–91; circuit judge, 1897; judge of U.S. District Court for the Western District of North Carolina, 1898–99, 1899–1900.

32. *Washington Evening Star,* Feb. 20, 1890.

33. *Washington Post,* Apr. 3, 1891. Herman Lehlbach (1845–1904). Born in Germany. Republican. Member of New Jersey state legislature, 1884; U.S. representative from New Jersey Sixth District, 1885–91.

34. Ibid., Feb. 20, Mar. 5, 1890.

35. Ibid., Mar. 1, 1890.

36. E. Morris, *Rise of Theodore Roosevelt,* 422; *Washington Evening Star,* May 3, 1890.

37. 51st Cong., 1st sess., 1890, *Report of the House Committee on Civil Service Reform,* Serial 2823, Document 2445.

38. James, *American Scene,* 353.

39. Jan. 13, 1890, Roosevelt, *Letters,* 1:211.

40. Blum, "Theodore Roosevelt," 1485.

41. L. D. White, *Republican Era,* 304.

42. *Civil Service Record,* Feb. 1884, 32.

43. Sageser, *First Two Decades,* 194.

44. Aron, *Ladies and Gentlemen of the Civil Service,* 3.

45. House Subcommittee on the Legislative, Executive, and Judicial Appropriation Bill, testimony by Roosevelt, Mar. 30, 1890, *Congressional Record.*

46. TR and George Johnston to Cleveland, June 24, 1893, GCP.

47. Blum, *Republican Roosevelt,* 18.

48. TR to American Institute of Architects, May 1891, TRC.

49. Roosevelt, *Letters,* 1:209.

50. Roosevelt, *An Autobiography,* 135.

51. Albert Bierstadt (1830–1902). Emigrated from Germany to Bedford, Massachusetts, when he was three. Became internationally renowned for his beautiful and enormous paintings of the American West. His works found their way into public and private collections at staggeringly high prices. His popularity and wealth rose to tremendous heights, only to fade as the interest in impressionism turned public taste away from his highly detailed landscapes suffused with golden light. By 1895 declared himself bankrupt.

52. McCullough, *Mornings on Horseback,* 180.

53. Roosevelt, *An Autobiography,* 7.

54. Quote attributed to George William Curtis, from Burton, *Learned Presidency,* 41; McCullough, *Mornings on Horseback,* 151.

55. Hagedorn, *Boy's Life of Theodore Roosevelt,* 9.

56. Roosevelt, *An Autobiography,* 9.

57. McCullough, *Mornings on Horseback.*

58. Renehan, *Lion's Pride,* 17.

59. Dalton, *Theodore Roosevelt,* 26.

60. Renehan, *Lion's Pride,* 23; the German immigrant supposedly died in battle. Dalton writes that Thee paid $300 each for two substitutes (*Theodore Roosevelt,* 26).

61. N. Roosevelt, *A Front Row Seat,* 17; Jeffers, *Theodore Roosevelt, Jr.,* 10; Dalton, *Theodore Roosevelt,* 27.

62. Martha "Mittie" Bulloch Roosevelt (1835–84). Ancestors emigrated from Scotland in 1729. Great-granddaughter of Archibald Bulloch, who served as gov-

ernor of Georgia during the Revolution. As an Atlanta journalist, Margaret Mitchell researched Martha Bulloch's younger life on the plantation at Bulloch Hall, and evidence suggests that many of Mittie's looks and mannerisms may have contributed to the character of Scarlett O'Hara in Mitchell's epic *Gone With the Wind.*

63. Norton, *Theodore Roosevelt,* 15.

64. Renehan, *Lion's Pride,* 14.

65. Ibid., 18.

66. Nelson, "A Short, Ironic History," 762.

67. Sageser, *First Two Decades,* 32.

68. Roosevelt, *Letters,* 1:29, 30.

69. Ibid., 30.

70. McCullough, *Mornings on Horseback,* 180.

71. Robinson, *My Brother,* 105.

72. Roosevelt, *Diaries of Boyhood and Youth,* 364.

73. TR to Henry Davis Minot, Feb. 20, 1878, Roosevelt, *Letters,* 1:31.

74. McCullough, *Mornings on Horseback,* 187.

75. Josephson, *Politicos,* 249; Teplin, "Theodore Roosevelt," 165.

76. John Steinbeck, *Travels with Charley* (New York: Penguin, 1961), 118.

77. Roosevelt, *An Autobiography,* 96–97.

78. Hagedorn, *Boy's Life of Theodore Roosevelt,* 83.

79. Roosevelt, *An Autobiography,* 96.

80. George Cabot Lodge (1873–1909), nicknamed Bay, who in a few years would become one of the more admired American poets of the era.

81. South and North Dakota gained statehood the previous fall.

82. S. J. Morris, *Edith Kermit Roosevelt,* 127.

83. Roosevelt, *An Autobiography;* McCullough, *Mornings on Horseback;* Caroli, *Roosevelt Women,* 90.

84. TR to Charles Collins, Jan. 21, 1891, Hagan, "Civil Service Commissioner," 191.

85. TR to Joseph Gilbert Thorp, Feb. 9, 1891, Roosevelt, *Letters,* 1:238; E. Morris, *Rise of Theodore Roosevelt,* 432.

86. Hagedorn, *Roosevelt in the Bad Lands,* 235.

87. Hagan, "Civil Service Commissioner," 188.

88. U.S. Civil Service Commission, *Eighth Annual Report;* Socolofsky and Spetter, *Presidency of Benjamin Harrison,* 41.

CHAPTER 3

1. B Street is now Constitution Avenue. The Baltimore and Potomac station was destroyed after the completion of Union Station in 1907.

2. In his murder trial, Guiteau was one of the first to argue a defense of insanity. Unsuccessful, he was found guilty and hanged in the Washington, D.C., city jail on June 30, 1882.

3. Fuess, *Carl Schurz,* 318; Bishop, *Charles Joseph Bonaparte;* G. H. Putnam, *Memories of a Publisher,* 141.

4. Goldman, *Charles J. Bonaparte,* 24.

5. U.S. Civil Service Commission, *Ninth Annual Report,* 262; Williams, "Theodore Roosevelt," 43–62.

6. Williams, "Theodore Roosevelt," 46.

7. Oct. 10, 1891, Roosevelt, *Letters,* 1:261.

8. *Washington Post,* Apr. 3, 1891; E. Morris, *Rise of Theodore Roosevelt,* 435.

9. E. Morris, *Rise of Theodore Roosevelt,* 435; *Washington Post* clipping dated July 1891, TRC.

10. Scrapbook, TRC; Bishop, *Theodore Roosevelt and His Time,* 1:50.

11. Roosevelt, *Works,* 20:12.

12. July 31, 1889, Roosevelt, *Letters,* 1:177.

13. U.S. Civil Service Commission, *Eleventh Annual Report,* 236.

14. Minutes of the U.S. Civil Service Commission, July 1, 1989–Dec. 31, 1889, Record Group 146, entry dated Oct. 24, 1889, p. 99, National Archives, College Park, Maryland.

15. E. Morris, *Rise of Theodore Roosevelt,* 437, 442; *Civil Service Chronicle,* May 1892, 48.

16. U.S. Congress, 52nd Cong., 1st sess., H. Rpt. 1669, *Violations of the Civil Service Law at Baltimore,* 44–58.

17. TR to Harrison, May 16, 1892, BHP.

18. *New York Times,* May 26, 1892; *Plymouth Free Press* clipping dated June 10, 1892, Scrapbook, TRC.

19. *Washington Post* clipping dated June 18, 1892, Scrapbook, TRC.

20. U.S. Civil Service Commission, *Ninth Annual Report,* 262; Busch, *T.R.,* 90; Williams, "Theodore Roosevelt," 46.

21. TR to Brander Matthews, June 23, 1891, from Oliver, *Letters of Theodore Roosevelt and Brander Matthews,* 26.

22. *New York Times,* Jan. 2, 1891.

23. The Tiffany screen stood in the White House entrance from 1882 until 1902. President Roosevelt, during the 1902 remodeling of the White House, ordered many of the late-nineteenth-century Victorian interiors stripped from the mansion, including the garish but priceless screen. In 1903 the screen was sold at auction for $275. Monkman, *White House,* 169.

24. Foraker, *I Would Live It Again,* 133.

25. TR to Taft, June 9, 1903, Roosevelt, *Letters,* 3:485.

26. Feb. 1, 1891, ibid., 1:237n. 1. Levi Morton (1824–1920). American banker, twenty-second vice president under Benjamin Harrison (1889–93). Founded New York banking firm of Morton, Bliss & Company, 1863. Served in House of Representatives (1879–81), minister to France (1881–85), governor of New York (1895–96), worked for civil service reform and consolidation of New York City. Remained independent of the Republican state machine.

Charles J. Bonaparte (1851–1921). U.S. cabinet official, Baltimore lawyer, and political leader. Identified with reform causes. Appointed secretary of the navy, 1905. Appointed attorney general, 1906. Active in suits brought against the trusts and helped break up the tobacco monopoly. President of the National Municipal League.

James Cardinal Gibbons (1834–1921). Appointed archbishop of Baltimore, 1877. Appointed cardinal by Pope Leo XIII, 1886. Became first chancellor of

Catholic University, 1889. Sought peace between immigrating Catholic groups, particularly Irish and German. Emphasized to Rome the separation of church and state in the United States.

27. William McKinley (1843–1901). Twenty-fifth president of the United States, practiced law in Canton, Ohio, U.S. congressman, 1877–91, governor of Ohio, 1891–96. As president supported civil service reform and the protective tariff. When assassinated in 1901, then–vice president Roosevelt became president.

28. Morgan, *Gilded Age*, 149.

29. Feb. 1, 1891, Roosevelt, *Letters*, 1:236.

30. Thomas B. Reed (1839–1902). Attorney, attorney general of Maine, 1870–72; U.S. congressman from Maine, 1879–99; Speaker of the House, 1889–91, 1895–99. Sometimes called "Czar Reed" because of the blunt, powerful way he controlled the House.

31. Feb. 8, 1891, Roosevelt, *Letters*, 1:237.

32. Charles H. Grosvenor (1833–1917). Civil War general, Republican congressman from Ohio, 1885–91, 1893–1907.

33. Roosevelt, *An Autobiography*, 137.

34. Joseph Gurney Cannon (1836–1926). U.S. congressman from Illinois, 1873–91, 1893–1913, 1915–23; Speaker of the House (1903–11) during the Roosevelt and Taft presidencies. Regarded as one of Congress's most powerful legislators and the personification of centralized authority and partisan strength.

Louis Emory McComas (1846–1907). Republican. U.S. representative from Maryland Sixth District, 1883–91; defeated, 1876, 1890; justice of District of Columbia Supreme Court, 1892–99; U.S. senator from Maryland, 1899–1905; appointed by Roosevelt as judge of U.S. Court of Appeals for the D.C. Circuit, 1905–7.

Benjamin Butterworth (1837–98). Republican member of Ohio legislature; U.S. representative, 1879–83, 1885–91.

35. *Washington Evening Star*, Feb. 14, 1891. Nelson Dingley Jr. (1832–99). Republican. Governor of Maine, 1874–76; U.S. representative from Maine, 1881–99. Died in office.

36. Ibid.

37. *House Report 4038*, 51st Cong., 2nd sess., Aug. 23, 1890.

38. *Washington Evening Star*, Aug. 23, 1890.

39. Aug. 27, 1890, Roosevelt, *Letters*, 1:231.

40. Nov. 10, 1878, ibid., 35.

41. Owen Wister (1860–1938). Harvard-educated lawyer from Philadelphia, American writer whose Westerns helped establish the cowboy as archetypical folk hero. In 1885 first ventured west to Wyoming and began writing of his experiences, later used to write his first novel, *The Virginian* (1902). "Smile when you say that" was the novel's most famous line.

42. Wister, *Roosevelt*, 4.

43. McCullough, *Mornings on Horseback*; G. H. Putnam, *Memories of a Publisher*.

44. Norton, *Theodore Roosevelt*, 20.

45. Hagedorn, *Boy's Life of Theodore Roosevelt*, 66.

46. TR to Charles Grenfill Washburn, Nov. 10, 1881, Roosevelt, *Letters*, 1:55.

47. Foraker, *Notes of a Busy Life*, 1:167–68.

48. Stoddard, *As I Knew Them,* 312.

49. Lorant, *Life and Times of Theodore Roosevelt,* 196.

50. DiNunzio, *Theodore Roosevelt,* 1.

51. During Roosevelt's presidency, Alice Roosevelt (1884–1980) married Nicholas Longworth, a second-term Ohio congressman fifteen years her senior. Alice became a Washington social legend and lived an energetic life of ninety-six years, meeting every president from Benjamin Harrison to Gerald Ford.

52. Renehan, *Lion's Pride,* 106.

53. Norton, *Theodore Roosevelt,* 23.

54. Feb. 21, 1884, Roosevelt, *Letters,* 1:66.

55. Pringle, *A Biography,* 52.

56. George Bird Grinnell (1849–1938). Naturalist, anthropologist, Indian rights advocate. Studied at Yale. Editor of *Forest and Stream* (1876–1911), the leading natural history magazine in North America; founder of the Audubon Society and Boone and Crockett Club. Glacier National Park came about largely through his efforts.

57. TR to Captain George Anderson, Mar. 30, 1894, unfiled letter, TRC.

58. E. Morris, *Rise of Theodore Roosevelt,* 384.

59. Miller, *A Life,* 196.

60. Roosevelt, *Letters,* 1:306n. 1. William Hallett Phillips (d. 1897). Noted environmentalist, intimate friend of John Hay, Henry Adams, and Roosevelt, instrumental in passage in 1894 of law establishing efficient administration of Yellowstone Park.

61. Apr. 7, 1894, Roosevelt, *Letters,* 1:371.

62. In 1883, John Hay and Henry Adams acquired the property at the corner of H and Sixteenth Streets, the present site of the Hay-Adams Hotel. Adams and Hay commissioned the most celebrated architect of the day, Henry Hobson Richardson, to build Adams's town house at 1603 H Street and Hay's turreted and fortresslike residence at 800 Sixteenth Street. Both homes were completed late in 1885.

63. Stevenson, *Henry Adams,* 192.

64. O'Toole, "What They All Had in Common," 132; Stevenson, *Henry Adams,* 197.

65. Berkelman, "Clarence King," 314.

66. Henry Brooks Adams (1838–1918). Historian, editor, author, and educator. After settling in Washington, D.C., plunged into the capital's social and political life. Supported civil service reform and retention of the silver standard. Editor of the *North American Review* (1870–76), professor of medieval history at Harvard (1870–77). Most impressive achievement as a historian was nine-volume *History of the United States of America during the Administrations of Thomas Jefferson and James Madison* (1889–91). Also published two biographies, *The Life of Albert Gallatin* (1879) and *John Randolph* (1882); two novels, *Democracy* (1880) and *Esther* (1884); a story about New York City society; and an autobiography, *The Education of Henry Adams* (1931).

67. Berkelman, "Clarence King," 313; Adams, *Education,* 6.

68. A letter from Adams's wife, Clover, to her father, written on Dec. 5, 1872,

from the *Isis* off Cairo, mentions a "Mr. Roosevelt of New York, who came to see us today." From M. Adams, *The Letters of Mrs. Henry Adams,* 62. During the Nile trip, the Roosevelt family lunched with another *dahabeah* traveler, the aging Ralph Waldo Emerson. See Dalton, *Theodore Roosevelt,* 54.

69. TR to Martha Bulloch Roosevelt, Jan. 18, 1877, Roosevelt, *Letters,* 1:22.

70. May 15, 1889, Adams, *Letters* (1982), 3:175.

71. McCullough, *Mornings on Horseback,* 383.

72. Shumate, "Political Philosophy," 599; O'Toole, "What They All Had in Common," 135.

73. Blum, "Theodore Roosevelt," 1491; TR to Alfred Thayer Mahan, May 12, 1890, Roosevelt, *Letters,* 1:222.

74. Adams, *Education,* 7.

75. Dalton, *Theodore Roosevelt,* 136.

76. Adams to Elizabeth Cameron, June 13, 1892, Adams, *Letters* (1982), 4:22.

77. Adams to Cameron, Sept. 5, 1891, Adams, *Letters* (1930), 1:521, and Adams to Sir Ronald Lindsay, Jan. 16, 1909, ibid., 2:515.

78. McCullough, *Mornings on Horseback,* 59; Dalton, *Theodore Roosevelt,* 28. John Hay (1838–1905). American author and statesman. Practiced law at Springfield, Illinois, where he met Abraham Lincoln. Accompanied Lincoln to Washington as his private secretary until the president's death. Appointed assistant secretary of state in 1878. After ten years of work, published with John Nicolay the monumental *Abraham Lincoln: A History* (1890). Appointed ambassador to Great Britain in 1897. Served as secretary of state under McKinley and Roosevelt from 1898 until his death. Remarkably, he served three presidents who were assassinated—Lincoln, Garfield, and McKinley. Died in 1905, a few months after the beginning of Roosevelt's second term.

79. E. Morris, *Theodore Rex,* 238; Burton, *Learned Presidency,* 64.

80. O'Toole, "What They All Had in Common," 134.

81. Jan. 28, 1909, Roosevelt, *Letters,* 6:1489–90.

82. O'Toole, *Five of Hearts,* 145, xvi.

83. Marian Hooper "Clover" Adams (1843–85); O'Toole, "What They All Had in Common."

84. Adams, *Education,* vi.

85. Berkelman, "Clarence King," 315. Clarence King (1842–1901). Gifted geologist and moving spirit behind the great *Report of the Geological Exploration of the Fortieth Parallel.* Author of *Mountaineering in the Sierra Nevada* (1872), a collection of essays written during his years as a geologist in the American West. First to use relief-contour lines for the mapping of large areas. Director of U.S. Geological Survey, 1879 to 1881.

86. O'Toole, *Five of Hearts,* xvii; Berkelman, "Clarence King," 304.

87. Adams, *Education,* 311.

88. O'Toole, *Five of Hearts;* O'Toole, "What They All Had in Common."

89. O'Toole, "What They All Had in Common," 132.

90. TR to Spring-Rice, from Washington, Dec. 25, 1892, Roosevelt, *Letters,* 1:304. Henry Adams, along with John LaFarge, visited the South Seas the previous year. There they met Tati Salmon and invited him to the United States.

91. Brands, *Last Romantic,* 228.

92. O'Toole, *Five of Hearts,* 91.

93. John LaFarge (1835–1910). Born in New York City into a cultured French family. Leading figure in New York arts in the late nineteenth century, known for exquisite murals, stained-glass designs, and innovative techniques. Traveled to Europe, where he was influenced by the stained glass in medieval architecture. In Paris, studied with Thomas Couture, and in London, influenced by Pre-Raphaelites, who focused on importance of art's being morally and spiritually uplifting. After returning to the United States, completed first window commission in 1874. Discovered that layering of two or more pieces of glass, rather than painting on it, created exotic effects; thus became inventor of opalescent glass, which he patented in 1880.

94. Augustus Saint-Gaudens (1848–1907). Born in Ireland to a French shoemaker and Irish housewife. Family immigrated to New York City. Studied art at Cooper Union and the National Academy of Design. At nineteen, traveled to Paris and studied at the Ecole des Beaux-Arts. Beginning in 1870, spent five years in Rome studying classical art and architecture. Returning to the United States, he received his first major commission in 1876, a monument to Admiral David Farragut in New York's Madison Square. Artistic adviser and contributor to the Columbian Exposition of 1893, avid supporter of the American Academy in Rome, and made recommendations for the architectural preservation of the nation's capital.

95. O'Toole, *Five of Hearts,* 166; "as hard and sharp" quotation attributed to Clarence King.

96. Adams, *Education,* 329.

97. James, *American Scene,* 343.

98. Foraker, *I Would Live It Again,* 195.

99. Josephson, *Politicos,* 448.

100. Sir Arthur Cecil Spring-Rice (1859–1918). British diplomat, graduate of Oxford, secretary at the Washington legation, 1887–88, 1889–92, 1894–95; minister to Teheran, 1906–8; ambassador to the United States, 1913–18. Poet, author of the patriotic "I Vow to Thee, My Country" (1918).

101. S. J. Morris, *Edith Kermit Roosevelt,* 99.

102. Caroli, *Roosevelt Women,* 83.

103. Renehan, *Lion's Pride,* 55; DiNunzio, *Theodore Roosevelt,* 10.

104. Roosevelt, *An Autobiography,* 118.

105. Caroli, *Roosevelt Women,* 83.

106. May 3, 1892, Roosevelt, *Letters,* 1:277.

107. July 1, 1891, ibid., 256.

108. Blake, "Ambassadors at the Court," 181.

109. May 15, 1891, Roosevelt, *Letters,* 1:245.

110. TR to George Otto Trevelyan, Feb. 4, 1907, ibid., 5:579.

111. Blake, "Ambassadors at the Court," 179.

112. Fenton, "Theodore Roosevelt," 370.

113. TR to Brander Matthews, Dec. 6, 1892, Roosevelt, *Letters,* 1:299.

114. John William Fox (1863–1919). Novelist, adventurer, Rough Rider, and

Harper's Weekly correspondent. Most famous works were *The Little Shepherd of Kingdom Come* (1903) and *The Trail of the Lonesome Pine* (1908).

115. Burton, *Theodore Roosevelt,* 77.
116. Norton, *Theodore Roosevelt,* 64.
117. Ibid., 25.
118. July 13, 1889, Roosevelt, *Letters,* 1:172.
119. Oliver, "Theodore Roosevelt, Brander Matthews," 94.
120. Cook, *Book of Positive Quotations,* 436.
121. *Washington Star* clipping, July 2, 1891, Scrapbook, TRC.
122. *Washington Post* clippings, ibid.
123. N. Roosevelt, *A Front Row Seat,* 23.
124. Dalton, *Theodore Roosevelt,* 134.
125. Roosevelt, *Letters,* 1:187.
126. Pinchot, *Breaking New Ground,* 317.
127. Oct. 10, 1891, Roosevelt, *Letters,* 1:262.
128. Unfiled letter, Dec. 29, 1891, TRC.

CHAPTER 4

1. *New York Times,* Jan. 10, 1892.
2. McCullough, *Mornings on Horseback,* 144.
3. Lash, *Eleanor and Franklin,* 7.
4. Pringle, *A Biography,* 45.
5. Roosevelt, *Letters,* 1:46.
6. Ibid., 74.
7. McCullough, *Mornings on Horseback,* 226.
8. Ibid., 243.
9. July 1, 1883, Roosevelt, *Letters,* 1:61.
10. TR to HCL, Oct. 10, 1886, ibid., 109.
11. July 28, 1889, ibid., 174.
12. June 17, 1888, ibid., 140.
13. Caroli, *Roosevelt Women,* 92.
14. Ibid., 93; E. Morris, *Rise of Theodore Roosevelt,* 438.
15. Low, "Washington," 778.
16. TR to ARC, Jan. 23, May 10, 1891, TRC.
17. *New York Sun,* Aug. 17, 1891.
18. S. J. Morris, *Rise of Theodore Roosevelt,* 445.
19. Roosevelt, *An Autobiography.* Cushman K. Davis (1838–1900). Republican lawyer. Served in the Union army during the Civil War; member of Minnesota state house of representatives, First District, 1867; U.S. district attorney for Minnesota, 1868–73; governor of Minnesota, 1874–76; U.S. senator from Minnesota, 1887–1900; died in office, 1900. Helped negotiate the Treaty of Paris, which ended the Spanish-American War and gave Puerto Rico and the Philippines to the United States.

Orville Platt (1827–1905). Republican lawyer. Secretary of state of Connecticut, 1857–58; member of Connecticut state senate, Sixth District, 1861–62;

member of Connecticut state house of representatives, 1864, 1869; speaker of the Connecticut state house of representatives, 1869; U.S. senator from Connecticut, 1879–1905; died in office, 1905.

Francis Cockrell (1834–1915). Democrat. General in the Confederate army during the Civil War; U.S. senator from Missouri, 1875–1905; candidate for Democratic nomination for president, 1904.

George Dargan (1841–98). Democrat. U.S. representative from South Carolina, Sixth District, 1883–91.

20. E. Morris, *Rise of Theodore Roosevelt,* 393; McCall, *Life,* 110.

21. TR to Henry Childs Merwin, Dec. 18, 1894, Roosevelt, *Letters,* 1:412.

22. TR to George W. Jolley, Jan. 5, 1892, ibid., 270.

23. U.S. Civil Service Commission, *Eleventh Annual Report,* 21.

24. Ibid., 277–301.

25. May 3, 1892, Roosevelt, *Letters,* 1:276.

26. U.S. Civil Service Commission, *Seventeenth Annual Report,* 61.

27. Hoogenboom, "Pendleton Act," 309.

28. May 7, 1892, Roosevelt, *Letters,* 1:280. Lucius Burrie Swift. Lawyer, civil service reformer, helped found Indiana Civil Service Reform Association, editor of *Civil Service Chronicle,* 1889–96.

29. Aron, *Ladies and Gentlemen of the Civil Service,* 111.

30. U.S. Department of Commerce, Bureau of the Census, *Historical Statistics of the United Sates, 1789–1945* (Washington, D.C.: Government Printing Office, 1949); Hoogenboom, *Outlawing the Spoils,* 268; U.S. Civil Service Commission, *Tenth Annual Report,* 140.

31. TR to C. W. Watson, Feb. 25, 1895, Roosevelt, *Letters,* 1:428; Hoogenboom, "Pendleton Act," 308.

32. Pringle, *A Biography,* 129.

33. Roosevelt, *Works,* 20:143; Hoogenboom, "Pendleton Act," 313.

34. TR to Arthur Pue Gorman, Mar. 1, 1891, Roosevelt, *Letters,* 1:239.

35. J. R. Lambert, *Arthur Pue Gorman,* 250.

36. *Baltimore Sun,* Oct. 15, 1895.

37. Quote attributed to Senator John Sherman, from Sageser, *First Two Decades,* 57.

38. William Dudley Foulke (1848–1935). Author, newspaper editor, biographer, president of the Indiana Civil Service Reform Association, and president of National Civil Service Reform League (1923–24). Served as civil service commissioner during Roosevelt's presidency.

39. Feb. 10, 1894, Roosevelt, *Letters,* 1:362.

40. Williams, "Theodore Roosevelt," 78.

41. Van Riper, *United States Civil Service,* 144.

42. TR to James T. Young, June 25, 1894, Roosevelt, *Letters,* 1:386.

43. Teplin, "Theodore Roosevelt," 199.

44. TR to Henry Childs Merwin, Dec. 18, 1894, Roosevelt, *Letters,* 1:417.

45. Teplin, "Theodore Roosevelt," 199. Interestingly, Roosevelt changed his policy when he became a supervisor. As New York City police commissioner he reversed the weighting, giving a maximum weight of 35 percent to the competitive exam and 65 percent to his own judgment as a commissioner.

46. Harrison issued an executive order on Dec. 4, 1891, directing each department to devise and implement a plan for maintaining efficiency records for all employees.

47. Harrison to Blaine, Dec. 4, 1891, BHP; Volwiler, *Correspondence between Harrison and Blaine*, 213.

48. Department of the Interior, circular, "Efficiency Record in Compliance with the President's Instructions on Dec. 4, 1891," Jan. 2, 1892, Miscellaneous Letters Received, Appointments Division, Interior Department Files, National Archives, College Park, Maryland; Aron, *Ladies and Gentlemen of the Civil Service*, 220n. 99.

49. Teplin, "Theodore Roosevelt," 201.

50. U.S. Civil Service Commission, *Eighth Annual Report;* Williams, "Theodore Roosevelt," 86.

51. Aron, *Ladies and Gentlemen of the Civil Service*, 107.

52. A. M. Dockery to Hoke Smith, Oct. 2, 1893, from Aron, *Ladies and Gentlemen of the Civil Service*, 215n. 32.

53. Commissioner of Patents John Seymour to Secretary of the Interior, Mar. 6, 1894, Miscellaneous Letters Received, Appointments Division, Department of Interior Files, National Archives, Washington, D.C.; Aron, *Ladies and Gentlemen of the Civil Service*, 218n. 55.

54. Roosevelt, *Works*, 11:230.

55. Spring-Rice, *Letters and Friendships of Sir Cecil Spring-Rice*, 437.

56. E. Morris, "As a Literary Lion," 93.

57. Leach, *Land of Desire*, 212.

58. Klein, "Gospel of Wanamaker," 28.

59. Leach, *Land of Desire*, 196.

60. Harbaugh, *Power and Responsibility*, 78; Williams, "Theodore Roosevelt," 26; Van Riper, *United States Civil Service*, 124; Josephson, *Politicos*, 440.

61. Socolofsky and Spetter, *Presidency of Benjamin Harrison*, 40.

62. Busch, *T.R.*, 89.

63. L. D. White, *Republican Era*, 262.

64. Leach, *Land of Desire*, 209.

65. Appel, *Business Biography of John Wanamaker*.

66. Licht, *Industrializing America*, 57; Leach, *Land of Desire*, 338.

67. L. D. White, *Republican Era*, 262.

68. Klein, "Gospel of Wanamaker," 39.

69. Williams, "Theodore Roosevelt," 28.

70. Gibbons, *John Wanamaker*, 302; Skowronek, *Building a New American State*, 76.

71. Cashman, *America in the Gilded Age*, 255.

72. Trachtenberg, *Incorporation of America*, 173.

73. Aug. 12, 1899, Roosevelt, *Letters*, 2:1054.

74. From Medora, Dakota Territory, May 15, 1886, ibid., 1:100.

75. Painter, *Standing at Armageddon*, 116.

76. Adams, *Education*, 320.

77. Gibbons, *John Wanamaker*, 328.

78. Oct. 10, 1891, Roosevelt, *Letters*, 1:261.

79. Lodge, *Correspondence*, 124.

80. Roosevelt, "Foreign Policy," 1113–15.

81. Morgan, *Gilded Age*, 124.

CHAPTER 5

1. *New York Times*, Mar. 5, 1893.

2. Steffens, *Letters*, 1:167. Joseph Lincoln Steffens (1866–1936). American journalist whose sensational articles on city and state government corruption made him one of the leading muckrakers of his era. Held successive editorial positions on *McClure's*, the *American*, and *Everybody's* magazines. Articles later collected in *The Shame of the Cities* (1904), *The Struggle for Self-Government* (1906), and *Upbuilders* (1909).

3. Painter, *Standing at Armageddon*, 116.

4. Roosevelt, *Works*, 14:79; Pringle, *A Biography*, 118.

5. TR to Cleveland, telegram, Oct. 15, 1892, GCP.

6. Dec. 5, 1892, Roosevelt, *Letters*, 1:298.

7. *New York Tribune*, Nov. 22, 1892.

8. Trefousse, *Carl Schurz.*

9. Sproat, *Best Men*, 137.

10. Dec. 29, 1892, Roosevelt, *Letters*, 1:304. Francis E. Leupp, journalist, at the time chief of the Washington bureau of the *New York Evening Post* and correspondent for the *Nation*. Also edited *Good Government*, official organ of the National Civil Service Reform League (1892–95). On Roosevelt's recommendation, Herbert Welsh hired Leupp as a lobbyist for the Indian Rights Association in 1895. In 1904, Roosevelt appointed Leupp commissioner of Indian affairs.

11. Schurz to TR, Jan. 4, 1893, TRP.

12. Jan. 5, 1893, Roosevelt, *Letters*, 1:305.

13. Schurz, *Speeches, Correspondence*, 126.

14. E. Morris, *Rise of Theodore Roosevelt*, 457; Bishop, *Theodore Roosevelt and His Time*, 1:52. Benjamin Tracy (1830–1915). Republican reformer, New York Court of Appeals judge, secretary of the navy (1889–93), former Union general, and Medal of Honor recipient.

15. *New York Daily Tribune*, Mar. 7, 1891.

16. Apr. 26, 1893, Roosevelt, *Letters*, 1:314.

17. May 27, 1893, ibid., 318.

18. Harvey, *Civil Service Commission*, 224.

19. May 24, 1891, Cowles, *Letters*, 117–18.

20. *House Report 4038*, 51st Cong., 2nd sess.

21. *Civil Service Record*, Apr. 1891, 107.

22. *House Report 4038*, 51st Cong., 2nd sess., 90.

23. Hagedorn, *Roosevelt Family of Sagamore Hill*, 23.

24. Rixey, *Bamie.*

25. Dec. 14, 1893, file CR-1, Vol. 4, TRC.

26. Dec. 17, 1893, Roosevelt, *Letters*, 1:343.

27. Roosevelt, *An Autobiography*, 55.

28. Busch, *T.R.*, 89.

29. In *Theodore Roosevelt: A Biography,* Pringle estimates that in 1880 Roosevelt's share of his father's estate assured him an income between $7,500 and $10,000 a year. When Roosevelt died in 1919, his wealth approximated $1 million. See Teplin, "Theodore Roosevelt," 4.

30. Renehan, *Lion's Pride,* 47.

31. Hagedorn, *Roosevelt Family of Sagamore Hill,* 26.

32. In 2000 dollars, Roosevelt's losses would approach a half million dollars.

33. Wagenknecht, *Seven Worlds of Theodore Roosevelt,* 211; Brands, *Last Romantic,* 231.

34. TR to Corinne, June 2, 1889, Robinson, *My Brother,* 132.

35. TR to ARC, Oct. 13, 1889, Cowles, *Letters,* 107.

36. Undated 1890 letter, file CR-1, TRC.

37. EKR, miscellaneous accounts, 1890, file CR-1, TRC.

38. Town of Oyster Bay Tax Receipt, Jan. 24, 1894, TRP. On the other hand, a $1,200-per-year government clerk in Washington, with a wife and three children, had monthly expenses that averaged $30 for rent, $15 for staple groceries, $27 for perishable foods, and $9.50 for wood, coal, and gas (Green, *Washington, Capitol City,* 80).

39. Green, *Washington, Capitol City;* Logan, *Thirty Years in Washington,* 518.

40. James, *American Scene,* 342. Henry James (1843–1916). American-born writer, gifted in literature, psychology, and philosophy. Wrote 20 novels, 12 plays, 112 short stories, and a number of works of literary criticism. Best-known work was *Daisy Miller* (1879). Models were Dickens, Balzac, and Hawthorne.

41. Foraker, *I Would Live It Again,* 215.

42. Sageser, *First Two Decades,* 177.

43. Fowler, *Cabinet Politician,* 228. Wilson Shannon Bissel (1847–1903). Buffalo, New York, attorney. Chancellor of University of Buffalo, 1902–3; law partner of Grover Cleveland, 1873–82; postmaster general, 1893–95.

44. Ibid., 233, from Postmaster General Letterbook, July 11, 1894.

45. June 8, 1893, Roosevelt, *Letters,* 1:322.

46. Aug. 9, 1893, ibid., 329.

47. June 25, 1894, ibid., 388.

48. TR to Lucius Swift, Feb. 27, 1895, ibid., 429.

49. TR to ARC, Feb. 25, 1895, ibid.

50. Sageser, *First Two Decades,* 178–79.

51. Walter Quintin Gresham (1832–95). Union army brigadier general; postmaster general, 1883–84; secretary of the treasury, 1884; switched from Republican to Democratic Party in 1892 to support Cleveland; appointed secretary of state in 1893.

52. TR to Carl Schurz, Aug. 23, 1893, Roosevelt, *Letters,* 1:334–35.

53. Josephson, *Politicos,* 521. John Griffin Carlisle (1835–1910). Attorney; lieutenant governor of Kentucky, 1871–75; editor of the *Louisville Daily Ledger;* Democratic congressman, 1877–90; Speaker of the House, 1883–89; U.S. senator, 1890–93; secretary of the treasury, 1893–97.

54. June 24, 1894, Roosevelt, *Letters,* 1:385.

55. Hoogenboom, "Pendleton Act," 307.

56. June 25, 1894, Roosevelt, *Letters,* 1:387.

57. Thomas Corwin Mendenhall (1841–1924). Physicist, meteorologist, expert in earthquakes. Appointed by Harrison to superintend the Coast and Geodetic Survey in 1889. Previously served as chair of physics at Ohio State University, chief of the Instrument Division in the U.S. Signal Corps, and president of Rose Polytechnic Institute, Terre Haute, Indiana.

58. TR to Hugh McKittrick, Feb. 21, 1895, Roosevelt, *Letters,* 1:427; Hoogenboom, "Pendleton Act," 307.

59. TR to Lucius Swift, Aug. 14, 1894, Roosevelt, *Letters,* 1:394.

60. Harbaugh, *Writings of Theodore Roosevelt,* 197.

61. DiNunzio, *Theodore Roosevelt,* xi.

62. Dyer, *Roosevelt and the Idea of Race,* 143.

63. Wagenknecht, *Seven Worlds of Theodore Roosevelt,* 230.

64. Dyer, *Roosevelt and the Idea of Race,* 27.

65. Roosevelt, *New York,* 527; Blum, *Republican Roosevelt,* 28.

66. Wagenknecht, *Seven Worlds of Theodore Roosevelt,* 231.

67. Dyer, *Roosevelt and the Idea of Race,* 112.

68. Ibid., 91.

69. Not until the Wilson administration did federal officials begin to establish racial segregation within Washington agencies, requiring separate offices, separate desks, and separate lunchrooms. Aron, *Ladies and Gentlemen of the Civil Service,* 30; C. Abbott, *Political Terrain,* 88.

70. Miller, *A Life,* 363.

71. TR to William Lyall, Jan. 13, 1890, Roosevelt, *Letters,* 1:212.

72. John Sharp Williams (1854–1932). Mississippi Democrat. U.S. representative, 1893–1909; U.S. senator, 1911–23.

73. Riis, *Roosevelt, the Citizen,* 119.

74. Roosevelt, *Works,* 2:238.

75. Ibid., 214.

76. E. Morris, "As a Literary Lion," 93.

77. Burton, *Learned Presidency,* 52.

78. DiNunzio, *Theodore Roosevelt,* xi.

79. Roosevelt, *An Autobiography,* 116.

80. Norton, *Theodore Roosevelt,* 28.

81. Pringle, *A Biography,* 54.

82. Robinson, *My Brother,* 128.

83. Norton, *Theodore Roosevelt,* 79.

84. Pringle, *A Biography,* 116–17.

85. Adams, *Letters* (1930), 2:521.

86. Fenton, "Theodore Roosevelt," 369.

87. E. Morris, *Rise of Theodore Roosevelt,* 410.

88. Miller, *A Life,* 198.

89. Oliver, "Theodore Roosevelt, Brander Matthews," 106.

90. Hart and Ferleger, *Theodore Roosevelt Cyclopedia,* 443.

91. Roosevelt, "Kidd's 'Social Evolution'"; Hofstadter, *Social Darwinism,* 99–102.

92. Feb. 7, 1886, Roosevelt, *Letters,* 1:93.

93. Mar. 27, 1886, ibid., 95.

94. June 27, 1892, ibid., 288.

95. Wister, *Roosevelt,* 41.

96. Hagedorn, *Boy's Life of Theodore Roosevelt,* 22.

97. Roosevelt, *Works,* 20:325.

98. Roosevelt, *An Autobiography,* 322.

99. James Brander Matthews (1852–1929). Essayist, drama critic, novelist, and professor of dramatic literature at Columbia University. A close friend of Roosevelt's, Matthews was influential in American letters for thirty years.

100. Oliver, "Theodore Roosevelt, Brander Matthews," 95.

101. Bishop, *Theodore Roosevelt and His Time,* 1:55.

102. Norton, *Theodore Roosevelt,* 29.

103. Blum, "Theodore Roosevelt," 1491.

104. Lodge, *Speeches and Addresses,* 103.

105. Oliver, "Theodore Roosevelt, Brander Matthews," 102.

106. Ibid., 95.

107. Ibid.

108. June 29, 1894, Roosevelt, *Letters,* 1:390.

109. Oliver, "Theodore Roosevelt, Brander Matthews," 97.

110. Ibid., 98.

111. July 31, 1889, Roosevelt, *Letters,* 1:177.

112. TR to Mrs. Lucius B. Swift, Aug. 21, 1894, ibid., 396.

113. Warner, *Generals in Gray,* 161.

114. Oliver, *Letters of Theodore Roosevelt and Brander Matthews,* 64.

115. TR and Lyman to Cleveland, Nov. 20, 1893, GCP.

116. Nov. 21, 1893, Roosevelt, *Letters,* 1:341.

117. Oct. 27, 1893, ibid.

118. TR to Lucius Swift, Nov. 28, 1893, file CR-1, TRC; Foulke, *Lucius B. Swift,* 69.

119. Roosevelt, *Letters,* 1:317n. 1.

120. *Chicago Tribune,* May 2, 1893.

121. Appelbaum, *Chicago World's Fair.*

122. Flinn, *Official Guide;* Burg, *Chicago's White City.*

123. O'Toole, *Five of Hearts,* 264.

124. S. J. Morris, *Edith Kermit Roosevelt,* 146.

125. Appelbaum, *Chicago World's Fair;* Burg, *Chicago's White City;* Flinn, *Official Guide.*

126. Hoxie, *A Final Promise,* 84.

127. The fair was not without its critics. The most vocal was Louis Sullivan, the talented Chicago architect who pioneered modern buildings designed from the inside out and first emphasized "form follows function." Sullivan labeled the White City an "appalling calamity" and charged that the fair, with its emphasis on neoclassicism and symmetry, set American architecture back an entire generation.

128. Adams, *Letters* (1930), 2:331.

129. June 8, 1893, Roosevelt, *Letters,* 1:320.

CHAPTER 6

1. TR to ARC, Jan. 7, 1894, Roosevelt, *Letters,* 1:345.
2. N. Roosevelt, *A Front Row Seat,* 25.
3. TR to ARC, Jan. 7, 1894, Roosevelt, *Letters,* 1:345.
4. Halloran, *Romance of the Merit System,* 64.
5. Teplin, "Theodore Roosevelt," 5.
6. Renehan, *Lion's Pride,* 15.
7. Caroli, *Roosevelt Women,* 73–77.
8. Rixey, *Bamie,* 181; Caroli, *Roosevelt Women,* 121.
9. Caroli, *Roosevelt Women,* 78.
10. Rixey, *Bamie,* vi.
11. Cowles, *Letters,* 120.
12. Caroli, *Roosevelt Women,* 119.
13. *Washington Evening Star,* Sept. 24, 1889.
14. Ibid., Mar. 20, 1894. Thomas R. Stockdale (1828–99). Democrat. U.S. representative from Mississippi Sixth District, 1887–95; justice of Mississippi state supreme court, 1899.
15. Benjamin A. Enloe (1848–1922). Democrat. Member of Tennessee state legislature; U.S. representative from Tennessee Eighth District, 1887–95.
16. *Congressional Record,* 53rd Cong., 2nd sess., 1894, 26, pt. 6, p. 5102.
17. *Washington Evening Star,* May 23, 1894. William Everett (1839–1910). Democrat. U.S. representative from Massachusetts Seventh District, 1893–95.
18. TR to Lucius Swift, Feb. 1, 1894, Roosevelt, *Letters,* 1:358.
19. TR to Henry Childs Merwin, Dec. 18, 1894, ibid., 416.
20. Feb. 7, 1894, ibid., 359.
21. Ibid. Hilary Herbert (1834–1919). Former Confederate colonel; Democratic congressman from Alabama, 1877–93; appointed secretary of the navy by Cleveland. As both congressman and navy secretary, advocated increases in the navy despite opposition in Congress.
22. TR to ARC, Jan. 7, 1894, ibid., 345. Hoke Smith (1855–1931). Georgia Democrat, owner and editor of the *Atlanta Journal,* credited with carrying his state for Cleveland's nomination in 1892. Secretary of the interior, 1893–96; governor of Georgia, 1907–9; U.S. senator, 1911–21.
23. TR to Schurz, Aug. 9, 23, 1893, ibid., 328, 334.
24. Aug. 9, 1893, ibid., 328.
25. May 27, 1894, ibid., 382.
26. *Washington Post,* Feb. 2, 1894.
27. EKR to ARC, Feb. 3, 1894, TRC; Gilder, *Grover Cleveland;* Gilder, *Letters;* S. J. Morris, *Edith Kermit Roosevelt,* 148.
28. Twain, *Gilded Age,* 183.
29. Monkman, *White House,* 172.
30. Gilder, *Letters,* 244. Richard Watson Gilder (1844–1909). A leading figure in the late-nineteenth-century world of arts and letters, author of three volumes of poetry, editor of *Century* (1881–1909), and friend of many American writers, artists, intellectuals, and leaders, including Roosevelt, Cleveland, Mark Twain,

and Augustus Saint-Gaudens. Active in efforts to reform housing conditions, municipal government, and civil service.

31. Josephson, *Politicos,* 437.

32. Dec. 31, 1893, Roosevelt, *Letters,* 1:344.

33. Hoogenboom, "Pendleton Act," 303.

34. Wheeler, "Rise and Progress of the Merit System," 487.

35. Stewart, *National Civil Service Reform League,* 37.

36. Pendleton Act, *U.S. Statutes at Large* 22 (1883): 403.

37. *Washington Evening Star,* Oct. 31, 1889.

38. Williams, "Theodore Roosevelt," 42.

39. U.S. Civil Service Commission, *Eleventh Annual Report,* 230; Sageser, *First Two Decades,* 118.

40. TR, Proctor, and Lyman to Cleveland, Aug. 1, 1894, GCP.

41. *Washington Evening Star,* Aug. 4, 1894.

42. *Boston Herald,* Feb. 21, 1893.

43. Hoogenboom, "Pendleton Act," 315.

44. Dec. 18, 1894, Roosevelt, *Letters,* 1:416.

45. Logan, *Thirty Years in Washington,* 250; C. Abbott, *Political Terrain,* 94.

46. Skowronek, *Building a New American State,* 82.

47. Sageser, *First Two Decades,* 235.

48. Hoogenboom, "Pendleton Act," 310.

49. TR to Edward Porritt, Jan. 12, 1895, TRC.

50. TR to Judson Grenell, Apr. 29, 1895, Roosevelt, *Letters,* 1:449.

51. TR to Carl Schurz, Dec. 26, 1894, ibid., 418.

52. Hansen, "Theodore Roosevelt and Civil Service Reform," 3.

53. Roberts, "A History of the Federal Civil Service," 26.

54. Hoogenboom, "Pendleton Act," 304.

55. Ingraham, *Foundation of Merit,* 33.

56. D. H. Smith, *United States Civil Service Commission,* 18.

57. Nelson, "A Short, Ironic History," 767.

58. TR to Carrie Harrison, Dec. 18, 1894, file CR-1, TRC; Harvey, *Civil Service Commission,* 118.

59. Harbaugh, *Power and Responsibility,* 77.

60. Dalton, *Theodore Roosevelt,* 74.

61. C. Abbott, *Political Terrain,* 93. Francis Elias Spinner (1802–90). Born in upstate New York, started life making harnesses and candy. Served in the New York State Militia and ultimately achieved the rank of major general before being appointed sheriff and a commissioner of a mental institution. Served in the U.S. House (1855–61) as a Republican. Appointed by Lincoln as treasurer of the United States (1861–75). While there, he signed our money—literally—slowly, deliberately, artfully, note by note. Obviously, this was before the signature was printed directly onto the notes.

62. Aron, *Ladies and Gentlemen of the Civil Service,* 5.

63. Not until the passage of the Classification Act of 1923 were female government employees guaranteed equal pay for equal work.

64. Aron, *Ladies and Gentlemen of the Civil Service,* 67.

65. *Revised Statutes 27,* July 12, 1870; L. D. White, *The Civil Service,* 188.

66. John Noble to Appointment Clerk, July 31, 1890, Miscellaneous Letters Received, Appointments Division, Interior Department Records, National Archives, College Park, Maryland; see Aron, *Ladies and Gentlemen of the Civil Service,* 220n. 90.

67. Aron, *Ladies and Gentlemen of the Civil Service,* 109.

68. C. Abbott, *Political Terrain,* 94.

69. Dyer, *Roosevelt and the Idea of Race,* 164; Wagenknecht, *Seven Worlds of Theodore Roosevelt,* 88.

70. Roosevelt, *Works,* 14:177.

71. Higham, *Strangers in the Land,* 73–82. In 1887, Henry F. Bowers founded the APA, one of many repressive organizations that flourished during the 1890s and whose purpose was to root out internal "enemies."

72. Oct. 15, 1894, Roosevelt, *Letters,* 1:405.

73. TR to C. P. Connolly, Apr. 11, 1894, ibid., 373.

74. TR to T. T. Hudson, Oct. 12, 1894, ibid., 403.

75. Oct. 15, 1894, ibid., 405.

76. TR to Spring-Rice, May 3, 1892, ibid., 277.

77. TR to Spring-Rice, Jan. 25, 1892, ibid., 270; "pistol" from Pinchot, *Breaking New Ground,* 315.

78. Mackintosh, *C&O Canal.*

79. Roosevelt, *Works,* 20:329.

80. Apr. 1, 1894, Roosevelt, *Letters,* 1:370.

81. Hagedorn, *Roosevelt Family of Sagamore Hill,* 25.

82. Logan, *Thirty Years in Washington,* 524.

83. Kent, *America in 1900,* 9.

84. Dalton, *Theodore Roosevelt,* 143.

85. Schwantes, *Coxey's Army.*

86. Hoffman, *Depression of the Nineties,* 262.

87. Lorant, *Life and Times of Theodore Roosevelt,* 257.

88. Merrill, *Bourbon Leader,* 32.

89. Morgan, *Gilded Age,* 142.

90. Kent, *America in 1900,* 9; Hoffman, *Depression of the Nineties,* 262; Pollack, *Populist Mind,* 330–42.

91. Eugene V. Debs (1855–1926). American labor leader and Socialist candidate for president (1900, 1904, 1908, 1912, and 1920). Turned to radical politics to express dissatisfaction with economic and social conditions. In 1893 founded the American Railway Union, destroyed in 1894 in the violent Pullman strike. Convicted for contempt of a court injunction during the strike, served six months in jail. Opposed U.S. entry into World War I, convicted in 1918 under the Espionage Act and sentenced to ten years in prison.

92. Lorant, *Life and Times of Theodore Roosevelt,* 264.

93. Trachtenberg, *Incorporation of America,* 232.

94. Morgan, *Gilded Age,* 143.

95. Roosevelt, *American Ideals,* 6–7.

96. July 22, 1894, Roosevelt, *Letters,* 1:391.

97. Oct. 22, 1894, ibid., 407.

98. Oct. 24, 1894, ibid., 408.

99. EKR to ARC, Sept. 28, 1894, TRC.

100. TR to ARC, Aug. 18, 1894, ibid.

101. TR to ARC, Feb. 13, 1892, ibid.; Lash, *Eleanor and Franklin,* 38–39.

102. Cowles, *Letters,* 121.

103. Roosevelt, *Letters,* 1:375.

104. July 29, 1894, ibid., 392.

105. Sept. 30, 1894, ibid., 399.

106. EKR to Gertrude Carow, Aug. 10, 1894, TRC.

107. Roosevelt, *Letters,* 1:393.

108. E. Morris, *Rise of Theodore Roosevelt,* 474.

109. Aug. 18, 1894, TRC.

110. Aug. 29, 1894, Roosevelt, *Letters,* 1:397.

CHAPTER 7

1. Twain, *Gilded Age,* 182.

2. Crichton, *America 1900,* 150.

3. During the same period, Baltimore had 31 murders; New Orleans, 60; San Francisco, 43; and New York, 223. On a per capita basis all of these cities had a higher murder rate than Washington. Statistics from National Criminal Justice Reference Center.

4. James, *American Scene,* 355.

5. *Washington Star,* May 13, 1889; Green, *Washington, Capitol City;* Latimer, *Your Washington and Mine.* Although informally called the White House, the presidential mansion would not officially take that name until Roosevelt's presidency.

6. Carpenter, *Carp's Washington,* 5.

7. Dalton, *Theodore Roosevelt,* 135.

8. Latimer, *Your Washington and Mine,* 597; Carpenter, *Carp's Washington,* 9.

9. Green, *Washington, Capitol City,* 97; Latimer, *Your Washington and Mine,* 597.

10. *Washington Evening Star,* May 26, 1894.

11. TR to ARC, Dec. 31, 1893, Roosevelt, *Letters,* 1:344.

12. Gilmour, *The Long Recessional,* 71.

13. Oliver, *Letters of Theodore Roosevelt and Brander Matthews,* 96.

14. Pringle, *A Biography,* 129.

15. S. J. Morris, *Edith Kermit Roosevelt,* 154.

16. Gilmour, *The Long Recessional,* 101.

17. May 31, 1892, Roosevelt, *Letters,* 1:286.

18. Apr. 1, 1894, ibid., 370.

19. Mar. 11, 1893, ibid., 43.

20. Aug. 11, 1899, ibid., 1053.

21. E. Morris, *Rise of Theodore Roosevelt,* 477.

22. Kipling, *Something of Myself,* 73; Gilmour, *The Long Recessional,* 129n.

23. Kipling, *Something of Myself,* 72; Carrington, *Life of Rudyard Kipling,* 175.

24. Sept. 13, 1898, Kipling, *Letters,* 350.

25. Kipling, *Something of Myself,* 74.
26. Dyer, *Roosevelt and the Idea of Race,* 123.
27. Lorant, *Life and Times of Theodore Roosevelt,* 167.
28. Roosevelt, *Fear God,* 27.
29. Oliver, *Letters of Theodore Roosevelt and Brander Matthews,* 212.
30. Sept. 25, 1892, Roosevelt, *Letters,* 1:290.
31. TR to Kipling, Nov. 1, 1904, Dyer, *Roosevelt and the Idea of Race,* 140.
32. Diary, Jan. 12, 1882, TRC.
33. Mar. 21, 1891, Cowles, *Letters,* 116.
34. Blum, "Theodore Roosevelt," 28.
35. Wagenknecht, *Seven Worlds of Theodore Roosevelt,* 229.
36. Burton, *Learned Presidency,* 38.
37. Mar. 19, 1895, Roosevelt, *Letters,* 1:436.
38. Aug. 10, 1886, ibid., 108.
39. Renehan, *Lion's Pride,* 25.
40. Blum, "Theodore Roosevelt," 1490.
41. Ibid., 31.
42. James Tanner (1844–1927). Teacher in rural New York schools when the Civil War began. After his wounding, learned to walk with wooden legs and in 1863 became doorkeeper of the New York Legislature. In 1864 obtained clerkship in the War Department. On the evening of April 14, 1865, hurried to Ford's Theater on hearing that Lincoln had been shot, remained throughout the night, and took shorthand notes as the search for the assassin was carried out. His notes remain the most comprehensive record of the tragic events. Admitted to the New York Bar in 1869. Active in Republican politics, the Grand Army of the Republic (GAR), and lobbied Congress for veterans. In 1888 made national tours for Harrison's candidacy. Appointed in March 1889 as commissioner of pensions, forced to resign in September 1889. In 1904, President Roosevelt appointed him as register of wills for the District of Columbia. A year later, Tanner became national commander of the GAR.
43. *Nation,* Sept. 12, 1889, 205.
44. Malone, *The New Nation,* 141.
45. TR to HCL, July 11, 1889, Roosevelt, *Letters,* 1:170.
46. McMurry, "Political Significance of the Pension Question," 23.
47. Quotation attributed to General Benjamin Butler at the national encampment of the GAR, Boston, Aug. 11, 1890. From ibid., 23.
48. Teplin, "Theodore Roosevelt," 177.
49. TR to Congressman Alexander Dockery, Jan. 8, 1894, Roosevelt, *Letters,* 1:348.
50. *U.S. Statutes at Large* 22 (1883): 403.
51. Sageser, *First Two Decades,* 104, 116.
52. Ibid., 151.
53. Ibid., 163, 201.
54. During Cleveland's second administration there was a decline in the number of proposals for veteran's preference. Ten such bills were introduced between 1893 and 1897, less than half the number presented in the Harrison administration. With McKinley turning a blind eye to the spoilsmen, the

Spanish-American War opened further possibilities for patronage and veterans' inroads. During McKinley's administration, over four hundred removals had been made by July 1897 to give places to veterans. During the first session of the Fifty-sixth Congress, fifteen veteran's preference bills were introduced. Sageser, *First Two Decades*, 225.

55. Pringle, *A Biography*, 171; May 12, 1890, Roosevelt, *Letters*, 1:221.

56. Gilmour, *The Long Recessional*, 248.

57. Burton, *Learned Presidency*, 48.

58. Turk, *Ambiguous Relationship*, 2.

59. Brooks Adams (1848–1927). American historian. Brother of Henry and Charles Francis, married Evelyn Davis, sister of Henry Cabot Lodge's wife. His theory that civilization rose and fell according to growth and decline of commerce first developed in *The Law of Civilization and Decay* (1895). Adams applied it to his own capitalistic age, of which he was a militant critic. In *America's Economic Supremacy* (1900), said that Western Europe had already begun to decline and that Russia and the United States were the only potential great powers left. His other chief works include *The Emancipation of Massachusetts* (1887), *The New Empire* (1902), and *Theory of Social Revolutions* (1913).

60. Lepawsky, *Administration*, 10.

61. Hirschfield, "Brooks Adams," 384.

62. Renehan, *Lion's Pride*, 24.

63. Mar. 1, 1896, Roosevelt, *Letters*, 1:520.

64. Ibid., 570n. 2.

65. Hirschfield, "Brooks Adams," 375.

66. Blum, *Republican Roosevelt*, 34.

67. TR to HCL, Apr. 27, 1899, Roosevelt, *Letters*, 2:998.

68. May 29, 1897, ibid., 1:620.

69. Hirschfield, "Brooks Adams," 380.

70. Blum, *Republican Roosevelt*, 34; Hirschfield, "Brooks Adams," 374.

71. Roosevelt, "Present State of Civil Service Reform," 354.

72. Roosevelt, *Works*, 10:538.

73. Jacob Riis (1849–1914). Journalist, immigrated to New York from Denmark in 1870. Police reporter for *New York Evening Sun*, 1888–99. His *How the Other Half Lives* (1890) documented the sordid conditions of New York tenements. Roosevelt and Riis developed a close friendship when Theodore later served as police commissioner.

74. Brands, *Last Romantic*, 269.

75. Dalton, *Theodore Roosevelt*, 149.

76. Lemuel Quigg (1863–1919). New York City journalist and Republican power broker. Served in Congress from 1894 to 1899. Editor of the *New York Press*, 1895–96. Influential in Roosevelt's nomination for New York governor in 1898.

77. Mar. 26, 1895, Roosevelt, *Letters*, 1:437.

78. Ibid., 441.

79. Ibid., 444.

80. July 4, 1893, Lodge, *Correspondence*, 130.

81. Roosevelt, *Administration*, 13.

82. L. D. White, *Jacksonians,* 281.

83. Roosevelt, *Works,* 14:134.

84. Pringle, *A Biography,* 134.

85. Twain, *Gilded Age,* 183.

86. Stoddard, *As I Knew Them,* 7.

87. Ibid., 16.

88. E. Morris, *Theodore Rex,* 82.

89. *Washington Star,* May 13, 1889.

90. L. D. White, *Jacksonians,* 279.

91. Hoxie, *A Final Promise,* 103. Charles Fletcher Lummis (1859–1928). Author and explorer of the southwest United States, Mexico, and South America; city editor of the *Los Angeles Times,* 1885–87. Once walked from Cincinnati to Los Angeles "purely for pleasure."

92. Interview with TR, *Washington Evening Star,* Oct. 26, 1894.

93. Van Riper, *United States Civil Service,* 124.

94. U.S. Civil Service Commission, *Eighth Annual Report,* 8.

95. Harbaugh, *Power and Responsibility,* 77.

96. Unpublished bibliography composed by Robert Vail, TRC; Norton, *Theodore Roosevelt,* 28.

97. Van Riper, *United States Civil Service,* 180.

98. Harbaugh, *Power and Responsibility,* 243.

99. L. D. White, *Jacksonians,* 281.

100. Bishop, *Theodore Roosevelt and His Time,* 1:54.

101. *Washington Post,* Sept. 2, 1891. Hatton died in April 1894 at the age of forty-eight.

CHAPTER 8

1. A. Lambert, "Roosevelt the Companion," 382.

2. Teplin, "Theodore Roosevelt," 6.

3. Pringle, *A Biography,* 132.

4. Brands, *Last Romantic,* 377.

5. Stewart, *National Civil Service Reform League,* 64.

6. U.S. Civil Service Commission, *Nineteenth Annual Report,* 9–14; Van Riper, *United States Civil Service,* 201; Ingraham, *Foundation of Merit,* 36.

7. Fowler, *Cabinet Politician,* 269.

8. Stewart, *National Civil Service Reform League,* 65; Skowronek, *Building a New American State,* 178; Mowry, *Era of Theodore Roosevelt,* 167.

9. Aron, *Ladies and Gentlemen of the Civil Service,* 107.

10. Skowronek, *Building a New American State,* 72; Stewart, *National Civil Service Reform League,* 54.

11. Ingraham, *Foundation of Merit,* 36.

12. Skowronek, *Building a New American State,* 334.

13. Van Riper, *United States Civil Service,* 181.

14. Fowler, *Cabinet Politician,* 271.

15. Sept. 15, 18, 1903, Roosevelt, *Letters,* 3:601.

16. U.S. Civil Service Commission, *History of the Federal Civil Service,* 81.

17. Van Riper, *United States Civil Service,* 190.

18. Teplin, "Theodore Roosevelt," 153.

19. Foulke, *Fighting the Spoilsman,* 200.

20. Sageser, *First Two Decades,* 228.

21. U.S. Civil Service Commission, *Nineteenth Annual Report,* 147–64.

22. Ingraham, *Foundation of Merit,* 36.

23. Fowler, *Cabinet Politician,* 270.

24. Stewart, *National Civil Service Reform League,* 66.

25. Party bosses, especially those in Democratic machines in large eastern cities and in the Deep South, continued to levy political assessments at the state and local level well into the twentieth century. During the reign of Huey Long from 1928 to 1935, almost every state, municipal, and parish employee in Louisiana was forced to contribute 10 percent of his or her salary to Long's infamous "deduct box."

26. Skowronek, *Building a New American State,* 79, 180.

27. Van Riper, *United States Civil Service,* 193.

28. "Civil Service Chronology" (1956), typescript, National Civil Service Reform League Archives, Box 224, AHC.

29. Roberts, "A History of the Federal Civil Service," 27.

30. Fowler, "Precursors of the Hatch Act," 257.

31. Fowler, *Cabinet Politician,* 272.

32. Van Riper, *United States Civil Service,* 187.

33. Ibid., 204, as quoted in the *New York Evening Post,* Feb. 6, 1904.

34. Roosevelt, *Works,* 15:433.

35. Van Riper, *United States Civil Service,* 188; U.S. Civil Service Commission, *Twentieth Annual Report,* 147–50.

36. Teplin, "Theodore Roosevelt," 220.

37. L. F. Abbott, *Impressions of Theodore Roosevelt,* 118.

38. Stewart, *National Civil Service Reform League,* 53.

39. Marcus Alonzo Hanna (1837–1904). Prosperous American industrialist whose financial interests spanned coal, iron, banking, railroads, and publishing. Prominent in the Republican Party, Hanna successfully promoted the candidacy of William McKinley as Ohio governor (1892–96) and then as president (1897–1901). In 1896 he skillfully directed McKinley's $3.5 million campaign, the most costly and best-organized campaign the nation had witnessed. Once in office, McKinley appointed Senator John Sherman as secretary of state, thus creating a Senate vacancy to which Hanna was elected and in which he remained until his death.

40. Blum, *Republican Roosevelt,* 22.

41. Pringle, *A Biography,* 122.

42. Teplin, "Theodore Roosevelt," 47.

43. Blum, *Republican Roosevelt,* 14.

44. Schurz, *Speeches, Correspondence,* 264.

45. Foulke, *Fighting the Spoilsman,* 155.

46. Hansen, "Theodore Roosevelt and Civil Service Reform," 95; Foulke, *Roosevelt and the Spoilsmen,* 57.

47. Croly, *Marcus Alonzo Hanna,* 122.

48. Van Riper, *United States Civil Service,* 182.

49. Bishop, *Theodore Roosevelt and His Time,* 1:155.

50. Van Riper, *United States Civil Service,* 183.

51. Bishop, *Theodore Roosevelt and His Time,* 1:356–57.

52. Ibid., 184.

53. Mowry, *Era of Theodore Roosevelt,* 167.

54. Barry, *Forty Years in Washington,* 279.

55. May 5, 1902, Roosevelt, *Letters,* 3:256.

56. U.S. Civil Service Commission, *Nineteenth Annual Report,* 75.

57. U.S. Civil Service Commission, *Twentieth Annual Report,* 66.

58. Sageser, *First Two Decades,* 225; McMurry, "Bureau of Pensions," 345.

59. C. Abbott, *Political Terrain,* 87; King, *Separate and Unequal,* 7, 47, 221. Taft also showed little interest in the employment of blacks, and Wilson's later segregation policies further eroded attempts by African Americans to increase their presence in the federal bureaucracy.

60. Fowler, *Cabinet Politician,* 268.

61. Roosevelt, *An Autobiography,* 98.

62. Fenton, "Theodore Roosevelt," 373.

63. Sageser, *First Two Decades,* 188.

64. Gould, *Presidency of Theodore Roosevelt,* 198.

65. Pringle, *A Biography,* 199.

66. Teplin, "Theodore Roosevelt," 158.

67. Renehan, *Lion's Pride,* 132.

68. Burton, *Learned Presidency,* 59.

69. May 12, 1905, Roosevelt, *Letters,* 4:1145.

70. Wister, *Roosevelt,* 43.

71. Ibid.

72. Harbaugh, *Writings of Theodore Roosevelt,* 256.

73. Van Riper, *United States Civil Service,* 179.

74. L. D. White, *Jacksonians,* 281.

75. Blum, *Republican Roosevelt,* 17.

76. Lansford, *"Bully" First Lady,* ix.

77. Roosevelt, *Writings of Theodore Roosevelt,* 260.

78. Van Riper, *United States Civil Service,* 263.

79. Blum, *Republican Roosevelt,* 17.

80. Adams to Elizabeth Cameron, Jan. 27, 1902, Adams, *Letters* (1930), 2:370.

81. Teplin, "Theodore Roosevelt," 11.

82. Gatewood, *Roosevelt and the Art of Controversy,* 24.

83. Blum, *Republican Roosevelt,* 74; DiNunzio, *Theodore Roosevelt,* 15.

84. Van Riper, *United States Civil Service,* 180.

85. A.D. Chandler, "Roosevelt and the Panama Canal," 1547.

86. Teplin, "Theodore Roosevelt," 246.

87. R. D. White, "Civilian Management of the Military," 54.

88. Roosevelt, *Letters,* 2:840.

89. Pringle, *A Biography,* 188.

90. R. D. White, "Civilian Management of the Military," 44; 32 U.S. 830 (1903).

91. R. D. White, "Civilian Management of the Military," 50.

92. L. D. White, *Republican Era*, 88.

93. Skowronek, *Building a New American State*, 50.

94. L. D. White, *Republican Era*, 91.

95. L. D. White, *Jacksonians*, 282; Arnold, *Making the Managerial Presidency*, 20.

96. Pinkett, "The Keep Commission," 297.

97. Ibid., 299.

98. L. D. White, *Republican Era*, 92.

99. Van Riper, *United States Civil Service*, 192.

100. Pinkett, "The Keep Commission," 310.

101. Skowronek, *Building a New American State*, 185.

102. *House Report 4038*, 51st Cong., 2nd sess., 77.

103. Pringle, *A Biography*, 78.

104. U.S. Civil Service Commission, *Twenty-third Annual Report*, 11–12.

105. Pinkett, "The Keep Commission," 305.

106. Ibid., 309.

107. Gatewood, *Roosevelt and the Art of Controversy*, 11.

EPILOGUE

1. Gibbons, *John Wanamaker*, 236, 299; Appel, *Business Biography of John Wanamaker;* Ershkowitz, *John Wanamaker*.

2. Klein, "Gospel of Wanamaker," 27.

3. Wanamaker diary, June 22, 1912, Historical Society of Pennsylvania, Philadelphia.

4. Wanamaker diary, Nov. 6, 1912, ibid.

5. Wanamaker to Roosevelt, telegram, Oct. 24, 1916, ibid.

6. The remarriage lasted only four years. The 1920 Republican nomination of Warren Harding signaled the death of the Progressive Party. Beginning at that time, the GOP took its present-day conservative stance and was no longer split between progressive and old-guard elements.

7. Gibbons, *John Wanamaker*, 399.

8. Telegram, May 22, 1917, TRP.

9. TR to Kermit Roosevelt, Sept. 8, 1918, file CR-1, TRC.

10. In World War II, Ted received the Medal of Honor as a brigadier general for leading his division ashore at Normandy under heavy fire. He was the oldest American to make the landing. Near the front a month later, he died from a heart attack.

11. Quentin and Ted are buried in Normandy next to each other.

12. Appel, *Business Biography of John Wanamaker*, 255.

Bibliography

Abbott, Carl. *Political Terrain: Washington, D.C., from Tidewater Town to Global Metropolis*. Chapel Hill: University of North Carolina Press, 1999.

Abbott, Lawrence F. *Impressions of Theodore Roosevelt*. New York: Doubleday, 1923.

Adams, Henry. *Democracy: An American Novel*. New York: Henry Holt, 1908.

———. *The Education of Henry Adams*. New York: Modern Library, 1931.

———. *The Letters of Henry Adams*. 2 vols. Boston: Houghton Mifflin, 1930.

———. *The Letters of Henry Adams*. 6 vols. Cambridge: Harvard University Press, 1982.

Adams, Marian Hopper. *The Letters of Mrs. Henry Adams*. Boston: Little, Brown, 1936.

Adams, Richard P. "Architecture and the Tradition: Coleridge to Wright." *American Quarterly* 9, no. 1 (1957): 46–62.

Appel, Joseph H. *The Business Biography of John Wanamaker, Founder and Builder: America's Merchant Pioneer from 1861 to 1922*. New York: Macmillan, 1930.

Appelbaum, Stanley. *The Chicago World's Fair of 1893*. New York: Dover, 1980.

Arnold, Peri. *Making the Managerial Presidency: Comprehensive Reorganization Planning, 1905–1980*. Princeton, N.J.: Princeton University Press, 1986.

Aron, Cindy Sondik. *Ladies and Gentlemen of the Civil Service: Middle-Class Workers in Victorian America*. New York: Oxford University Press, 1987.

Barry, David S. *Forty Years in Washington*. Boston: Little, Brown, 1924.

Berkelman, Robert. "Clarence King: Scientific Pioneer." *American Quarterly* 5, no. 4 (1953): 301–24.

Bishop, Joseph B. *Charles Joseph Bonaparte: His Life and Public Services*. New York: Scribner, 1922.

———. *Theodore Roosevelt and His Time*. 2 vols. New York: Scribner, 1919.

Blake, Nelson M. "Ambassadors at the Court of Theodore Roosevelt." *Mississippi Valley Historical Review* 42, no. 2 (1955): 179–206.

Blodgett, Geoffrey. "The Mugwump Reputation, 1870 to the Present." *Journal of American History* 66, no. 4 (1980): 867–87.

Blum, John M. *The Republican Roosevelt*. New York: Atheneum, 1970.

——. "Theodore Roosevelt: The Years of Decision." In *The Letters of Theodore Roosevelt*, ed. Elting E. Morison, 2:1484–94. Cambridge: Harvard University Press, 1951.

Brands, H. W. *TR: The Last Romantic*. New York: Basic Books, 1997.

Burg, David F. *Chicago's White City of 1893*. Lexington: University of Kentucky Press, 1976.

Burrows, Edward G., and Mike Wallace. *Gotham: A History of New York City to 1898*. New York: Oxford University Press, 1999.

Burton, David H. *The Learned Presidency: Theodore Roosevelt, William Howard Taft, Woodrow Wilson*. Rutherford, N.J.: Fairleigh Dickinson Press, 1988.

——. *Theodore Roosevelt: American Politicians, An Assessment*. Madison, N.J.: Fairleigh Dickinson University Press, 1997.

Busch, Noel F. *T.R.: The Story of Theodore Roosevelt and His Influence on Our Times*. New York: Reynal, 1963.

Caroli, Betty Boyd. *The Roosevelt Women*. New York: Basic, 1998.

Carpenter, Frank G. *Carp's Washington*. New York: McGraw-Hill, 1960.

Carrington, C. E. *The Life of Rudyard Kipling*. Garden City, N.Y.: Doubleday, 1956.

Cashman, Sean D. *America in the Gilded Age*. New York: New York University Press, 1988.

Chandler, Alfred D., Jr. "Theodore Roosevelt and the Panama Canal." In *The Letters of Theodore Roosevelt*, ed. Elting E. Morison, 6:1547–57. Cambridge: Harvard University Press, 1951.

Chandler, Ralph C. *A Centennial History of the American Administrative State*. New York: Free Press, 1987.

Cleveland, Grover. *Grover Cleveland: Chronology, Documents, Bibliographical Aids*. Ed. Robert I. Vexler. Dobbs Ferry, N.Y.: Oceana, 1968.

——. *Letters of Grover Cleveland, 1850–1908*. Ed. A. Nevins. Cambridge, Mass.: Riverside Press, 1933.

Condrey, Stephen E., and Robert Maranto, eds. *Radical Reform of the Civil Service*. Lanham, Md.: Lexington, 2001.

Cook, John, ed. *The Book of Positive Quotations*. Minneapolis: Fairview Press, 1993.

Cowles, Anna Roosevelt. *Letters from Theodore Roosevelt, 1870–1918*. New York: Scribner, 1924.

Crichton, Judy. *America 1900*. New York: Henry Holt, 1998.

Croly, Herbert. *Marcus Alonzo Hanna: His Life and Work*. New York: Macmillan, 1912.

Cutright, Paul R. *Theodore Roosevelt: The Making of a Conservationist*. Urbana: University of Illinois Press, 1985.

Dalton, Kathleen. *Theodore Roosevelt: A Strenuous Life*. New York: Knopf, 2002.

Doughty, Howard. *Francis Parkman*. New York: Macmillan, 1962.

DiNunzio, Mario R., ed. *Theodore Roosevelt: An American Mind—Selected Writings*. New York: Penguin, 1994.

Dunning, William A. "Henry Adams on Things in General." *Political Science Quarterly* 34, no. 2 (1919): 305–11.

Durbin, Louise. *Inaugural Cavalcade.* New York: Dodd, Mead, 1971.

Dyer, Thomas G. *Theodore Roosevelt and the Idea of Race.* Baton Rouge: Louisiana State University Press, 1992.

Edwards, James A. *The Court Circle: A Tale of Washington Life.* Washington, D.C.: N.p., 1895.

Ershkowitz, Herbert. *John Wanamaker: Philadelphia Merchant.* Philadelphia: Combined, 1999.

Fenton, Charles. "Theodore Roosevelt as an American Man of Letters." *Western Humanities Review* 13 (1959): 369–74.

Fish, Carl R. *The Civil Service and the Patronage.* New York: Longmans, Green, 1905.

Flinn, John J. *Official Guide to the World's Columbian Exhibition.* Chicago: Columbian Guide, 1893.

Foraker, Joseph B. *Notes of a Busy Life.* Cincinnati: Stewart and Kidd, 1917.

Foraker, Julia B. *I Would Live It Again: Memories of a Vivid Life.* New York: Harper, 1932.

Foulke, William D. *Fighting the Spoilsman: Reminiscences of the Civil Service Reform.* New York: Putnam, 1919.

——. *A Hoosier Biography.* New York: Oxford University Press, 1922.

——. *Lucius B. Swift: A Biography.* Indianapolis: Bobbs-Merrill, 1930.

——. *Roosevelt and the Spoilsmen.* New York: National Civil Service Reform League, 1925.

Fowler, Dorothy G. *The Cabinet Politician: The Postmasters General, 1829–1909.* New York: Columbia University Press, 1943.

——. "Precursors of the Hatch Act." *Mississippi Valley Historical Review* 47, no. 2 (1960): 247–62.

Friedrich, Carl J. "The Rise and Decline of the Spoils Tradition." *Annals of the American Academy of Political and Social Science* 189 (1937): 10–18.

Fuess, Claude M. *Carl Schurz: Reformer (1829–1906).* New York: Dodd, Mead, 1932.

Gardner, Joseph L. *Departing Glory: Theodore Roosevelt as Ex-President.* New York: Scribner, 1973.

Garraty, John A. *Henry Cabot Lodge: A Biography.* New York: Knopf, 1953.

Gatewood, Willard B., Jr. *Theodore Roosevelt and the Art of Controversy.* Baton Rouge: Louisiana State University Press, 1970.

Gibbons, Herbert A. *John Wanamaker.* New York: Harper, 1926.

Gilder, Richard Watson. *Grover Cleveland: A Record of Friendship.* New York: Century, 1910.

——. *Letters of Richard Watson Gilder.* Ed. Rosamond Gilder. New York: Houghton Mifflin, 1916.

Gilmour, David. *The Long Recessional: The Imperial Life of Rudyard Kipling.* New York: Farrar, Straus, and Giroux, 2002.

Goldman, Eric F. *Charles J. Bonaparte: Patrician Reformer.* Baltimore: Johns Hopkins University Press, 1943.

Goodwin, Doris Kearns. *No Ordinary Time: Franklin and Eleanor Roosevelt: The Home Front in World War II.* New York: Simon and Schuster, 1994.

Gould, Lewis L. *The Presidency of Theodore Roosevelt.* Lawrence: University of Kansas Press, 1991.

Green, Constance. *Washington, Capitol City: 1879–1950*. Princeton, N.J.: Princeton University Press, 1963.

Hagan, William T. "Civil Service Commissioner Theodore Roosevelt and the Indian Rights Association." *Pacific Historical Review* 44, no. 2 (1975): 187–200.

Hagedorn, Hermann. *The Boy's Life of Theodore Roosevelt*. New York: Harper, 1918.

——. *The Roosevelt Family of Sagamore Hill*. New York: Macmillan, 1954.

——. *Roosevelt in the Bad Lands*. Boston: Houghton Mifflin, 1921.

——. *Theodore Roosevelt Treasury*. New York: Putnam, 1957.

Halford, E. W. "Roosevelt's Introduction to Washington." *Leslie's Illustrated Weekly Newspaper*, Mar. 1, 1919, 293.

Halloran, Matthew F. *The Romance of the Merit System: Forty-five Years' Reminiscences of the Civil Service*. Washington, D.C.: Judd and Detweiler, 1929.

——. "Theodore Roosevelt—Civil Service Commissioner." In *Roosevelt in the Bunk House and Other Sketches,* by William Chapin Deming. Laramie, Wyo.: Laramie Printing, 1930.

Hansen, Donald A. "Theodore Roosevelt and Civil Service Reform." M.A. thesis, University of San Francisco, 1956.

Harbaugh, William H. *Power and Responsibility: The Life and Times of Theodore Roosevelt*. New York: Farrar, Straus and Cudahy, 1961.

——, ed. *The Writings of Theodore Roosevelt*. New York: Bobbs-Merrill, 1967.

Harrison, Benjamin. *Speeches of Benjamin Harrison*. New York: John W. Lovell, 1892.

——. *Views of an Ex-President*. Indianapolis: Bowen-Merrill, 1901.

Hart, Albert, and Herbert R. Ferleger, eds. *Theodore Roosevelt Cyclopedia*. New York: Roosevelt Memorial Association, 1941.

Harvey, Donald R. *The Civil Service Commission*. New York: Praeger, 1970.

Higham, John. *Strangers in the Land: Patterns of American Nativism*. New Brunswick, N.J.: Rutgers University Press, 1955.

Hirschfield, Charles. "Brooks Adams and American Nationalism." *American Historical Review* 69, no. 2 (1964): 371–92.

Hoffman, Charles. *The Depression of the Nineties: An Economic History*. Westport, Conn.: Greenwood, 1970.

Hofstadter, Richard. *The Age of Reform: From Bryan to FDR*. New York: Vintage, 1959.

——. *Social Darwinism in American Thought*. Boston: Beacon Press, 1944.

Hoogenboom, Ari. *Outlawing the Spoils: A History of the Civil Service Reform Movement*. Urbana: University of Illinois Press, 1961.

——. "The Pendleton Act and the Civil Service." *American Historical Review* 64, no. 2 (1959): 301–18.

——. "Thomas A. Jenckes and Civil Service Reform." *Mississippi Valley Historical Review* 47, no. 4 (1961): 636–58.

Hoxie, Frederick E. *A Final Promise: The Campaign to Assimilate the Indians, 1880–1920*. Lincoln: University of Nebraska Press, 1984.

Humes, James C. *The Wit and Wisdom of Abraham Lincoln*. New York: Gramercy, 1996.

Huntington, Samuel P. *The Soldier and the State: The Theory and Politics of Civil Military Relations.* Cambridge: Harvard University Press, 1957.

Ingraham, Patricia W. *The Foundation of Merit: Public Service in American Democracy.* Baltimore: Johns Hopkins University Press, 1995.

James, Henry. *The American Scene.* New York: Horizon Press, 1967.

———. *The Correspondence of Henry James and Henry Adams.* Ed. George Monteiro. Baton Rouge: Louisiana State University Press, 1992.

Jeffers, H. Paul. *An Honest President: The Life and Presidencies of Grover Cleveland.* New York: HarperCollins, 2000.

———. *Theodore Roosevelt, Jr.: The Life of a War Hero.* Novato, Calif.: Presidio Press, 2002.

Josephson, Matthew. *The Politicos, 1865–1896.* New York: Harcourt, Brace, 1938.

Jusserand, Jules. *What Me Befell: The Reminiscences of J. J. Jusserand.* Boston: Houghton Mifflin, 1934.

Kehl, James A. *Boss Rule in the Gilded Age: Matt Quay of Pennsylvania.* Pittsburgh: University of Pittsburgh Press, 1981.

Kent, Noel Jacob. *America in 1900.* Armonk, N.Y.: M. E. Sharpe, 2000.

King, Desmond S. *Separate and Unequal: Black Americans and the U.S. Federal Government.* New York: Oxford University Press, 1995.

Kipling, Rudyard. *The Letters of Rudyard Kipling.* 3 vols. Iowa City: University of Iowa Press, 1990.

———. *Something of Myself.* New York: Cambridge University Press, 1937.

Klein, Maury. "The Gospel of Wanamaker." *Audacity: The Magazine of Business History* 4, no. 4 (1996): 26–39.

Lambert, John R. *Arthur Pue Gorman.* Baton Rouge: Louisiana State University Press, 1953.

———. "Roosevelt the Companion." In Roosevelt, *Works,* 2:375–89.

Lansford, Tom. *A "Bully" First Lady: Edith Kermit Roosevelt.* Huntington, N.Y.: Nova History, 2001.

Lash, Joseph. *Eleanor and Franklin.* New York: New American Library, 1973.

Latimer, Louise Payson. *Your Washington and Mine.* New York: Scribner, 1924.

Leach, William. *Land of Desire: Merchants, Power, and the Rise of a New American Culture.* New York: Pantheon, 1993.

Lepawsky, Albert. *Administration: The Art and Science of Organization and Management.* New York: Knopf, 1960.

Leupp, Francis E. *Walks About Washington.* Boston: Little, Brown, 1921.

Licht, Walter. *Industrializing America: The Nineteenth Century.* Baltimore: Johns Hopkins University Press, 1995.

Lodge, Henry Cabot. *Speeches and Addresses, 1884–1909, by Henry Cabot Lodge.* New York: Houghton Mifflin, 1909.

———. "Why Patronage in Offices Is Un-American." *Century Illustrated Monthly Magazine* 40 (1890): 837–44.

———, ed. *Selections from the Correspondence of Theodore Roosevelt and Henry Cabot Lodge, 1884–1918.* New York: Scribner, 1925.

Logan, Mrs. John A. *Our National Government.* Minneapolis: H. L. Baldwin, 1908.

——. *Thirty Years in Washington or Life and Scenes in Our National Capitol.* Hartford, Conn.: A.D. Worthington, 1901.

Lorant, Stefan. *The Life and Times of Theodore Roosevelt.* New York: Doubleday, 1959.

Low, A. Maurice. "Washington: The City of Leisure." *Atlantic Monthly,* Dec. 1900, 767–68.

Lyman, Charles. "Ten Years of Civil Service Reform." *North American Review* 157 (1893): 571–79.

Mackintosh, Barry. *C&O Canal: The Making of a Park.* Washington, D.C.: National Park Service, 1991.

Malin, James C. "Roosevelt and the Elections of 1884 and 1888." *Mississippi Valley Historical Review* 14, no. 1 (1927): 25–38.

Malone, Dumas. *The New Nation: 1865–1917.* New York: Appleton-Century-Crofts, 1964.

Marcus, Robert D. *Grand Old Party: Political Structure in the Gilded Age, 1880–1896.* New York: Oxford University Press, 1971.

Marszalek, John F. *Grover Cleveland: A Bibliography.* Westport, Conn.: Meckler, 1988.

McCaleb, Walter F. *Theodore Roosevelt.* New York: A. and C. Boni, 1931.

McCall, Samuel W. *The Life of Thomas Brackett Reed.* Boston: Houghton Mifflin, 1914.

McCullough, David. *Mornings on Horseback.* New York: Touchstone, 1981.

McElroy, Robert. *Grover Cleveland: The Man and the Statesman.* New York: Harper, 1923.

McFarland, Gerald W. "The New York Mugwumps of 1884: A Profile." *Political Science Quarterly* 78, no. 1 (1963): 40–58.

McMurry, Donald L. "The Bureau of Pensions during the Administration of President Harrison." *Mississippi Valley Historical Review* 13, no. 3 (1926): 343–64.

——. "The Political Significance of the Pension Question: 1885–1897." *Mississippi Valley Historical Review* 9, no. 1 (1922): 19–36.

Merrill, Horace S. *Bourbon Leader: Grover Cleveland and the Democratic Party.* Boston: Little, Brown, 1957.

Miller, Nathan. *Theodore Roosevelt: A Life.* New York: William Morrow, 1992.

Monkman, Betty C. *The White House: Its Historic Foundations and First Families.* New York: Abbeville Press, 2000.

Moore, Charles. *Washington Past and Present.* New York: Century, 1929.

Morgan, H. Wayne, ed. *The Gilded Age.* Syracuse, N.Y.: Syracuse University Press, 1970.

Morris, Edmund. "As a Literary Lion, Roosevelt Preached What He Practiced." *Smithsonian* 14 (1983): 86–93.

——. *The Rise of Theodore Roosevelt.* New York: Coward, McCann, and Geoghegan, 1979.

——. *Theodore Rex.* New York: Random House, 2001.

Morris, Sylvia J. *Edith Kermit Roosevelt.* New York: Coward, McCann, and Geoghegan, 1980.

Morstein Marx, Fritz, ed. *Elements of Public Administration.* Englewood Cliffs, N.J.: Prentice-Hall, 1959.

Mowry, George E. *The Era of Theodore Roosevelt, 1900–1912.* New York: Harper, 1958.

Murphy, Lionel V. "The First Federal Civil Service Commission, 1871–1875." *Public Personnel Review* 3 (Jan., July, and Oct. 1942): 29–39, 218–31, 299–323.

Muzzey, David S. *James G. Blaine: A Political Idol of Other Days.* New York: Dodd, Mead, 1935.

Nelson, Michael. "A Short, Ironic History of American National Bureaucracy." *Journal of Politics* 44, no. 3 (1982): 747–78.

Nevins, Allan. *Grover Cleveland: A Study in Courage.* New York: Dodd, Mead, 1932.

Norton, Aloysius A. *Theodore Roosevelt.* Boston: Twayne, 1980.

Oliver, Lawrence J. "Theodore Roosevelt, Brander Matthews, and the Campaign for Literary Americanism." *American Quarterly* 41, no. 1 (1989): 93–111.

———, ed. *The Letters of Theodore Roosevelt and Brander Matthews.* Knoxville: University of Tennessee Press, 1995.

O'Toole, Patricia. *The Five of Hearts: An Intimate Portrait of Henry Adams and His Friends.* New York: Clarkson Potter Publishers, 1990.

———. "What They All Had in Common Was Wit and Friendship." *Smithsonian* 21, no. 3 (1990): 132–44.

Painter, Nell Irvin. *Standing at Armageddon: United States, 1877–1919.* New York: Norton, 1987.

Pearson, Edmund L. *Theodore Roosevelt.* New York: Macmillan, 1920.

Pinchot, Gifford. *Breaking New Ground.* Seattle: University of Washington Press, 1947.

Pinkett, Harold T. "The Keep Commission, 1905–1909: A Rooseveltian Effort for Administrative Reform." *Journal of American History* 52, no. 2 (1965): 297–312.

Pinney, Thomas, ed. *Rudyard Kipling: Something of Myself and Other Biographical Writings.* New York: Cambridge University Press, 1990.

Pollack, Norman. *The Populist Mind.* Indianapolis: Bobbs-Merrill, 1967.

Pringle, Henry F. *Theodore Roosevelt: A Biography.* Norwalk, Conn.: Easton Press, 1931.

Putnam, Carleton. *Theodore Roosevelt: The Formative Years.* New York: Scribner, 1958.

Putnam, George Haven. *Memories of a Publisher.* New York: Putnam, 1915.

Renehan, Edward J. *The Lion's Pride: Theodore Roosevelt and His Family in Peace and War.* New York: Oxford University Press, 1998.

Reps, John W. *Monumental Washington: The Planning and Development of the Capitol Center.* Princeton, N.J.: Princeton University Press, 1967.

Riis, Jacob A. *Theodore Roosevelt, the Citizen.* New York: Macmillan, 1904.

Rixey, Lillian. *Bamie: Theodore Roosevelt's Remarkable Sister.* New York: David McKay, 1963.

Roberts, Gary E. "A History of the Federal Civil Service." In *Radical Reform of the Civil Service,* ed. Stephen E. Condrey and Robert Maranto. Lanham, Md.: Lexington, 2001.

Robinson, Corinne. *My Brother, Theodore Roosevelt*. New York: Scribner, 1921.

Roosevelt, Nicholas. *A Front Row Seat*. Norman: University of Oklahoma Press, 1953.

Roosevelt, Theodore. *Administration: Civil Service*. New York: Putnam, 1900.

———. *American Ideals, and Other Essays, Social and Political*. New York: AMS Press, 1897.

———. "The Common Sense of Civil Service Reform." *Century* 26 (1894): 154–55.

———. *Fear God and Take Your Own Part*. New York: Scribner, 1915.

———. "The Foreign Policy of President Harrison." *Independent* 44 (1892): 1113–15.

———. "Kidd's 'Social Evolution.'" *North American Review* 161 (1895): 94–109.

———. *The Letters of Theodore Roosevelt*. Ed. Elting E. Morison. 8 vols. Cambridge: Harvard University Press, 1951.

———. *Letters of Theodore Roosevelt*. Washington, D.C.: U.S. Civil Service Commission, 1958.

———. "The Merit System in Government Appointments." *Cosmopolitan* 13 (1892): 66–71.

———. "The Merit System versus the Patronage System." *Century* 17 (1890): 632–33.

———. "National Life and Character." *Sewanee Review* 2 (1894): 353–76.

———. *New York*. New York: Longmans, Green, 1891.

———. "An Object Lesson in Civil Service Reform." *Atlantic Monthly*, 1891. In Roosevelt, *Works* 14:115.

———. "The Present State of Civil Service Reform." *Atlantic Monthly* 75 (1895): 239–46.

———. *Presidential Papers and State Addresses*. New York: Review of Review, 1910.

———. "Six Years of Civil Service Reform." *Scribner's Magazine* 18 (1895): 242.

———. *Theodore Roosevelt: An Autobiography*. New York: Macmillan, 1913.

———. *Theodore Roosevelt's Diaries of Boyhood and Youth*. New York: Scribner, 1928.

———. *The Wilderness Hunter*. New York: Putnam, 1893.

———. *The Works of Theodore Roosevelt*. Ed. Hermann Hagedorn. 20 vols. New York: Scribner, 1925.

———. *The Writings of Theodore Roosevelt*. Ed. William H. Harbaugh, New York: Bobbs-Merrill, 1967.

Rosenbloom, David H. *Centenary Issues of the Pendleton Act of 1883: The Problematic Legacy of Civil Service Reform*. New York: Marcel Dekker, 1982.

———. *Federal Service and the Constitution*. Ithaca: Cornell University Press, 1971.

Rugoff, Milton. *America's Gilded Age: Intimate Portraits from an Era of Extravagance and Change, 1850–1890*. New York: Holt, 1989.

Sageser, A. Bower. *The First Two Decades of the Pendleton Act: A Study of Civil Service Reform*. Lincoln: University Studies of the University of Nebraska, 1935.

Schurz, Carl. *The Autobiography of Carl Schurz*. New York: Scribner, 1961.

———. *The Reminiscences of Carl Schurz*. New York: McClure, 1908.

——. *Speeches, Correspondence, and Political Papers of Carl Schurz*. Ed. Frederic Bancroft. New York: Putnam, 1913.

Schwantes, Carlos. *Coxey's Army: An American Odyssey*. Lincoln: University of Nebraska Press, 1985.

Shaw, Albert. *A Cartoon History of Roosevelt's Career*. New York: Review of Reviews Company, 1910.

Shumate, Roger V. "The Political Philosophy of Henry Adams." *American Political Science Review* 28, no. 4 (1934): 599–610.

Sievers, Harry J. *Benjamin Harrison: Hoosier President, the White House and After*. New York: Bobbs-Merrill, 1968.

——. *Benjamin Harrison: Hoosier Statesman, from the Civil War to the White House, 1865–1888*. New York: University Publishers, 1959.

——, ed. *Benjamin Harrison: Chronology, Documents, Bibliographical Aids*. Dobbs Ferry, N.Y.: Oceana, 1969.

Sinkler, George. *The Racial Attitudes of American Presidents, from Abraham Lincoln to Theodore Roosevelt*. Garden City, N.Y.: Doubleday, 1971.

Skowronek, Stephen. *Building a New American State: The Expansion of National Administrative Capacities, 1877–1920*. New York: Cambridge University Press, 1982.

Smith, Darrell H. *The United States Civil Service Commission: Its History, Activities, and Organization*. Baltimore: Johns Hopkins Press, 1928.

Smith, Theodore C. *The Life and Letters of James Abram Garfield*. New Haven: Yale University Press, 1925.

Socolofsky, Homer E., and Allan B. Spetter. *The Presidency of Benjamin Harrison*. Lawrence: University of Kansas Press, 1987.

Spring-Rice, Cecil Arthur. *The Letters and Friendships of Sir Cecil Spring-Rice: A Record*. London: Constable, 1929.

Sproat, John G. *The Best Men: Liberal Reformers in the Gilded Age*. New York: Oxford University Press, 1968.

Steffens, Lincoln. *The Letters of Lincoln Steffens*. Ed. Ella Winter and Granville Hicks. 2 vols. New York: Harcourt, Brace, 1938.

Stevenson, Elizabeth. *Henry Adams: A Biography*. New York: Macmillan, 1955.

Stewart, Frank Mann. *The National Civil Service Reform League*. Austin: University of Texas Press, 1929.

Stoddard, Henry L. *As I Knew Them: Presidents and Politics from Grant to Coolidge*. New York: Harper, 1927.

Teplin, Joseph. "Theodore Roosevelt: A Study in Administrative Thought and Behavior." Ph.D. diss., University of Chicago, 1949.

Thayer, William R. *Theodore Roosevelt: An Intimate Biography*. New York: Grosset and Dunlap, 1919.

Thomas, Flora McDonald. "Art in the White House." *Harper's Bazaar* 34 (1901): 143–48.

Trachtenberg, Alan. *The Incorporation of America: Culture and Society in the Gilded Age*. New York: Hill and Wang, 1982.

Trefousse, Hans Louis. *Carl Schurz: A Biography*. Knoxville: University of Tennessee Press, 1982.

Turk, Richard W. *The Ambiguous Relationship: Theodore Roosevelt and Alfred Thayer Mahan.* New York: Greenwood Press, 1987.

Twain, Mark, and Charles Dudley Warner. *The Gilded Age: A Tale of To-Day.* New York: Bobbs-Merrill, 1972.

United States Civil Service Commission. *Sixth Report of the United States Civil Service Commission: July 1, 1888–June 30, 1889.* Washington, D.C.: Government Printing Office, 1889.

———. *Seventh Report of the United States Civil Service Commission: July 1, 1889–June 30, 1890.* Washington, D.C.: Government Printing Office, 1890.

———. *Eighth Report of the United States Civil Service Commission: July 1, 1890–June 30, 1891.* Washington, D.C.: Government Printing Office, 1891.

———. *Ninth Report of the United States Civil Service Commission: July 1, 1891–June 30, 1892.* Washington, D.C.: Government Printing Office, 1892.

———. *Tenth Report of the United States Civil Service Commission: July 1, 1892–June 30, 1893.* Washington, D.C.: Government Printing Office, 1893.

———. *Eleventh Report of the United States Civil Service Commission: July 1, 1893–June 30, 1894.* Washington, D.C.: Government Printing Office, 1894.

———. *Twelfth Report of the United States Civil Service Commission: July 1, 1894–June 30, 1895.* Washington, D.C.: Government Printing Office, 1895.

———. *Seventeenth Report of the United States Civil Service Commission: July 1, 1899–June 30, 1900.* Washington, D.C.: Government Printing Office, 1900.

———. *Nineteenth Report of the United States Civil Service Commission: July 1, 1901–June 30, 1902.* Washington, D.C.: Government Printing Office, 1902.

———. *Twentieth Report of the United States Civil Service Commission: July 1, 1902–June 30, 1903.* Washington, D.C.: Government Printing Office, 1903.

———. *Twenty-third Report of the United States Civil Service Commission: July 1, 1905–June 30, 1906.* Washington, D.C.: Government Printing Office, 1906.

———. *History of the Federal Civil Service: 1789 to the Present.* Washington, D.C.: Government Printing Office, 1941.

Van Riper, Paul. *History of the United States Civil Service.* Evanston, Ill.: Row, Peterson, 1958.

Volwiler, Albert T., ed. *The Correspondence between Benjamin Harrison and James G. Blaine, 1882–1893.* Philadelphia: American Philosophical Society, 1940.

Wagenknecht, Edward. *The Seven Worlds of Theodore Roosevelt.* New York: Longmans, Green, 1958.

Warner, Ezra J. *Generals in Gray.* Baton Rouge: Louisiana State University Press, 1959.

Weber, Max. *From Max Weber: Essays in Sociology.* New York: Oxford University Press, 1958.

Welling, Richard. *As the Twig Is Bent.* New York: Putnam, 1942.

Welsh, Herbert. *Civilization among the Sioux Indians.* Philadelphia: Indian Rights Association, 1893.

Wheeler, Everett P. "The Rise and Progress of the Merit System." *Political Science Quarterly* 34, no. 3 (1919): 486–92.

White, Leonard D. *The Civil Service in the Modern State.* Chicago: University of Chicago Press, 1930.

———. *The Jacksonians.* New York: Macmillan, 1954.

———. "The Public Life of T.R." *Public Administration Review* 14 (1954): 278–82.

———. *The Republican Era: 1869–1901.* New York: Macmillan, 1958.

White, Richard D. "The Bullmoose and the Bear: Theodore Roosevelt and John Wanamaker Struggle over the Spoils." *Pennsylvania History: A Journal of Mid-Atlantic Studies* (forthcoming).

———. "Civilian Management of the Military: Elihu Root and the Reorganization of the Army General Staff." *Journal of Management History* 4, no. 1 (1998): 43–59.

———. "Muckrakers." In *The International Encyclopedia of Public Policy and Administration,* ed. Jay Shafritz. Boulder, Colo.: Westview Press, 1997.

———. "Theodore Roosevelt as Civil Service Commissioner: Linking the Influence and Development of a Modern Administrative President." *Administrative Theory and Praxis* 22, no. 4 (2000): 696–713.

Wiebe, Robert H. *The Search for Order.* New York: Hill and Wang, 1967.

Williams, Cleveland A. "Theodore Roosevelt: Civil Service Commissioner." M.A. thesis, University of Chicago, 1955.

Wilson, Woodrow. "Cleveland's Cabinet." *American Review of Reviews* 7, no. 39 (1893): 286–97.

———. "The Study of Administration." *Political Science Quarterly* 2 (1887): 197–222.

Wister, Owen. *Roosevelt: The Story of a Friendship, 1880–1919.* New York: Macmillan, 1930.

Ziff, Larzer. *The American 1890s: Life and Times of a Lost Generation.* New York: Viking, 1966.

Acknowledgments

THE ASSISTANCE provided by Wallace Dailey, the curator of the Theodore Roosevelt Collection at Harvard, was essential and greatly appreciated. William Andrew, a doctoral student at Virginia Polytechnic Institute, researched the National Civil Service Reform League Archives files and kindly provided his notes. Victoria Kalamaris, a National Park Service curator at Sagamore Hill, was quite helpful in guiding me through the records and providing a unique glimpse into how the Roosevelts lived during the 1890s. Penny McMillan provided a fascinating tour of Bulloch Hall, the childhood home of Roosevelt's mother, Mittie Bulloch, which is located near Atlanta, Georgia.

A number of scholars lent valuable assistance and advice to this research project. Professor Paul Van Riper of Texas A&M, the premier historian of the American civil service, kindly reviewed the manuscript. Nathan Miller, a noted Roosevelt biographer, also provided valuable guidance. Jim Richardson, Dan Marin, and Lamar Jones of Louisiana State University, Lanny Keller of Baton Rouge, Jim Bowman of Florida State, and Jeremy Plant of Penn State made important contributions. The LSU Council of Research provided two summer research grants to help complete this book.

This project could not have been completed without the outstanding support and guidance of the staff of the University of Alabama Press.

Index